This Book Comes With Lots of
FREE Online Resources

Nolo's award-winning website has a page dedicated just to this book. Here you can:

KEEP UP TO DATE. When there are important changes to the information in this book, we'll post updates.

GET DISCOUNTS ON NOLO PRODUCTS. Get discounts on hundreds of books, forms, and software.

READ BLOGS. Get the latest info from Nolo authors' blogs.

LISTEN TO PODCASTS. Listen to authors discuss timely issues on topics that interest you.

WATCH VIDEOS. Get a quick introduction to a legal topic with our short videos.

And that's not all.
Nolo.com contains thousands of articles on everyday legal and business issues, plus a plain-English law dictionary, all written by Nolo experts and available for free. You'll also find more useful **books, software, online apps, downloadable forms,** plus a **lawyer directory.**

Get updates and more at
www.nolo.com/back-of-book/BHCA.html

16th Edition

How to
Buy a House
in California

Real Estate Broker Ira Serkes,
George Devine & Ilona Bray J.D.

Sixteenth Edition	JANUARY 2017
Editor	ILONA BRAY
Production	SUSAN PUTNEY
Proofreading	SUSAN CARLSON GREENE
Index	CYNTHIA DARLING LANDEEN
Printing	BANG PRINTING

Names: Serkes, Ira, 1949- author. | Devine, George, 1941- author. | Bray, Ilona M., 1962- author.
Title: How to buy a house in California / Real Estate Broker Ira Serkes, George Devine & Ilona Bray J.D.
Description: 13th Edition. | Berkeley, CA : Nolo, 2017. | Revised edition of the authors's How to buy a house in California, 2015.
Identifiers: LCCN 2016031813 (print) | LCCN 2016036596 (ebook) | ISBN 9781413323337 (pbk.) | ISBN 9781413323344 (ebook)
Subjects: LCSH: House buying--California. | Real property--California. | Mortgages--California. | Housing--California--Finance. | Real estate business--California.
Classification: LCC HD266.C2 S47 2017 (print) | LCC HD266.C2 (ebook) | DDC 643/.1209794--dc23
LC record available at https://lccn.loc.gov/2016031813

Acknowledgments

Collecting and organizing the material for this book turned out to be a daunting task, one that might have defeated us had it not been for the enthusiastic help of Nolo legal editors Ilona Bray, Mary Randolph, Alayna Schroeder, and Marcia Stewart.

For help with this latest edition, enormous thanks go to Rainey Gray-Gross, senior mortgage consultant with Stonecastle Land and Home Financial, in Danville, California (www.stonecastle-lhf.com). Rainey went above and beyond the call of duty in updating facts and figures, rethinking what guidance would be of most value to readers, and making sure the discussion reflects current market conditions.

Tim Devaney also was a central figure in developing this work. A fine geographer and writer, he contributed much of the original research and writing in Appendix A, Welcome to California.

A number of real estate professionals contributed their good ideas and constructive criticisms. Recognizing that they don't necessarily agree with some of our conclusions or points of emphasis, many thanks to John Murphy, Guy Berry, John Pinto, Terry Moerler, Rob Bader, Judy Cranston, Shel Givens, Elizabeth Hughes, Donald Pearman (author of *The Termite Report*), Martin Reutinger, Temmy Walker, Gene Fama, Robert Jackson, and Judy Rydell.

Our heartfelt thanks to all those house buyers who shared their purchase experiences with us. Many of their stories appear throughout the book, though sometimes slightly edited and with fictitious names. Contributors (and general reviewers) include Mack Babitt, Mike and Carmella Boschetti, Valerie Brown, David Cole, the late Steve Elias, Jo and Don Gallo, Mary Glaeser, Rose Green, Barry Gustin, Ann Heron, Barbara Hodovan, Wendy Lewis, Jackie and Tony Mancuso, Ken Norwood, Mary Randolph, Barbara Kate Repa, and Ed Shelton.

Thanks, too, to Twila Slesnick, Ph.D., enrolled agent, for information on borrowing against retirement plans; Adrianne Peixotto, personal insurance specialist with ProInsurance; and Mike Mansel, certified insurance counselor; Michael Cohen, Berkeley-based loan broker with Schnell Investment Company; Marjo Diehl, loan agent with RPM Mortgage in Alamo, California; Kathy Fuller, loan adviser with RPM Mortgage in Orinda, California; Mark Adams, senior escrow officer at First American Title Company in San Francisco; Sue Giesberg of the California Attorney General's Office; Xavier Guerrero, senior exam policy analyst, Internal Revenue Service, for tax information; David

Meyers, real estate editor of the *Los Angeles Times;* Susan Tubbesing, executive director of the Earthquake Engineering Research Institute in Oakland; and Brian Moggan, senior loan officer at Union Trust Mortgage Services, Inc.

Special thanks to Terri Hearsh, whose creative book design, financial savvy, and cheerful nature made a tremendous difference to this book.

Finally, the work of several prominent real estate writers especially inspired us, including Peter G. Miller, Jack Reed, and Leigh Robinson, and the late Robert Bruss.

Dedications

To Carol Serkes, who showed me how to buy a home when I'd only known how to acquire houses.

To Snidely and Gouger, furry felines and now just beloved memories, who kept me company in the wee hours of the night and helped give birth to the book by sleeping on the manuscript whenever possible; and Lucy The Cat who diligently helped in the revisions on previous editions, plopping herself on my chest whenever I'd lie down on the sofa.

To those of you willing to open your mind to new ideas, especially when your friends tell you that you're dreaming. At 20, I had my entire life planned; at 40, I had no idea what opportunities lay ahead! I'm now past 60 (and 60 is the new 30!). The day after Thanksgiving a few years ago, Puddy Maximus, our cat, strolled away—we did all we could to find her, but she seems to have adopted a new family. It was time to give another fur person a new home, and so Baby T came into our lives to join her sister, Poudini (the escape artist).

So our four-legged children continue to rule the roost, the garden is blooming, a 15" MacBook Pro is our tool of choice, and we continue to live a wonderful life in Berkeley, California, the center of the universe.

Thanks to John and Ellen Pinto, pioneers and experts in the field of buyer brokerage. John and Ellen have also set the standard for living La Dolce Vita.

And thanks to Al Gore for inventing the Internet. Without it, I would have never been able to create Berkeleyhomes.com and Berkeleyhomes.com/blog.

—Ira Serkes

To my daughter and Realtor-associate extraordinaire, Annemarie Devine Kurpinsky.

—George Devine

About the Authors

Ira Serkes is a Berkeley Realtor and broker with Pacific Union/Christie's International Real Estate. He and his wife, Carol, represent Berkeley, Albany, Kensington, El Cerrito, Rockridge, Piedmont, and other (San Francisco) East Bay home buyers and sellers, and offer nationwide referrals to other buyer brokers (email ira@berkeleyhomes.com). Both Ira and Carol have been awarded the certified residential specialist (CRS) designation by the National Association of Realtors. This is the highest professional designation of residential specialty in the industry. Ira is also a certified luxury home marketing specialist (CHLMS), an accredited buyer representative (ABR®), seniors real estate specialist (SRES®), and one of the first 500 Realtors to receive the electronic real estate professional certification (e-PRO) designation. He is coauthor of *Get the Best Deal When Selling Your Home*, is an Allen Hainge CyberStar of the year, and hosts neighborhood information, homes for sale, his amazing super-moon-over-Berkeley photograph, videos, and social networking connections at berkeleyhomes.com and berkeleyhomes.com/blog.

George Devine was, until his recent passing, a licensed real estate broker and a widely respected educator in the real estate field. He earned a B.A. from the University of San Francisco and an M.A. from Marquette University and pursued additional studies at San Francisco State University, Seton Hall University, Fordham University, New York University, and the University of California at Berkeley. He taught real estate at the School of Management at the University of San Francisco, where he was named outstanding adjunct professor. He was also the author and principal instructor of a course on San Francisco rent control for New Technologies Institute and taught at Seton Hall University, Marquette University, Manhattan College, and St. John's University.

George authored Nolo's *For Sale by Owner in California,* and for several years wrote the popular "Real Estate Handbook" column in the weekly Real Estate Guide section of the *San Francisco Progress.* He served on a California state task force to study the code of ethics and professional conduct for real estate licensees, and on another concerning real estate continuing education.

Ilona Bray is an author and legal editor at Nolo, specializing in real estate, immigration law, and nonprofit fundraising. She is a member of the National Association of Real Estate Editors (NAREE) and coauthor of *Nolo's Essential Guide to Buying Your First Home*,
First-Time Landlord: Your Guide to Renting Out a Single-Family Home, and numerous other top-selling books. Bray also blogs about real estate at Nolo.com.

Bray's working background includes solo practice, nonprofit, and corporate stints, as well as long periods of volunteering, including an internship at Amnesty International's main legal office in London. She received an A.B. in philosophy from Bryn Mawr College and her law degree and a master's degree in East Asian (Chinese) Studies from the University of Washington.

Table of Contents

Your Legal Companion to Buying a Home in California 1

1 Describe Your Dream Home 3

You Know the House You Want to Buy 4

Don't Be Talked Into Buying the Wrong House 4

Identify Your Ideal House Profile 5

Create a House Priorities Worksheet 8

Prepare a House Comparison Worksheet 11

2 How Much House Can You Afford? 15

The Basics of Determining Housing Affordability 16

Prepare a Family Financial Statement 18

How Much Down Payment Will You Make? 21

Estimate the Mortgage Interest Rate You'll Likely Pay 23

Calculate How Much House You Can Afford 24

Tips on Improving Your Financial Profile 25

Get Loan Preapproval 33

3 Narrowing the Affordability Gap: How to Afford Buying a House 35

Why California Houses Are Expensive 36

Rent and Wait? 36

Fix Up the House You Already Own 39

Strategies for Buying an Affordable House 41

4 Raising Money for Your Down Payment 71

Assisted No and Low Down Payment Plans 72

Five and Ten Percent Down Payment Mortgages 73

Will You Have to Buy Private Mortgage Insurance? 73

How Much Should Your Down Payment Be?..75

Using Equity in an Existing House as a Down Payment
on a New One 77

Using a Gift to Help With the Down Payment................................77

Borrowing Down Payment Money From a Relative or Friend......80

Is It a Gift or a Loan? Sometimes It Pays to Be Vague.................80

Borrowing From Your 401(k) Plan 81

Tapping Into Your IRA...82

5   Working With Real Estate Professionals....................................83

Best and Worst Aspects of Working With a Real Estate Professional........84

Who Your Real Estate Agent Really Works For 90

Hiring an Agent by the Hour..93

Finding a Good Agent 93

How Not to Find an Agent...98

Getting Rid of a Broker or Agent You Don't Like 100

6   How to Find a House 103

The Best Time to Look for Houses 104

Organizing Your House Search 104

Where to Look for Houses... 105

Use an Agent With Good Technical Skills 110

Enlist the Help of Personal Contacts.. 111

Finding a House When You're New to an Area............................. 114

Finding a Newly Built House 116

7   New Houses, Developments, and Condominiums........................ 117

Pitfalls and Pluses of Buying a New House 118

Choose the Developer, Then the House... 121

Using a Real Estate Agent or Broker 123

Financing a New House 124

Optional Add-Ons and Upgrades... 126

Choosing Your Lot 132

Restrictions on the Use of Your Property: CC&Rs......................... 134

Dealing With Delays 139

Inspect the House Before Closing 142

Guarantees and Warranties 143

8 Financing Your House: An Overview 145

How Mortgage Lenders Think 146

Who Lends Mortgage Money? 147

Standardized Loans: Fannie Mae, Freddie Mac,
  and the Secondary Mortgage Market 147

Mortgage Types 148

Comparing Fixed Rate and Adjustable Rate Mortgages 149

The Cost of Getting a Loan 150

Which Mortgage Is Best for You? 152

9 Fixed Rate Mortgages 155

Should You Choose a Fixed Rate Mortgage If You Can Afford One? 156

Not All Fixed Rate Mortgages Are the Same: Points,
  Interest Rates, and Other Variables 157

Mortgages Lengths and Payment Schedules 158

10 Adjustable Rate Mortgages 161

When Should You Finance With an ARM? 162

Loan and Payment Caps 163

ARM Indices and Margins 163

Assumability 165

Hybrid Adjustable Rate Mortgage 165

Summing Up—What Good ARMs Look Like 166

11 Government-Assisted Loans 167

Veterans Affairs Loans 168

Federal Housing Administration Financing 170

California Housing Finance Agency Programs 172

CalVet Loans 172

Down Payment Assistance Programs (DAP) 173

12 Private Mortgages..175
Advantages of Private Mortgages............................176
Getting a Loan From Friends or Relatives...............177
Shared Equity Transactions......................................182
Second Mortgages—Financing by Sellers...............182
Second Mortgages—Financing by Private Parties
    Other Than the Seller..184

13 Obtaining a Mortgage...187
Gather Information on Mortgage Rates and Fees.....188
Researching Mortgages Online.................................188
Work With a Mortgage Broker..................................189
Interview Lenders..191
Credit and Income Preapproval................................192
Get the House Appraised..194

14 Buying a House When You Already Own One.......195
Check the Housing Market Carefully........................197
How to Briefly Own Two Houses...............................200
Tax Breaks for Selling Your Home............................203

15 What Will You Offer?...207
How a Contract Is Formed..208
Decide What You Will Offer.......................................208
What Is the Advertised Price?...................................209
How Much Can You Afford?......................................211
What Are Prices of Comparable Houses?.................211
Is the Local Real Estate Market Hot or Cold?...........213
Is the House Itself Hot or Cold?...............................214
What Are the Seller's Needs?....................................215
Is the House Uniquely Valuable to You?...................216
How Much Are You Willing to Pay?...........................216
Making the Final Price Decision...............................217
Other Ways to Make Your Offer Attractive...............217

16 Putting Your Offer in Writing.. 221

What Makes an Offer Legally Valid... 222

How California Offers and Counteroffers Are Made................................... 223

What Your Purchase Agreement Should Cover... 224

17 Presenting Your Offer and Negotiating.. 239

Notify the Seller of Your Offer.. 240

Present Your Offer..243

The Seller's Response to Your Offer... 244

Negotiate by Counteroffers 250

An Offer Is Accepted—A Contract Is Formed 252

Revoking an Offer or Counteroffer 252

Making a Backup Offer 252

18 After the Contract Is Signed:
Escrow, Contingencies, and Insurance.. 255

Open Escrow... 256

Remove Contingencies.. 262

Obtain Homeowners' Insurance..271

Obtain Title Report and Title Insurance.. 279

Conduct Final Physical Inspection of Property.. 282

Closing Escrow.. 286

19 Check Out a House's Condition.. 289

Evolution of California's Disclosure Requirements....................................... 290

Real Estate Transfer Disclosure Statement... 291

Natural Hazard Disclosure Statement... 303

Earthquake and Seismic Disclosures 306

Environmental Hazards 307

Lead... 308

Disclosure of Deaths... 308

Disclosure of Military Ordnance... 309

Local Disclosures... 309

Inspecting the Property Yourself...310

Arranging Professional Inspections...311

Are the Repairs Really Needed?...321

Who Pays for Defects?...322

Ask for a Home Warranty...322

20 Legal Ownership: How to Take Title.......................................325

One Unmarried Person..326

Two or More Unmarried People..326

Couple or Domestic Partners Owning Together..331

Married Person Owning Alone..335

Partnership...336

Avoiding Having the Property Go Through Probate....................................339

21 If Something Goes Wrong During Escrow............................341

The Seller Backs Out...342

The Seller Refuses to Move Out...342

You Back Out...343

The Seller Dies..344

You Discover a Defect in the Property...344

The House Is Destroyed by Natural Disaster
(Fire, Earthquake, Flood)...345

House-Hungry Martians Take Possession of the House............................345

Finding a Lawyer..346

Appendixes

A Welcome to California..349

Climate and Geography..350

Natural Hazards..352

Pollution...357

Nuclear Plants...360

Schools..360

Traffic..362

Crime...363

B Real Estate Websites... 367

Top Real Estate Websites.. 368

How to Find a California Statute Online 375

C Planning Your Move... 377

Tax-Deductible Moving Expenses and Costs of Sale... 378

Moving Checklist: Two Weeks Before Moving.. 379

Things to Remember While Packing.. 380

Who Should Get Changes of Address.. 381

Things to Do After Moving In 382

D Using the Downloadable Forms... 383

Editing RTFs.. 384

List of Forms 385

Index.. 387

Your Legal Companion to Buying a Home in California

Buying a house should be fun. A good house not only provides shelter, warmth, and a place to lay your head, it has the potential to come to life and be a true friend to you and your family.

Unfortunately, locating an affordable California house that suits your needs isn't always easy. And even if you find your dream house, that's only the first step to making it yours: You must still bargain with the seller for favorable terms, arrange for a good deal on a mortgage, have the house inspected for physical defects, and make decisions regarding dozens of other potentially daunting issues.

This book gives you the information you need to understand how California houses are negotiated over, financed, inspected, and, finally, purchased. If you've previously bought a house in another part of the United States, the lessons you've learned may be helpful—or may be misleading. While the fundamentals of home sales are similar nationwide, California's fast growth and geographic diversity have resulted in many unique and surprising home sale customs. Some of these even vary regionally within the state of California.

Some of the concerns that may be on your mind, however, are universal. Maybe you're worried you won't be able to afford a decent house, or you'll pay too much. Or perhaps you wonder whether the dings on your credit record will keep you from getting a loan, whether you'll be taken advantage of by aggressive real estate salespeople, or that you'll hit hard times and be foreclosed on.

Fortunately, this book will help you educate yourself about the process, and overcome those fears. But first, you must commit yourself to doing three things:

- **Understand all the important aspects of the purchase process.** That's what this book is all about—giving you a thorough, practical discussion of the steps necessary to find and purchase a California house. We recommend reading this whole book, so you can take informed action on dozens of matters, such as finding a suitable agent, deciding how big a down payment you can afford, choosing the best mortgage, and arranging for an inspection that will reveal hidden problems.

- **Be patient.** By learning all the house-buying basics, you can plan carefully so that you will have time on your side at each stage of the purchase process—and for the sale of your old house, if you have one. Being relaxed while others are anxious and hurried is often the key to saving money.
- **Trust yourself.** The traditional approach to buying a house is to trust brokers, agents, mortgage lenders, and other "experts" to protect your interests. While many good, helpful people work in real estate, even the good ones must navigate potential conflicts of interest that are part of the purchase process. No one knows how to meet your needs better than you do. Draw on their advice, but don't blindly follow their lead.

Whether you're looking for a luxury beachfront home in Southern California, a bungalow in the San Francisco Bay Area, or an affordable new build in Fresno, this book shows you how to buy a house in California.

Get Worksheets, Updates, and More Online

This book offers various worksheets to help you with the homebuying process, such as a House Priorities Worksheet and a Family Financial Statement. They're not only shown within the book, but can be downloaded from Nolo's website.

When there are important changes to the information in this book, we'll also post updates online. To find these items, go to a page dedicated to this book:

www.nolo.com/back-of-book/BHCA.html

You'll find other useful information there, too, including author blogs and articles on related topics.

Describe Your Dream Home

You Know the House You Want to Buy 4

Don't Be Talked Into Buying the Wrong House 4

Identify Your Ideal House Profile 5

    Must Haves: Mandatory Priorities 7

    Hope to Haves: Secondary Priorities 7

    Absolute No Ways 8

Create a House Priorities Worksheet 8

Prepare a House Comparison Worksheet 11

You Know the House You Want to Buy

Given your family's needs, tastes, and finances, you probably already have a good idea of the type of house you want. We'll therefore skip the typical first chapter in home buyers' books, in which the author compares such things as the joys of living on a dusty road in outer suburbia to the convenience of living in a townhouse in a major city. If you haven't already thought these things through, you may need to do some critical self-evaluation before beginning your home search.

> **SKIP AHEAD**
> **Already found the house you want and mainly interested in the ins and outs of financing?** Skip ahead to Chapter 2, "How Much House Can You Afford?"

Don't Be Talked Into Buying the Wrong House

Many California buyers face an affordability gap between the house they'd like to buy and the one they can afford. "After years of declining prices, California has become a strong seller's market," says Ira Serkes. Without an organized house-buying approach, you might be talked into compromising on the wrong house by friends, relatives, a real estate agent, or even yourself.

"Not me. I know my own mind," you say. "Don't be too sure," we reply. Every day, confident and knowledgeable home seekers become so anxious and disoriented that they leap into deals they later come to regret.

Here is our method to ensure that you buy a house you'll enjoy living in:

- Firmly establish your priorities before looking at houses.
- Insist that any house you offer to buy meets at least your most important priorities (even if you must compromise in other areas).

In the following sections, we help you consider a range of house features, establish your priorities, and compare potential houses.

Tips on Searching New Places

Perhaps you've heard it said that choosing a house's location wisely is as important as picking a good house. In a state the size of California, it's a vast understatement to say you have a lot of locations to choose from. To help you think about specific California areas, we include Appendix A, "Welcome to California."

Despite the title, Welcome to California isn't meant only for newcomers to the state. Whether you're a San Franciscan moving closer to a San Ramon job, a New Yorker relocating to Los Angeles, or simply someone unfamiliar with certain California areas, you'll find a wealth of information. In addition, in Chapter 5 we discuss working with a local real estate agent to get essential information on neighborhoods.

But there's still no substitute for your own legwork. Chat with friends and colleagues, walk and drive around neighborhoods, talk to local residents, read local newspapers, check the library's community resources files, visit the local planning department, and do whatever else will help you get a better sense of a neighborhood or city.

Identify Your Ideal House Profile

It's easy to become overwhelmed by the array of home choices, from size to style to floor plan and fixtures. Then, there's the issue of location—houses come in all sorts of neighborhoods, school districts, and potential hazard zones (fire, earthquake, and flood, to name a few). And, of course, price and purchase terms are crucial considerations. To cope with all these and at least a dozen other relevant variables, it's essential to establish your priorities in advance and stick to them.

Identify house features most important to you by completing our Ideal House Profile, which lists all major categories such as upper price limit, number and type of rooms, and location. A sample is shown below.

Ideal House Profile

Upper price limit: $1.3 million
Maximum down payment: $400,000
Special financing needs: N/A

	Must Have	Hope to Have
Neighborhood or location:		
Northern Berkeley	✓	
Near Oxford Street		✓
School needs:		
Berkeley High School	✓	
Desired neighborhood features:		
Quiet street with little traffic	✓	
Walking distance to Solano Avenue	✓	
Neighborhood association		✓
Lots of trees		✓
Length of commute:		
Maximum of 15 minutes drive to Berkeley office	✓	
Access to public transportation:		
Walking distance to S.F. express buses	✓	
Size of house:		
Minimum 1,600 square feet	✓	
Number and type of rooms:		
3 bedrooms/2 baths	✓	
Modern kitchen	✓	
Family room for kids		✓
Eat-in kitchen or breakfast nook		✓
Condition, age, and type of house:		
Good shape, less than 100 years old	✓	
Type of yard and grounds:		
Fenced-in yard	✓	
Private yard		✓
Other desired features:		
Easy parking	✓	
Lots of light		✓
Absolute no ways:		
House in an active or potential slide zone		

FORM

You can download a copy of the Ideal House Profile. Go to the companion Web page for this book; you'll find the URL in Appendix D.

If you're buying with another person, prepare your list of priorities together, so that each person's strong likes and dislikes are respected and you have any arguments before you're with a real estate agent.

Must Haves: Mandatory Priorities

First, use the Ideal House Profile to name what you must have in a house, such as a particular city or neighborhood. Since price is an obvious consideration, fill in the top section first. For example, under *Upper price limit* you might note $800,000, with a *Maximum down payment* of $160,000. Then fill in the rest of the form.

TIP

Pay close attention to the *School needs* category. If you have children, buying a great house at a great price in a lousy school district may mean years of paying for private schools. By contrast, paying more for an okay house in an excellent school district may be a bargain in the long run. And if you plan to move in a few years, it will be easier to sell a house in a good school district, because that feature is important to many potential buyers.

If you have two kids, you might note that three bedrooms, excellent public schools, and a street with lots of children are must haves. If you plan to live in the house after retirement, a minimal number of stairs and short distances to shops and services may be must haves.

Hope to Haves: Secondary Priorities

Once you've compiled your list of must haves, jot down features that you'd like but aren't crucial to your decision of whether to buy. For example, under *Type of yard and grounds,* you might note patio and flat backyard in the Hope to Have column. Or under *Number and type of rooms,* you might list finished basement or master bedroom with bath.

Take a second look at your Must Have column. You may wonder how you will ever afford a house with the features you've listed. Don't despair—at least, not until you understand the strategies (discussed in Chapter 3) to help you buy an affordable house. For now, you might need to change a couple of must haves to hope to haves.

Absolute No Ways

Be sure to list your Absolute No Ways (you will not buy a house that has any of these features) at the bottom of the Ideal House Profile. Avoiding things you'll always hate—such as a house in a flood zone, poor school district, or high-crime area—can be even more important than finding a house that contains all your mandatory priorities.

If you're moving into a new-house development or condominium, think about what rules you can and can't cope with. Its covenants, conditions, and restrictions (CC&Rs) may be quite detailed and restrict everything from the color of your house to your landscaping. (CC&Rs are discussed in more detail in Chapter 7.)

Once you've completed your Ideal House Profile, you're ready to create a House Priorities Worksheet, which will help you see how each house stacks up.

Create a House Priorities Worksheet

Now use the information collected in your Ideal House Profile to create a master House Priorities Worksheet.

Enter the relevant information under each major category—Must Have, Hope to Have, and Absolute No Ways. A sample is shown below.

FORM

You can download a copy of the House Priorities Worksheet. Go to the companion Web page for this book; you'll find the URL in Appendix D.

House Priorities Worksheet

Date visited: September 15, 2015   List price: $ 1.2 million

Address: 5 Marin Way, Berkeley

Contact: Jo Tulare, Berkeley Homes   Phone #: 525-5555

Must Have:
- ☑ North Berkeley neighborhood
- ☑ Berkeley High School
- ☐ Quiet street with little traffic
- ☑ Walking distance to Solano Avenue
- ☑ Maximum of 15 minutes drive to Berkeley office
- ☑ Walking distance to S.F. express buses
- ☑ Minimum 1,600 square feet
- ☑ 3 bedrooms/2 baths
- ☐ Modern kitchen
- ☑ Good shape, less than 100 years old
- ☐ Fenced-in yard
- ☑ Easy parking

Hope to Have:
- ☐ Oxford or Spruce Street
- ☑ Neighborhood association
- ☑ Lots of trees
- ☐ Family room for kids
- ☑ Eat-in kitchen or breakfast nook
- ☐ Private yard
- ☑ Lots of light
- ☐ _____

Absolute No Ways:
- ☐ House in an active or potential slide zone
- ☐ _____
- ☐ _____

Comments about the particular house:
This house is terrific! Our agents found out there are five other interested bidders, so it will probably go for well above the list price, but well worth trying for. Street is pretty busy, but the house and location meet most of our needs. Neighbors seem very nice.

Once you have completed your House Priorities Worksheet to your (and your partner's) satisfaction, make several copies to carry with you on home visits.

For each house you see, fill in the top of the House Priorities Worksheet. As you walk around and talk to the owner or agent, enter a check mark if the house has a desirable or undesirable feature. Also, make notes next to a particular feature if it can be changed to meet your needs (for example, an okay kitchen that could be modernized for $45,000).

Don't Be Fooled by Staged Homes

House "staging" is now a regular practice in home sales. The right paint, furniture, music, and smells can create illusions that would make Martha Stewart and Houdini jealous. Furniture is often extra small to make the house look large. The point is to optimize the charms of a house. As Carol Serkes says, "No one ever watches TV in a staged home."

Also, notes coauthor Ira Serkes, "Your first impression of the home is likely to come from online photos; but keep in mind that one reason sellers stage their homes is that photos of staged homes look far better than those of vacant ones."

So if you visit a house that just reeks of charm—look behind, above, and below. Imagine it empty, or with your own furniture, office equipment, kids' toys, and toothbrushes.

Add comments at the bottom, such as "potential undeveloped lot next door" or "neighbors seem friendly." If you look at a lot of houses, taking notes such as these will help make sure you don't forget important information.

You should seriously consider only those houses with all or most of your must haves and none of your no ways. If you visit a nice, reasonably priced house that doesn't come close to matching your list and can't be easily changed to do so, say no. Take the time to find a more suitable house; you'll be glad you did.

TIP

Set up a good filing system. Failing to adopt a good system may lead to revisiting houses you've already seen and rejected or making decisions based on half-remembered facts. For each house that seems like a possible prospect, make a file that includes a completed House Priorities Worksheet, the information materials provided when you toured the home, the Multiple Listing Service information, ads, and your notes. Or, set up a simple database with key details on each house you visit. (For advice, see "Organizing Your House Search" in Chapter 6.)

Prepare a House Comparison Worksheet

If, like many people, you look at a considerable number of houses over an extended period of time—or even in the space of a week—you may soon have trouble distinguishing or comparing their features. That's where our House Comparison Worksheet comes in.

Across the top of the form, list the addresses of the three or four houses you like best. In the left column, fill in your list of priorities and no ways from your Ideal House Profile and House Priorities Worksheet. Then put a check mark on the line under each house that has that feature to allow for a quick comparison.

A sample is shown below.

FORM

You can download a copy of the House Comparison Worksheet.
Go to the companion Web page for this book; you'll find the URL in Appendix D.

House Comparison Worksheet

House 1 __257 Loving Avenue, Berkeley__

House 2 __1415 Gaylord Street, Berkeley__

House 3 __999 Spruce Street, Berkeley__

House 4 __5 Marin Way, Berkeley__

	1	2	3	4
Must have:				
North Berkeley neighborhood	✓	✓	✓	✓
Berkeley High School	✓	✓	✓	✓
Quiet street with little traffic	✓	✓		
Walking distance to Solano Avenue		✓	✓	✓
Maximum of 15 minutes drive to Berkeley office	✓		✓	✓
Walking distance to S.F. express buses	✓			✓
Minimum 1,600 square feet	✓	✓		✓
3 bedrooms/2 baths	✓	✓		✓
Modern kitchen			✓	
Good shape, less than 100 years old		✓		✓
Fenced-in yard	✓	✓	✓	
Easy parking			✓	✓
Hope to have:				
Oxford or Spruce Street		✓		
Neighborhood association		✓	✓	
Lots of trees	✓		✓	✓
Family room for kids	✓			
Eat-in kitchen or breakfast nook	✓	✓	✓	
Private yard	✓	✓	✓	
Lots of light		✓	✓	✓
Absolute no ways:				
House in an active or potential slide zone	✓	✓	✓	

True
Story

Ellen: How Not to Buy a House

I was a first-time buyer on a relatively tight budget when I set out to buy an older, attached row house in San Francisco. I wanted two bedrooms, no (or a very small) yard, proximity to a downtown bus route, and walking access to a neighborhood market and bookstore. I looked for many months at houses that were completely unsuitable, far too expensive, or, with depressing regularity, both. So I broadened my search by reading the classifieds. When I saw that prices were more reasonable in the suburbs, I spent a sunny Sunday afternoon browsing in Contra Costa County.

At the first open house I visited, I met an energetic real estate agent who spun a wonderful word picture of the joys of suburban life: lots of sun, room for a tomato garden, and friendly neighbors. She showed me a split-level house with an apple tree in full bloom in my price range. Almost before I realized what I was doing, I signed on the bottom line.

That was the fun part. Soon I was getting up at 6:00 a.m., driving to the train station, and standing for the 40-minute ride to San Francisco. My fantasy about the joy of suburban life was just that. It's hard to believe now, but I seemed to have temporarily overlooked the fact that I'm allergic to direct sun, detest tomatoes, and moved out of the suburbs to get away from overly involved neighbors.

Fortunately, I sold the house six months later, at a small profit. I went in with a friend and together we bought a house in San Francisco that meets my needs perfectly.

How Much House Can You Afford?

The Basics of Determining Housing Affordability 16

Prepare a Family Financial Statement 18

How Much Down Payment Will You Make? 21

Estimate the Mortgage Interest Rate You'll Likely Pay 23

Calculate How Much House You Can Afford 24

Tips on Improving Your Financial Profile 25

    Pay Off Debts 25

    Convert Assets to Cash 27

    Emphasize Imminent Income Raises 28

    If You Work for Yourself, Show a Profit or Make a Big Down Payment 28

    Borrow From Friends or Family 29

    Check Your Credit Rating and Clean Up Your File 29

Get Loan Preapproval 33

t's essential to determine how much you can afford to pay before you look for a house—first off, for your own planning and peace of mind. Crunching a few numbers is also important, however, to help you be either cautious when lenders offer you larger loans than you should realistically take on or assertive with lenders who don't realize that you're a better credit risk than your records show.

> **SKIP AHEAD**
> **If money is no object or you already know how much house you can afford, skip this chapter.**

Like most readers, you will find this chapter useful to:
- help you determine your price range before you go house hunting, and
- explain some techniques that experienced mortgage brokers use to help borrowers qualify for loans from banks or other lenders.

The Basics of Determining Housing Affordability

As a broad generalization, most people can afford to purchase a house worth about three times their total (gross) annual income, assuming a 20% down payment and a moderate amount of other long-term debts. With no other debts, they can afford a house worth up to four or five times their annual income.

A much more accurate way to determine how much house you can afford is to compare your monthly carrying costs plus your monthly payments on other long-term debts to your gross (total) monthly income. Carrying costs are the money needed to make a monthly payment (both principal and interest) plus one-twelfth of the yearly bill for property taxes and homeowners' insurance. In real estate industry jargon, monthly carrying costs are often referred to as "PITI" (pronounced "pity"), which stands for principal, interest, taxes, and insurance.

How Credit Scores Affect Loan Qualification

When reviewing loan applications and making financing decisions, lenders will look at a prospective homebuyer's credit score and sometimes also review the homebuyer's credit report. While many companies provide credit scores, most lenders use the FICO score. They usually request your FICO score from each of the three nationwide credit reporting agencies—Equifax, Experian, and Transunion.

Your FICO score is a numerical calculation that's supposed to predict how likely you are to default on credit obligations. Scores are based on information contained in your credit report, including your history of paying bills on time, outstanding debt (how much debt you have compared to your credit limit), how long you've been using credit (the longer the better), whether you've applied for new credit recently, and the types of credit you have (a mix is good). Scores don't take into account your race, national origin, gender, marital status, age, religion, income, employment status, or where you live.

In 2012, FICO introduced the FICO Mortgage Score. Some lenders may use this instead of, or in addition to, your regular FICO scores. The goal of the FICO Mortgage Score is to capture more information than does the regular FICO score, such as child support payments, rental payments, and other information gleaned from public records.

FICO scores range from 300 to 850. A high score means you are a low risk for default—so the higher the score, the better. If you routinely pay your bills late, have defaulted on debts, or otherwise have a poor credit history, expect a low score. If you have a low score, a lender might reject your loan application, require a high down payment, or offer you a loan with a relatively high interest rate.

Be sure to check your credit report so that you can clean up or fix any errors (remember, your credit score is based on information in your report). (How to do this is discussed below.) You can get a free copy of your credit report from each of the nationwide credit reporting agencies at www.annualcreditreport.com. In California, credit reporting agencies must provide you with your credit score if you request it. (Cal. Civ. Code Ann. § 1785.15.1.)

Assuming you have a decent credit score, lenders traditionally want your regular monthly payments (of all kinds) to total less than 36% of your gross monthly income. (Your credit score is a numerical measure that reflects how well you've managed credit in the past.) The lower your other monthly debts, the more of your 36% can be applied to your mortgage payment.

Using these percentages, if your monthly income is $4,000, you should not pay more than $1,440 (0.36 x $4,000) toward your debts. This is called the "debt-to-income ratio."

Some lenders will accept a higher debt-to-income ratio if you'll take a less-attractive loan, such as one with a higher-than-market interest rate or higher-than-usual points. (Points are an up-front loan fee figured as a percentage of the loan, discussed in Chapter 8.)

 TIP

Here's what the California Association of Realtors (CAR) says you can afford: According to CAR's statistics for the first quarter of 2016, the minimum household income needed to purchase a median-priced home costing $465,280 in California was $97,571 based on obtaining a 30-year fixed rate mortgage at 4.01% interest and paying 20% down. (Of course, typical homes may cost more or less than that amount within the area of California where you're looking.)

Prepare a Family Financial Statement

The first step in determining the purchase price you can afford is to prepare a Family Financial Statement, which should include:

- your monthly income
- your monthly expenses, and
- your net worth (assets minus liabilities).

(We use the word "family" as shorthand for the economic unit that will buy a house. For our purposes, an unmarried couple or a single person is just as much a family as a married couple with ten kids.)

Below is a sample Family Financial Statement.

Family Financial Statement

	Borrower	Coborrower
Name and address:	_____	_____
Home phone number:	_____	_____
Email address:	_____	_____
Employer's name & address:	_____	_____
Work phone number:	_____	_____

WORKSHEET 1: INCOME AND EXPENSES

	Borrower ($)	Coborrower ($)	Total ($)
I. INCOME			
A. Monthly gross income			
1. Employment	_____	_____	_____
2. Public benefits	_____	_____	_____
3. Dividends	_____	_____	_____
4. Royalties	_____	_____	_____
5. Interest & other investment income	_____	_____	_____
6. Other (specify):	_____	_____	_____
B. Total monthly gross income	_____	_____	_____
II. MONTHLY EXPENSES	_____	_____	_____
A. Nonhousing	_____	_____	_____
1. Child care	_____	_____	_____
2. Clothing & personal expenses	_____	_____	_____
3. Food	_____	_____	_____
4. Insurance (auto, life, medical, & dental)	_____	_____	_____
5. Medical & dental care (not insurance)	_____	_____	_____
6. Taxes (nonhousing)	_____	_____	_____
7. Education	_____	_____	_____
8. Transportation	_____	_____	_____
9. Other (specify):	_____	_____	_____
B. Current housing	_____	_____	_____
1. Mortgage payment or rent	_____	_____	_____
2. Taxes	_____	_____	_____
3. Insurance	_____	_____	_____
4. Utilities	_____	_____	_____
C. Total monthly expenses	_____	_____	_____

WORKSHEET 2: ASSETS AND LIABILITIES

	Borrower ($)	Coborrower ($)	Total ($)
I. ASSETS (Cash or Market Value)			
A. Cash & cash equivalents			
1. Cash			
2. Deposits (list):			
B. Marketable securities			
1. Stocks & bonds (bid price)			
2. Other securities			
3. Mutual funds			
4. Life insurance			
5. Other (specify):			
C. Total cash & marketable securities			
D. Nonliquid assets			
1. Real estate			
2. Retirement funds			
3. Business			
4. Motor vehicles			
5. Other (specify):			
E. Total nonliquid assets			
F. Total all assets			
II. LIABILITIES			
A. Debts			
1. Real estate loans			
2. Student loans			
3. Motor vehicle loans			
4. Child or spousal support			
5. Personal loans			
6. Credit cards (specify):			
7. Other (specify):			
B. Total liabilities			
III. NET WORTH (Total assets minus total liabilities)			

 CAUTION

This statement is solely for you. No matter how much debt a lender ultimately says you can handle, this form's purpose is to help you develop your own realistic picture of what buying a house will mean for your monthly cash flow. The information you collect will help you fill out your loan application, but you won't give this statement directly to the lender. So now is not the time to exaggerate your income or underestimate your expenses—you'll only be fooling yourself. (And if you were to compound your error by putting incorrect information on your actual loan application, you'd be committing fraud against the lender.)

FORM

You can download a copy of the Family Financial Statement. Go to the companion Web page for this book; you'll find the URL in Appendix D.

How Much Down Payment Will You Make?

The larger the percentage of the total price of a house you can put down, the easier it will likely be for you to qualify for a mortgage and find a willing seller.

As we discuss below, the monthly mortgage payment (plus taxes and insurance) is the major factor in determining the purchase price of the house you can afford. And with a higher down payment, those payments are lower. That also means that the lender's financial interests are better protected: If you default on your mortgage (which is less likely anyway, because the payment is more affordable), a lender has more room to sell the property and recover its investment.

For now, you need down payment money. How much do you have by way of liquid and nonliquid assets? If you have a house or another property you plan to sell, estimate what you're likely to receive after subtracting costs of sale. If necessary, think about other ways to reasonably raise cash.

Can you liquidate other assets or get a gift or loan from a relative or friend? (These and other money-raising techniques are discussed in Chapter 4.)

Once you've calculated the total amount of your liquid assets, do a quick and dirty calculation of how much home you can afford. Start by assuming that you'll pour all these assets into the standard 20% down payment. For example, if you've got $120,000 in assets, that would work as a 20% down payment on a $600,000 home.

But, as we said, these calculations are quick and dirty—you'll never be able to pour all your liquid assets into the down payment, because this would leave you nothing for closing costs and financial reserves. Closing costs can vary from approximately 2% to 5% of the purchase price. And, a lender will want to see that you have at least two to three months of reserve money left over after you've bought the house, so yours may insist that you spend less on a down payment to achieve this. (However, reserve money doesn't have to be liquid; it can also be in the form of retirement money.)

You'll likely need to fiddle with the figures a bit to arrive at a realistic combination of down payment, closing costs, and home price. If a 20% down payment would deplete your resources, look into government-assisted loans, discussed in Chapter 11.

Remember, in addition to the down payment, you must be able to afford the monthly mortgage, insurance, and property tax payments. If your income is relatively low, it may actually help if you increase your down payment to 25%–30% of the price of a house, to bring down the monthly payments.

If, however, you have both a good income and enough money set aside for a larger-than-required down payment, you have a choice: You can put more money into the down payment or invest it elsewhere. We discuss your options in Chapter 4.

Once you've completed your Family Financial Statement and done the basic calculations described above, you should have a good sense of what-priced a house you can realistically hope to buy.

Estimate the Mortgage Interest Rate You'll Likely Pay

Over the life of your mortgage, you will probably pay as much or more in interest as you will in principal. A relatively small difference in interest rate will amount to a big difference in your total debt, and hence the amount of your monthly payments.

	Paying Back a $100,000 Fixed Rate Loan:			
	Monthly and Total Amounts			
	15-year period		30-year period	
Interest Rate (%)	Mo. pmt.	Total pmts.	Mo. pmt.	Total pmts.
3.0	691	124,304	422	151,777
3.5	715	128,679	449	161,656
4.0	740	133,144	477	171,870
4.5	765	137,699	454	212,335
5.0	790.80	142,344	536.83	193,259
5.5	817.09	147,076	567.79	204,404
6.0	843.86	151,895	599.56	215,842
6.5	871.11	156,799	632.07	227,544
7.0	898.83	161,789	665.30	239,509
7.5	927.01	166,862	699.21	251,717
8.0	955.65	172,017	733.76	264,155
8.5	984.74	177,253	768.91	276,809
9.0	1,014.27	182,569	804.62	298,664
9.5	1,044.22	187,960	840.85	302,708

The table above illustrates the differences by interest rate and mortgage term, using the example of a $100,000 mortgage. (Simply subtract $100,000 from the numbers in the "Total pmts." columns to see the total interest owed.) Even at 5% interest, you would end up paying over $93,000 in interest!

Because different mortgage types carry different interest rates, start by deciding the mortgage type you want. If you haven't yet decided, read Chapters 8–12 for a thorough review of mortgage options.

Calculate How Much House You Can Afford

When you have a pretty good idea of the size of your down payment and the interest rate you expect to pay, you can calculate how much house you can afford.

The easiest way to do that is to use an online calculator, like those listed in "Website Resource" below. These calculators use your income and debts, along with the basic terms of the mortgage you expect or hope to get, to determine how much you can afford to borrow.

If you'd rather do the calculation yourself, follow the steps below:

1. **Estimate the amount you need to borrow.** First, you'll have to estimate the purchase price for the home you hope to buy. Reduce that by the amount of the down payment you expect to make (hopefully 20%). That's the amount you'll need to borrow.

2. **Estimate your monthly mortgage payment.** Begin by estimating the mortgage interest rate you expect to pay, based on up-to-date rate information. (See Chapter 13 for a discussion of gathering information on mortgage rates.) Then, using the Amortization Chart below, find the corresponding mortgage factor. Multiply this number by the number of thousands you'll need to borrow. The result is your estimated monthly principal and interest payment.

3. **Estimate insurance and property taxes.** Add the following factors together: homeowners' insurance (expect to pay close to $1,000 per year) and property taxes (approximately 1.2% to 1.8% of the purchase price). Divide that number by 12 to calculate a monthly cost for insurance and taxes.

4. **Estimate other house-related expenses.** If you're making a down payment of less than 20%, estimate monthly payments for "private mortgage insurance" or PMI. (See Chapter 4 for more information on PMI.) Also, if you expect to pay fees to a homeowners' association, estimate that monthly fee. Add these numbers together.

5. **Calculate your other fixed monthly debt.** This should include any other monthly debt you have, such as a car loan, student loan, or credit card debt. Add these monthly debt obligations together.

6. **Add Items 2–5.** These are your monthly expenses.

7. **Estimate lender qualification.** Generally, lenders will allow your monthly mortgage obligation to be up to 0.43 of your gross monthly income (the fewer your debts, and the higher your credit score, the higher the number you use can be).

8. **Divide Item 6 by Item 7.** That number is the amount of monthly gross income you'll need to get the loan that you want. You can multiply that number by 12 to calculate the yearly gross income you'll need to qualify.

Tips on Improving Your Financial Profile

Bringing your housing costs and monthly debts within the generally acceptable debt-to-income range of 28%–36% should allow you to get a home loan. Many people find, however, that it requires more than 36% of their monthly income to make house payments as well as pay their other debts. If you fit this description, here are some ways to bring yourself within the acceptable range.

Pay Off Debts

The best way to improve your debt-to-income ratio is to pay off some debts. Not only will this reduce your total monthly payments and thus, in the eyes of lenders, leave more of your income to be used for mortgage payments, it will also result in other savings.

Amortization Chart
Mortgage Principal & Interest Payment Factors (Per $1,000)

Interest rates (%)	15-year mortgage	30-year mortgage
3.50	7.14	4.49
3.75	7.27	4.63
4.00	7.39	4.77
4.25	7.52	4.91
4.50	7.64	5.06
4.75	7.77	5.21
5.00	7.90	5.36
5.25	8.03	5.52
5.50	8.18	5.68
5.75	8.31	5.84
6.00	8.44	6.00
6.25	8.58	6.16
6.50	8.72	6.33
6.75	8.85	6.49
7.00	8.99	6.65
7.25	9.13	6.82
7.50	9.27	6.99
7.75	9.41	7.16
8.00	9.56	7.34
8.25	9.70	7.51
8.50	9.85	7.69
8.75	9.99	7.87
9.00	10.14	8.05
9.25	10.29	8.23
9.50	10.44	8.41

Because the interest rates on consumer debts (such as credit cards) are almost always higher than the rate on mortgage debts, paying them off first can result in substantial savings. And you'll be shifting your debt to a type that's tax deductible: The interest paid on consumer debts is not tax deductible, while the interest portion of your mortgage is. (For more on the tax deductibility of mortgage interest, see Chapter 4.)

Check with your lender before deciding which (and how much) of your debts to pay off. You don't want to improve your ratio and then discover you've lowered your credit score or wiped out most of your down payment.

Convert Assets to Cash

If you need a few thousand extra dollars to pay off debts or increase your down payment, look for it in your garage, basement, or attic. If you're like most people, you may have many saleable items you don't really need.

Also look at your investments as a source of cash. Consider cashing in whole life insurance policies (if the cash value is significantly high) or withdrawing money from a retirement account or plan.

Online Mortgage and Financial Calculators

Dozens of websites offer calculators to help you determine monthly payments on different-sized mortgages and how much house you can afford. Sample different ones until you find the calculator that gives you the information you're looking for in the format you prefer.

 WEBSITE RESOURCE
Nolo's website has a variety of real estate calculators to help you, at www.nolo.com/legal-calculators. A few others that appear to have staying power are at www.homes.com, www.mortgage101.com, www.quickenloans.com, and www.mortgage-calc.com.

> **TIP**
>
> **Keep records to show "source of funds."** Lenders may suspect that any new savings with a less than two- to three-month history is really a loan.

Emphasize Imminent Income Raises

Lenders commonly require proof that you've been employed, without interruption, for the last two years or so. Exceptions, however, may be made in rare and compelling cases.

For example, if you have just graduated from college, and started a new, salaried position within your field of expertise, a lender may waive the minimum employment requirement. If you worked part-time within the field you're studying, or worked as an intern, it will help to add that to your employment record on the application.

If future raises are given at the discretion of your employer, consider discussing your house purchase with your boss. If the boss believes that your future with the company is bright, he or she may commit to a pay raise now or, in some cases, even arrange for your employer to make you a loan at a lower-than-market rate of interest.

If You Work for Yourself, Show a Profit or Make a Big Down Payment

Millions of Americans work for themselves, or supplement their income by operating small business on the side. Few of these businesses show large taxable profits; rather, most owners take advantage of the Internal Revenue Code rules that make it reasonably easy for small business owners to minimize their taxable earnings. Unfortunately, when a small business owner wishes to borrow money, doing everything legally possible to minimize income for tax purposes is likely to come back to haunt you.

Typically, a small business owner will try to convince a lender that the mere $28,000 of taxable income reported to the IRS was really closer to $50,000, if deductible business expenses such as transportation, meals, a home work space, depreciation, contributions to an IRA or Keogh plan, self-employment tax, contributions to medical insurance, and entertaining are added back in. But this may be difficult to do.

Lenders have heard it all before, and although they may privately acknowledge that an applicant's financial situation is likely to be better than reported to the IRS, they won't normally lend money in this situation unless the buyer can make a down payment of 25% or more. With a high down payment (and excellent credit rating), a borrower may qualify to purchase within accepted debt-to-income ratios even with relatively modest taxable income.

Normally, however, to qualify for a mortgage if your business shows an artificially low profit, you'll need to report a larger taxable profit. If your business really is quite profitable, this should take only a year or two. Instead of writing off every possible personal expense as a business expense while paying yourself a low salary, raise your pay, and treat more expenses as personal. You'll pay more federal income tax, but once you qualify for a mortgage loan, you can cut it back by deducting your mortgage interest and property tax payments.

Borrow From Friends or Family

We discuss ways to raise money from family and friends in Chapter 12, Private Mortgages. For purposes of showing lenders that you're able to make a solid down payment, you'll need an outright gift, or a loan that doesn't need to be paid back for a considerable period of time, and you may need to get it into your bank account a few months (usually three) prior to loan approval. This is called "seasoning" the funds. A lender wants you to have the money necessary to qualify, not to create another debt that will compete for repayment with your mortgage.

A gift made at the time you're purchasing a house requires documentation that it is a gift, not a loan. (See Chapter 4 for a sample gift letter.)

Check Your Credit Rating and Clean Up Your File

Your credit report, in particular your credit score, will affect the type and amount of mortgage loan lenders offer you.

Prospective buyers should check their credit files, kept by credit reporting agencies (also called credit bureaus), before applying for a loan.

Unfortunately, credit files often contain out-of-date or just plain wrong information. Sometimes they confuse names, addresses, Social Security numbers, or employers. If you have a common name (say John Brown), don't be shocked if you find information in your credit file on other John Browns, or John Brownes, or Jon Browns. Obviously, you don't want this incorrect information given to prospective lenders, especially if the person you're being confused with is in worse financial shape than you are.

A few credit problems doesn't mean you'll never get a loan. It may mean that you'll have to pay a higher interest rate or make a larger down payment. Talk to your mortgage broker—it's the best way to find out how or if you'll qualify for a loan.

> **TIP**
>
> **In the past, lenders liberally offered "stated income loans."** To get one, you simply told the lender your annual income, without tax returns or pay stubs to back it up. In exchange, you'd pay a higher interest rate. Don't count on getting one of these loans now. Some borrowers were taking advantage of these "liar loans," artificially inflating their income, and qualifying for large mortgages they later defaulted on. This made lenders pull the plug on such loan options.

How to Get a Copy of Your Credit Report

You can get a free copy of your credit report once a year from each of the three major credit bureaus, which adds up to three free reports per year if you time things right.

You can request your report at www.annual creditreport.com, by phone (877-322-8228), or by mail (Annual Credit Report Request Service, P.O. Box 105281, Atlanta, GA 30348-5281). If you request service by mail, you'll need to include a request form (available on the above website).

You can also contact any of the three major national credit bureaus directly:

- Equifax, www.equifax.com
- Experian, www.experian.com, and

- TransUnion, www.transunion.com.

If you need to request more than one credit report per company in the course of a year, you may need to pay.

You are also entitled to a copy of your credit report for free, however, if:

- You have been denied credit because of information in your credit file. You must request your copy within 60 days of being denied credit.

- You are unemployed and planning to apply for a job within 60 days following your request for your credit report.

- You receive public assistance.

- You believe your credit file contains errors due to someone's fraud, such as opening up accounts by using your name or Social Security number.

How to Correct Errors in Your Credit File

If you find any wrong information, take steps to correct the errors. You have the right to insist that the credit bureau review any wrong, inaccurate, or out-of-date information. Once the credit bureau receives your request, it has 30 days to reinvestigate and tell you its findings. If you need a faster answer, tell them. Items that can't be verified must be removed.

If the credit reporting agency insists on retaining inaccurate, wrong, or outdated information, or lists a debt you refused to pay because of a legitimate dispute with the creditor, you have the right to place a brief statement in your file giving your version of the situation.

How to Clean Up Your Credit

If the information in your file is accurate but unfavorable, your best strategy is to clean up your credit before seriously trying to purchase a house. Here are some tips:

- **Remove delinquencies.** Fully pay off small debts ($500 or less). For larger accounts, contact the creditor and attempt to work out a payment plan so that you're no longer listed as delinquent. Then stay current on the account.

Some creditors you've owed for a while may accept less than the total amount owed as payment in full. A creditor who has given up on collecting may jump at a lump sum payment of two-thirds of what's due. If so, make sure the creditor acknowledges in writing that you've satisfied the debt in full. If the creditor has a court judgment, make sure a "satisfaction of judgment" is filed with the court that issued the judgment. Show the satisfaction of judgment to the credit reporting agency. Be aware that the IRS considers cancelled debt to be income to you, and you may have to pay income taxes on it.

• **As a last resort, get professional assistance.** If you owe several creditors varying sums and can't figure out how much to pay whom, you might contact a nonprofit credit advisory group such as the National Foundation for Credit Counseling (NFCC) at www. nfcc.org. Be warned, however: There are many different consumer credit counseling organizations, and not all are created equal. Some charge high fees for little service. To find out more about consumer credit counseling, visit the National Consumer Law Center at www.nclc.org.

• **Rebuild your credit.** If you've suffered a major financial setback in the past few years (repossessed automobile, judgment against you for a large debt, foreclosed home, or bankruptcy), you'll need to rebuild your credit, unless a creditworthy person will cosign your mortgage loan, you have cash, or you can borrow from friends or family. It normally takes two to three years to rebuild your credit.

CAUTION

Exaggerating or listing bogus information on your loan application won't help anything. A lender can and will check the accuracy of your application. Your falsifications will very likely be discovered and held against you—that is, you could be prosecuted for fraud.

 **RESOURCE**

For information on credit files and rebuilding credit after a financial setback: See *Credit Repair,* by Robin Leonard, J.D. (Nolo).

Get Loan Preapproval

As an essential step toward purchasing a good house at a reasonable price, it's important to be preapproved for a loan. This means (in most cases) that a lender actually does a credit check on you and evaluates your financial situation, rather than simply relying on your own statement about your income and debts. Preapproval means that the lender would actually fund the loan, pending an appraisal of the property, title report, purchase contract, and any last verifications of your employment and financial resources.

Get a preapproval letter as soon as you start househunting. Sellers often accept offers from purchasers who can successfully or quickly close the deal (that is, have already arranged financing and have a preapproval letter), even if they don't make the highest offer. A seller who has had earlier deals fall through because of a buyer's financing problems may simply reject offers not backed by a loan preapproval.

And even if the seller hasn't seen previous deals fall through, his or her real estate agent no doubt has. The agent will be carefully scrutinizing your financial paperwork to make sure that accepting an offer from you won't be more trouble than it's worth.

CAUTION

Preapproval isn't a guarantee. Some buyers who got preapproved have found that their lenders got cold feet at the last minute and demanded lots of extra documentation or simply refused to make the loans.

For preapproval, your lender will ask you to pull together various documents, which usually include:

- pay stubs for the last two pay periods
- your last two years' tax returns and W-2 forms
- proof of nonsalary income, such as rental income or alimony
- three months of bank statements for every account you have (all pages)
- proof of assets such as pension funds, stocks, or life insurance
- the source of your down payment, including documentation for any gift funds involved
- the names, addresses, and phone numbers of your employers for the last two years, and
- the names, addresses, and phone numbers of your landlords for the last two years.

Prequalification Versus Preapproval

As soon as you've completed your financial statement, a lender or loan broker can prepare a prequalification letter saying that loan approval for a specified amount is *likely* based on your income and credit history. Unlike preapproval, however, prequalification is not even close to a commitment by the lender to lend you that amount, or to lend you money at all. Prequalifying will just help you determine how much you're able to borrow and how much you'll need for a down payment and closing costs.

If you are preparing the application yourself, complete every section. Don't leave any blanks. If an item doesn't apply, write "not applicable" or "N/A."

The lender will review and approve your file, subject to some conditions, such as—but not limited to—an acceptable property appraisal, a copy of your purchase contract, and clear title to the property. Your loan officer will review the lender conditions with you to make sure that you will be able to satisfy the lender's requests.

Be ready for follow-up requests right up until the day your house purchase closes. Lenders are still nervous. ●

Narrowing the Affordability Gap: How to Afford Buying a House

Why California Houses Are Expensive 36

Rent and Wait? 36

Fix Up the House You Already Own 39

Strategies for Buying an Affordable House 41

    Don't Buy Until You've Saved More Money 42

    Move to a More Affordable Part of the State 43

    Buy a Less Desirable House Than You Really Want 44

    Buy a Fixer-Upper 47

    Buy a Small House and Add On Later 48

    Buy a House at a Probate Sale 49

    Buy a House With a Structural Problem 51

    Buy a House Subject to Foreclosure 52

    Buy a House With Someone You'll Live With 55

    Buy a House With an Investor's Help 57

    Rent Out Part of the House 58

    Buy a Duplex, Triplex, or House With an In-Law Unit 58

    Lease a House You Can't Afford Now With an Option to Buy Later 60

    Buy a Condominium 63

    Buy a Town House 64

    Buy a Tenant-in-Common (TIC) Interest 64

    Buy Into a Cohousing or Cooperative Arrangement 65

    Buy a House at an Auction 67

SKIP AHEAD

No money worries. Those few readers with enough money to purchase the house of their dreams and no inclination to bargain hunt can safely skip this chapter. The other 99% should stick around and learn how to overcome the affordability gap.

Why California Houses Are Expensive

The concept of the affordability gap is simple—many house buyers can't afford to buy their ideal house. Some can't afford any house at all. The gap, while particularly acute in urban coastal areas of California, exists in many parts of the state, for several reasons:

- Millions of baby boomers have entered their prime house-buying years, creating heavy demand.
- Historically, more people have tended to move to California than leave it.
- Rising construction and lumber costs and, in many areas, restrictive government regulations and taxes, have made it expensive or even impossible, to build new housing.
- Recently, interest rates have been at historic lows, allowing more people to enter the real estate market.
- Houses are looked upon as a relatively sound investment.

Fortunately, as this chapter shows, there are many creative ways Californians have found to beat affordability problems.

Rent and Wait?

If you're happy renting and think you'll continue to be for years, think twice before stretching your finances to the breaking point. In fact, if you live in an area where monthly rents are less than mortgage payments on the same house would be, renting might be a good strategy—though such places have become hard to find.

California House Prices

In late-2016, the median sales price of an existing California single-family detached house was over $500,000, according to the California Association of Realtors. The median price is the middle point of all sales prices, meaning that one-half of all houses sold for more and one-half sold for less. This is different from the average, which is considerably higher (because high-priced luxury homes pull the average up).

In much of the San Francisco Bay Area and Southern California, the median sales price was considerably higher, exceeding $1 million in wealthy communities, such as San Mateo and Marin.

 WEBSITE RESOURCE

For median prices of California houses, see the California Association of Realtors website at www.car.org.

There are advantages to renting: You don't tie up a lot of money in home equity and improvements, and someone else worries about (and pays for) property maintenance, repairs, insurance, and taxes. In addition, putting all your savings toward a house leaves you with no financial cushion to fall back on in case of an emergency.

A principal advantage of renting is that money not tied up in down payments and improvements can be invested in ways that may produce a better long-term return than a house will. Of course, this depends on interest rates and the housing market at the time you buy and sell.

The major disadvantage of renting is that your entire monthly payment vanishes. With home ownership, part of each mortgage payment goes toward equity in your home. The remainder (interest), along with local property taxes, is deductible from your income taxes. People in higher tax brackets obviously have the most to gain (in terms of the largest tax break) by buying a house versus renting.

So, what's the bottom line? Is it better to buy or rent? There's no definitive answer, but the following factors may, depending on your circumstances, tip the balance one way or the other:

- **The shorter the time you plan to stay put, the more financially advantageous it is to rent.** People who buy and sell often incur transaction costs, such as real estate commissions and closing fees. Commonly, a buyer must own a house for at least three to five years, and sometimes longer, for its increase in value to cover these costs. In other words, a home typically has to appreciate in value by at least 8% to 10% to recover the transaction costs, so if you think you'll sell within two to three years, you're almost always better off renting instead.

- **It's a lot easier to move from a rental unit than from a house.** With a house you own, you can't just give the landlord notice and pick up and leave.

- **Renters have no protection against rent increases beyond the term of their rental agreement or lease.** The exception, of course, is if you live in a rent-controlled area. If you have a fixed rate mortgage, your loan payments remain constant.

- **A house forces you to be a disciplined saver.** If you're not good at saving and investing money, buying a house is a good way for you to build up a financial nest egg, especially as compared to renting and spending your excess money. Consider increasing your payments by $100 to $200 each month, to pay the loan down faster and thus pay less interest overall.

RESOURCE

Rent versus buy: online calculators. To help with your "rent versus buy" decision, see www.homefair.com, www.nolo.com/legal-calculators, or online mortgage broker sites, such as www.eloan.com.

Fix Up the House You Already Own

If you own a house and plan to sell it to purchase a more expensive one in the same area, consider remodeling rather than selling. You often get more for your money and avoid transaction costs. And better yet, you avoid moving to a house that may be many miles from your job, your friends, or your children's school. Indeed, land prices are so high in some California cities that they dwarf the cost of construction to the point that buyers commonly purchase modest houses on desirable lots only to tear them down and build afresh.

However, it's easy to underestimate remodeling costs. Here's how to think about the cost of remodeling as compared with the cost of moving.

Moving

- Figure out how much cash you would net for your existing house, by subtracting what you owe from its likely sales price.
- From this amount, subtract around 8% of the sales price for real estate commissions and other sales costs.
- Now add any money you've saved up for housing. The total is the amount you can put down toward the purchase of a new house.
- Estimate how much you'll need to pay for a suitable new house.
- Add 5% for your share of closing costs and moving expenses.
- Add remodeling costs, if any.

Remodeling

- Estimate the cost of hiring an architect experienced in house remodeling to draw the plans you need.
- Get a hard-eyed contractor's estimate for work you decide on.
- Add 20%–33% to the estimate to cover things you haven't considered and inevitable cost overruns.
- Add these costs to what you already owe on your house plus any costs of temporarily moving out and renting another place while remodeling, if that will be necessary.

- Consider how much you've saved to pay for remodeling or moving. You'll have to borrow any difference between what you have and what you need. If mortgage interest rates have gone down since you bought your house, the cheapest way to borrow may be to get a short-term construction loan and then, when the work is done, refinance the entire loan and your mortgage together. If interest rates have risen, however, keep your original mortgage and take out a second mortgage to refinance the construction.

- Finally, estimate how much the house will be worth in its remodeled condition. Ask local real estate agents and appraisers for their opinions on the house's current value and estimated value after remodeling.

Now ask yourself some big questions. How do the out-of-pocket costs of moving versus remodeling compare? And when the work is done, how much will each house be worth? If the cost of fixing your existing house is only 20%–30% of the purchase price of the new house, you're probably better off staying put.

It's not usually financially wise to remodel an existing house if any of the following are true:

- **You plan to sell in a year or two.** Although remodeling will increase the house's value, and you'll get more when you sell it, you're unlikely to get enough more to pay for your investment and trouble. In short, your improvements will benefit the next owner, not you.

- **You live in a marginal area, and your renovated house will be substantially bigger and nicer than its neighbors.** It's always hard to get full value when selling the best house on the block. Then again, if you plan to stay in the home for a long time, resale value may not be tops on your priority list. Ira and Carol Serkes, for example, built an addition to their Thousand Oaks home that took longer and cost more than expected, and could have been considered an over-improvement. Nevertheless, they're delighted with it, and have stayed in the same home for over 30 years.

- **The work you plan won't substantially increase your house's sales price.** Remodeled kitchens, bathrooms, and extra bedrooms tend to increase the value of a house by 75%–100% of what the remodeling work costs. On the other hand, swimming pools and spas often increase the value by only 50% of what they cost to install—and can sometimes decrease a house's value, because they create maintenance and liability insurance costs. Improvements to the foundation, roof, wiring, or plumbing often result in an even smaller increase in house value, as purchasers assume they should be in good shape to begin with.

> **RESOURCE**
>
> **Online resources on remodeling.** Everything you need to know about remodeling —from choosing a contractor to setting a budget to design ideas—can be found at www.improvenet.com. Also see www.nari.org, the website of the National Association of the Remodeling Industry. And the website of *Remodeling* magazine, at www.remodeling.hw.net, offers an annual "Cost vs. Value Report," analyzing which home remodeling projects lead to the greatest rises in property value.

Strategies for Buying an Affordable House

One obvious way to beat the affordability gap is to find a good house at a comparatively reasonable price. Not only are there great differences among houses offered for sale, but the sellers and buyers, who often have little prior experience with real estate, have vastly different family situations, tastes, and even prejudices. For example, the house at 111 Maple St. may be offered for sale by a retired financial planner determined to get top value, while a similar house at 112 Maple may be offered for fast sale by a divorcing couple or an out-of-town seller who has just inherited it. Sometimes, homes sell to the first person who makes an offer, especially if the owner likes the person, without exposing the home to the entire real estate market.

Below we'll discuss many strategies to narrow the affordability gap. Most are practical in today's market. A few have less merit but are included because potential home buyers often ask about them. Some of these strategies won't be relevant to you, but skim through them to see if you find one that helps put an affordable home within reach.

Don't Buy Until You've Saved More Money

First-time purchasers often ask whether it's better to buy a less-than-perfect house now or to save like mad for a few years to afford a better one later. Traditionally, the answer has been "buy now." In California, house prices have tended to increase faster than savings.

However, if house prices in the area you are interested in are staying level, you may do better by saving your money and waiting a few years. But keep a careful eye on interest rates. They're at historic lows—and the rises, when they come, could wipe out your extra savings.

What You Can Afford Relates to Your Financing

The focus of this chapter is on how to purchase a good house for less than what many others will pay. A major consideration is how you finance the purchase—covered in the following chapters:
- Raising Money for Your Down Payment (Chapter 4)
- Financing Your House: An Overview (Chapter 8)
- Fixed Rate Mortgages (Chapter 9)
- Adjustable Rate Mortgages (Chapter 10)
- Government-Assisted Loans (Chapter 11)
- Private Mortgages (Chapter 12), and
- Obtaining a Mortgage (Chapter 13).

Move to a More Affordable Part of the State

There's no better strategy for buying an affordable house than moving from an area with high housing costs to an area where houses cost far less. A house that would cost $1.5 million in Los Angeles or San Francisco would sell for much less in some communities near Bakersfield or Sacramento.

However, unless you work at home or for an employer that pays the same wages no matter where the location (such as the state or federal government), you will probably make less money in low-cost areas. But the ratio of your earnings to local house prices is what's important to comparing the affordability of housing in different areas. For example, if you can make 60% of your Orange County salary in Merced, but comparable houses cost 35% as much, your ability to buy a nice house has increased greatly.

How Leveraging Can Work When Prices Start to Rise

In an up market, it's possible to trade up to a better house quickly, because investing in a house gives you a unique chance to make a big gain on a small investment. Let's say you buy a house for $800,000, putting $160,000 down and taking a $640,000 mortgage, and a few years later the house goes up in value 20%. In that case, you've doubled your $160,000 investment. Pros call this being "highly leveraged." If you put the same money into a bond fund earning a solid 6%, it would take you nearly 12 years to achieve the same result.

Of course, the flip side to being highly leveraged is that if the value of the property drops, your investment can be quickly wiped out. In the example above, if the property's value dropped 20%, the entire $160,000 would be gone.

Buy a Less Desirable House Than You Really Want

People caught in an affordability squeeze typically must scale down their new-house wish list. A good percentage either:

- buy a marginal house in a desirable area
- buy a desirable house in a marginal area, or even
- buy a marginal house in a marginal area.

Buy a Marginal House in a Desirable Area

In older residential areas, where houses were typically built one by one or in small groups, house size, construction techniques, and lot size often vary significantly. On the same block, house prices can differ by a hundred thousand dollars or more. This means that bargains can, and do, pop up where you might not expect to find them.

Here are some houses that seem undesirable but can be greatly improved at modest expense:

- **Houses with ugly exteriors but pleasant interiors.** You'd be amazed at how many prospective buyers won't even get out of the car to enter a truly homely house.

- **Houses on busy streets that can be "turned around" to focus on a backyard.** For example, you might spruce up the back by adding a deck or patio, plus a fountain, to mask noise.

- **Houses with run-down interiors that mostly need elbow grease and creative tinkering.** Not only is paint cheap, but replacing wallpaper, linoleum, formica, and light fixtures can normally be done at a reasonable cost.

- **Houses that can be screened from an undesirable outdoor feature.** If there's room (and zoning rules allow you) to build a stout redwood fence or plant a thick, tall hedge, you can often block the problem from view. Street noise can often be reduced by walls, fences, and certain types of vegetation (preferably drought tolerant). (See, for example, *Landscaping for Privacy* by Marty Wingate (Timber Press).)

Problem Houses in Good Areas Can Be a Bargain

Our friend Tim, a savvy real estate professional, conducted an experiment. He blindfolded Kim, an experienced agent, and drove her to a house for sale, telling her only that it was located in a particular upscale neighborhood. When Kim entered the house, Tim removed her blindfold and asked her to look around, but not to open the blinds covering the front windows. After ten minutes, Kim was asked how much the house was worth. She replied that if the house didn't have any major structural problems, she'd guess it would sell for about $875,000.

When Tim told her the actual asking price—$650,000—Kim was flabbergasted. She then opened the blinds and saw that the house was on a busy local street. Even so, she continued to maintain that the house was underpriced.

The point should be readily understood—problem houses in nice neighborhoods may be underpriced, even when a reasonable amount is subtracted to compensate for the problem.

Buy a Desirable House in a Marginal Area

One good way to maximize gain in the short term is to buy a good house in an up-and-coming area that will appreciate quickly after purchase. We don't have a sure-fire technique for spotting a marginal area about to improve. (If we did, this book would cost a lot more!) But we can give you a few useful hints:

- **Avoid the worst neighborhoods.** Prices in desperately poor areas with high crime rates may improve eventually, but not as soon as you'd like; in the meantime, you face the day-to-day reality of living in a dangerous environment.

- **Avoid marginal areas on the immediate periphery of the worst neighborhoods.** As long as the blighted area is there, the marginal area is unlikely to improve much.

- **Look for areas that have been substantially devalued by something no longer, or soon to be no longer, an issue.** For example, house values are likely to be depressed by the proximity of a large, loud, and filthy factory, cannery, or railroad spurline. If the offending feature is about to close and the surrounding area is otherwise desirable, you may have found a terrific place to buy.

- **Look for blighted areas where a few hardy middle-class pioneers have already settled.** Once these pioneers begin turning things around, small businesses often follow, restaurants and cafes open, and then, seemingly overnight, individuals and developers buy and transform the dilapidated housing stock in the area. If you think you have a good idea about such an area, check with local planning departments. Applications for building permits and plans can tell you a lot about future prospects for a particular area.

- **Look for lower-priced areas touching on more desirable ones.** Many affluent California cities have one or more poorer cousins nearby. Areas particularly likely to improve are pockets of larger old houses.

- **Look for affordable areas where transportation, especially public transportation, is good or will improve soon.** Much of California is experiencing almost terminal traffic gridlock. Thus, older residential areas convenient to rail or ferry systems increase in value faster than the average residential area.

- **Look for affordable areas within excellent school districts.** It's sometimes possible to find a pocket of affordable housing in an upscale school district.

TIP

A nice house in a poor school district is a poor investment. Even if you have no children, think twice about buying where schools are poor, because values will not appreciate as much.

- **Pay attention to where immigrants are locating.** Property values in many previously depressed areas have jumped substantially as large numbers of new Americans locate there.

Buy a Marginal House in a Marginal Area

There's not much positive to say about buying a relatively undesirable house in a bad neighborhood, even though you can do this comparatively cheaply. We purposely de-emphasize this approach, both because of immediate problems (high crime and run-down public and private services) and because property values in very poor areas usually appreciate far more slowly than in other neighborhoods.

But as with any general rule, there are exceptions. Again, the most obvious is an area where large numbers of immigrants move in and quickly change the neighborhood's character. Another involves areas with an extremely desirable location that the city or private developers have already targeted for improvement. For example, plans to build a new ballpark or convention center in an area are often a tip-off that other major changes for the better are likely to follow.

Buy a Fixer-Upper

The era when a dilapidated house in a reasonably decent area could be purchased dirt cheap and fixed up at a moderate cost is past. The demand for this type of house has risen steadily for at least the last two decades, resulting in comparatively high prices for remaining fixer-uppers in all but the most undesirable neighborhoods. Part of the reason is that buying distressed houses, fixing them up quickly, and either renting them out or reselling at a profit is a profitable business for many small contractors, which means house buyers face professional competition.

> **TIP**
>
> **How to judge whether a fixer-upper is a good deal.** If you're seriously interested in a particular fixer-upper, hire a reliable remodeling contractor to check it out carefully and give you an estimate of needed renovation costs. If the total cost of the rehabilitated house is 90% or more of the cost of a comparable house in good shape, keep looking. By the time you factor in the trouble you'll go through and the likelihood of cost overruns, you won't save anything.

While most fixer-uppers are no longer great deals, they still cost less than a comparable house in good shape. Ask your real estate agent about special loans available from the Federal Housing Administration for fixer-uppers. (See Chapter 11.) Also, consider purchasing a foreclosed property, which will often be a fixer-upper. (See "Buy a House Subject to Foreclosure," below.)

When you consider the time, effort, and cost of finding and renovating a house, however, a fixer-upper is unlikely to be a bargain. Indeed, many fixer-uppers sell above their fair market value when you take a hard-eyed approach to the real costs of repair. Fixer-upper bargains are more likely to be found in higher price ranges, where affluent buyers tend to look for houses already in good condition.

Clues to Help You Find an Ugly Duckling

Look for ads or write-ups that say "not a drive-by," "a diamond in the rough," "has potential," or "needs TLC." Also look for houses that have sat on the market for a long time.

Buy a Small House and Add On Later

If you find a small house on a relatively large lot priced comparably to, or only slightly above, similar houses on ordinary-sized lots, you pay little or nothing for the extra land. In addition to the added privacy and room to play and garden, you normally have the space to enlarge the house any time you can afford to hire a contractor or have the time to do the work yourself.

Even if the lot isn't that large, consider buying a smaller house with remodeling potential and adding a second story. Check first to be sure that local zoning laws allow the changes.

Keep in mind, though, that while this strategy will address a short-term lack of cash, it might not be the most cost-effective in the long term. It's always faster, and almost always less expensive, to buy a larger home in the first place than to build onto an existing home.

True
Story

Monica and Dave: Building Additions

Monica and Dave knew they wanted a three-bedroom, two-bath house in the Berkeley-Oakland area for a maximum of $875,000. They also dreamed of a large deck for weekend lounging and parties. But after 18 months of looking at nearly 200 houses, they had not found anything even marginally decent in their price range. So they took a new approach—they looked at smaller houses with expansion potential.

Within weeks, they found a house in North Berkeley with only two bedrooms and one bath (and no deck). At $825,000, the price was right. Best of all, the backyard was deep enough to leave plenty of room to add on to the back. After checking carefully and assuring themselves it was feasible to add on a bedroom later, they said yes. They quickly added a second bathroom (using a space that had been a closet/hallway) and a large deck. After five years, their new equity allowed them to qualify for a home equity loan to add a second-story master bedroom.

Buy a House at a Probate Sale

Probate sales occur when a homeowner dies leaving property to be divided among inheritors, or to be sold to pay debts or taxes. The sale is handled by the executor of the homeowner's will (or a court-appointed administrator if there is no will). It is often supervised by the probate court judge, through a bidding process. The highest bidder gets the property. Some probate sales are handled directly by the executor of an estate without going through the court bidding process.

Occasionally, it's possible to buy a house at an estate or probate sale for substantially less than the current market rate. The time and uncertainty involved in bidding discourages many potential buyers from participating. Less buyer competition can mean a lower-than-market price. Also, the cost of bidding (you will likely be required to include a cashier's check for 10% of the price you're offering) discourages people from making casual bids.

The downside is that probate sales aren't subject to disclosure laws (discussed in Chapter 19), so while agents must legally disclose all pertinent facts, many probate-sold houses are sold "as is." You won't have the benefit of knowing what defects the owner observed on the property. Your bid made in court cannot contain financing, inspection, or other contingencies.

How a Court-Supervised Probate Sale Works

Here are the basic steps in a court-supervised probate house sale:

1. The house is advertised for sale in a newspaper (often a legal or fairly obscure one) published in the county in which the property is located and, if listed with a broker, in a Multiple Listing Service.

2. An appraisal value is established.

3. Bids are accepted by a certain date.

4. During the court procedure, higher bids are accepted. A cashier's check may be required with each bid. The first higher bid (called an "overbid") must exceed the original highest bid by at least 10% of the first $10,000, plus 5% of the balance. For example, the first overbid on a $400,000 offer must be $420,500:

10% of $10,000	=	$1,000
5% of $390,000	=	19,500
	$	20,500

An alternate formula that will get you the same result is 5% of the offer price plus $500.

5. Subsequent overbids are allowed in amounts set by the probate judge. For example, the judge might require that each new bid exceed the previous one by $1,000.

6. The highest bid, if it is at least 90% of the property's court-appraised value, is accepted.

7. Purchase of the property is normally financed in the same way as any other purchase.

If you're considering buying a house at a probate sale, here are tips for getting the best deal:

- **Find a knowledgeable broker or salesperson who knows the ropes of probate sales.** There are a few in every community.

- **If you plan to bid at a court-supervised probate sale, line up a highly trustworthy and thorough inspector.** Have the inspector check out any house before the court confirmation procedure and give you a report. (See Chapter 19 for details on inspections.)

- **Find a house that has been appraised too low.** This may be less difficult than you imagine, since a good percentage of houses subject to probate sales are run-down. (Chapter 15 discusses how to evaluate sales prices.)

- **For court-supervised sales, consider holding off on your bid until the court procedure begins and the first round of bids are in.** (See "How a Court-Supervised Probate Sale Works," above.) At some probate sales, many bids are placed by investors hoping to pick up a house cheaply and quickly resell it for a profit. If you can figure out what professional investors will offer and bid just a little higher, you can sometimes save a bundle. Call the probate court clerk (it's part of your county's superior court) for a list of probate sales on the court calendar. Then check out the property carefully. If it looks like the first-round winning bidder got a great price, inspect the property, line up your financing, and hope to bid higher at the court confirmation. Contact the attorney handling the estate for the date and time of the confirmation hearing.

Buy a House With a Structural Problem

California law strictly requires that a seller and agent disclose all known problems with a house, using detailed forms entitled "Real Estate Transfer Disclosure Statement" and "Natural Hazard Disclosure Statement." (Copies are in Chapter 19.) In addition (as discussed in Chapter 19), most buyers and lenders insist on conducting careful prepurchase inspections before the sale.

Fear of lawsuits for sellers failing to disclose house defects has resulted in some inspectors' providing excruciating detail on flaws and generally emphasizing the negative. This can make some houses difficult to sell. If buyer interest dries up (as it often does when a house has a long list of problems), its asking price will almost surely drop. The house may go "stale" (hard to sell at any price). You may snag a bargain even after accounting for the house's physical problems.

Buy a House Subject to Foreclosure

Foreclosure normally begins when a homeowner misses several mortgage payments and receives a notice of default. During the three months following, a California homeowner can make the back payments and cure the default. If he or she does not pay up, the house proceeds to foreclosure. For some house hunters, purchasing a house subject to a foreclosure is a way to buy a bargain.

Home foreclosures aren't usually advertised through the online Multiple Listing Service (MLS) or other normal channels. The best place to check on your own is through websites such as www.realtytrac.com, though you have to pay a membership fee to get anything more than bare-bones details. Another membership-based service, which contains listings of government foreclosures, is www.ushud.com.

> **SEE AN EXPERT**
>
> **Hire a real estate agent who knows the foreclosure ropes.** Many foreclosure markets are dominated by savvy investors, and you'll be at a disadvantage if you aren't represented by someone familiar with the process.

The three broad approaches to buying a house subject to foreclosure are:

- **Purchase from the owner during the three-month period before the foreclosure sale.** During this period following default, the owner may want to sell the property to avoid foreclosure and severe credit damage. At this point, some owners are delighted to sell for little or nothing more than they owe to the lenders, because they've given up hope of keeping the house. Some owners may even sell the house for less than is owed on the mortgage—called a "short sale"—conditional on the lender's approval, which typically takes months to obtain.

- **Purchase at the foreclosure sale.** If no one brings the mortgage current or buys the house before the sale, the trustee holds a foreclosure sale and sells the house to the highest bidder. The trustee opens the bidding at the amount of the outstanding mortgage being foreclosed. Potential buyers (often investors) attend the sale or auction with cash or a cashier's check in hand for a little more than the amount they plan to bid (to allow for a small increase). This up-front cash requirement eliminates casual bidders from foreclosure sales.

- **Purchase after the foreclosure sale if no one bids.** If no one bids at the sale, the foreclosing mortgage holder gets the property back. In recent years, lenders have ended up with a large number of houses this way, most of which they want to sell quickly, even if it means taking a loss. (These properties are often called REOs, for "real estate-owned.") Some lenders sell the properties themselves (often with favorable prices and low down payments); the better properties, however, are commonly turned over to real estate brokers, who try to sell them as they would any other house. Even so, the fact that the foreclosed house wasn't prepared for sale by an owner, and thus may be in less than perfect shape, often means there are bargains to be had.

Before purchasing a home through a private or government foreclosure sale, find out:

- **Does it have major problems?** Like probate sales, foreclosure sales are an exception to California Civil Code § 1102 requiring sellers to disclose all known problems. Many foreclosed properties are sold as is, so (if possible) arrange your own thorough inspection for any structural, mold, or pest control problems before you commit to a purchase. You likely won't be able to negotiate over needed repairs, but at least you'll know more about what you're taking on. In fact, mold problems have been the cause of some fore-closures: Homeowners find themselves in situations where the mold remediation would cost tens or hundreds of thousands of dollars and the insurance company won't pay a cent—so their only choice is to hand their keys to the bank.

- **Are you taking clear title?** (Title is the history of ownership; see Chapter 18 for more information.) The owner may have had other financial problems, and creditors may have placed liens on the house. Normally, these are paid off or wiped out during the foreclosure process, but before agreeing to buy the house, you'll want to be sure all liens really have been removed.

Government Foreclosure

If the distressed house had financing guaranteed by the U.S. Department of Veterans Affairs or insured by the Federal Housing Administration (of the U.S. Department of Housing and Urban Development), bidding at a foreclosure sale must follow the agency's rules (typically, sealed bids submitted by mail). Buyers frequently must go through a time-consuming and bureaucratic process before the sale is final. But don't let this scare you—government agencies often have good-sized inventories of foreclosed properties and will sometimes offer bargain prices, low down payments, and attractive financing deals to move them.

A real estate agent experienced with government foreclosures can help you locate and buy these types of houses. For more information, contact the U.S. Department of Veterans Affairs or Department of Housing and Urban Development. (For contact information, see Chapter 11, Government-Assisted Loans.)

- **Are there tenants or former owners living in the house?** If so, you'll need to abide by a federal law known as the "Protecting Tenants at Foreclosure Act of 2009" as well as a similar state law. (California Code of Civil Procedure Section 1161(b)(b).) Prior to passage of these laws, most renters lost their leases upon foreclosure. But now, California leases survive a foreclosure, up to the end of the lease term or for month-to-month tenancies, up to 90 days. But there's an important exception. California home buyers who intend to live on the property (rather than, say, rent it out to someone else) may terminate the rights of tenants who signed their lease *after* the foreclosed-upon mortgage was recorded. The new owner must, however, give 90 days' notice before requiring the tenants to move out. You may very well have to assert your rights by evicting the existing tenants after you purchase. This may require help from a local real estate attorney who specializes in unlawful detainers (evictions). We also suggest *The California Landlord's Law Book: Evictions,* by David Brown (Nolo).

- **Has anyone else been hanging out in the house?** If it has been sitting empty, it may have become a target for squatters, thieves, or vandals.

Buy a House With Someone You'll Live With

In an arrangement called "equity sharing," two or more people with pooled resources buy a house—more house than each could afford alone. Equity sharing tends to be most popular among unmarried couples, although it's also reasonably common with relatives and friends not in romantic relationships. The latter legal property ownership arrangements are bound to be different, since California's marital property laws do not apply.

It goes without saying that if you own and live in a house with others, you'd better be personally compatible. Couple or not, you should have a written contract spelling out the percentage of the house each person owns; who pays how much each month for the mortgage, taxes, insurance, and other costs; what happens if the household breaks up or an owner dies; as well as a number of other practical ownership issues.

We discuss a few of these issues in Chapter 20, but to draw up an equity-sharing contract, you'll need additional information.

RESOURCE

Writing shared equity contracts. Nolo publishes the following books to help equity sharers cope with owning property together:

- *The Sharing Solution,* by Emily Doskow and Janelle Orsi, addresses sharing real estate and other property with friends.
- *Living Together: A Legal Guide for Unmarried Couples,* by Ralph Warner, Toni Ihara, and Frederick Hertz, contains several sample house purchasing contracts for unmarried couples.
- *A Legal Guide for Lesbian & Gay Couples,* by Attorneys Frederick Hertz and Emily Doskow, contains sample contracts similar to those in *Living Together* but adapted to address the special concerns of lesbian and gay couples and groups buying together.

True Story

Deborah, Doug, and Rose: The Joy of Living Near Grandma

Deborah and Doug have a two-year-old daughter. Both artists, they wanted at least 1,500 square feet to accommodate their family and need for studio space. Here's how they bridged their affordability gap:

"We wanted to stay in our long-time neighborhood, but, unfortunately, couldn't afford it. Then we heard about a place right around the corner that sounded great—except that it was more expensive and larger than we needed.

"Deborah's mother, Rose, provided an unexpected solution. She offered to help us with the down payment and monthly mortgage payments in exchange for living in one of the units. We quickly struck a two-thirds–one-third financial split. Our family took the three-bedroom unit on the top floor and converted the bottom-floor unit into a home for Rose and the middle unit into a fantastic studio space.

We now have our ideal house at a price we can afford, while still retaining our privacy. But the best part is the special relationship between our daughter and her grandma. We wouldn't miss it for the world."

Buy a House With an Investor's Help

Equity sharing between a resident owner and an investor is often touted as a good solution for people with affordability problems. The idea is for a nonresident investor to put up a chunk of the down payment in exchange for a share of profits when the house is sold.

Equity sharing is not the best way for one person to help another buy a house. From the house purchaser's point of view, it's usually better to simply borrow the money and own the entire property. Similarly, equity sharing is often a poor idea for the investor. When a house is viewed as an investment by a lender and as a home by its occupant, the potential conflicts are huge. What if the resident wants to make improvements that will enhance the house's livability but which won't increase its market value? What if the nonresident wants his or her money back, but the resident doesn't want to sell and can't afford to pay the nonresident his or her share? Or, even more serious from the investor's point of view, what if the resident owner ceases making payments and refuses to vacate the house? Yes, a written contract can and should deal with these and many other similar questions, but the possibilities for future conflict are still considerable.

If, despite these warnings, you want to pursue equity sharing with a nonresident because you've got no other way to raise enough money for a down payment, it may make the most sense to buy with someone who is not a relative or friend, so as to establish that it's clearly a business deal. A good real estate agent should be familiar with programs in your area that bring buyers and investors together.

Typically, the investor supplies all or most of the down payment while the buyer lives in the house, maintains it, and pays all or most of the mortgage, insurance, and tax payments. At an agreed-upon date, the home buyer refinances and pays the investor the down payment plus a specified share of the appreciation. A clear, written agreement is necessary to cover the following:

- the use of the home
- the amount of the initial investment and the percentage of ownership

- buy-out provisions
- the amount and type of insurance to carry, and allocation of the proceeds should the house be damaged or destroyed (for example, by fire)
- the responsibility for daily costs and capital improvements, and
- the details of any sale or refinance (such as time, price, and profit splits).

You will likely want to get an attorney's help in drafting this.

Rent Out Part of the House

Renting out a room in an urban area may bring in $800 per month or more and offers tax advantages. A homeowner can deduct only property taxes and mortgage interest on federal income taxes, while a rental owner can also deduct business expenses, such as repairs and utilities, and take depreciation on the portion of the home that is rented out.

If you're seriously considering renting out a room or two as part of your house-financing strategy, do some homework. Start by finding out how much rent you can reasonably charge—that is, what local tenants pay for similar space.

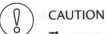 **CAUTION**

The prospect of rental income probably won't help you qualify for a loan. Conventional lenders don't count income from renting a room in a single-family home or taking in boarders when evaluating your loan eligibility. Fannie Mae does consider rental income under certain limited circumstances.

Buy a Duplex, Triplex, or House With an In-Law Unit

Another approach is to buy a duplex or triplex, then live in one unit while renting out the others. A variant of this approach is to buy a large house with a separate, smaller in-law unit.

True Story

Author Ira Serkes's Purchase of a Small Berkeley Multiunit Building

"When I first got interested in real estate, I couldn't afford a single-family home. Instead, I looked for a small apartment building where I could live in one unit and have rental income from the others subsidize the mortgage. I originally looked at triplexes but ended up buying a fixer-upper seven-plex. My family invested with the down payment and shared the appreciation. For the next five years, I lived in one of the units. With the help of some tenants, I renovated each apartment as it became vacant. As the value of the building went up, I borrowed against it and used the money for a down payment on another small building.

"My successes inspired a friend of mine to begin investing with me. Now I own a nice house and a number of investment properties, whose monthly rents helped put my nieces through college. And the best fringe benefit of buying this small apartment building is it was where I met my wife, best friend, and business partner, Carol! She rented an apartment from me, I broke my rule about going out with a renter, and the rest was history!"

However, there's considerable competition for these types of houses, which means prices are often marked up to the point that rental income is entirely eaten up by the extra monthly costs of the larger mortgage.

Your goal is to find a house selling for little more than if the second (or third) unit wasn't there. The more unconventional the second unit, the more likely you are to be able to accomplish this. For example, if an in-law unit is tucked under a hillside house with access down a driveway and around two trees and a rosebush (as opposed to being attached to your unit, with a door facing the street), the real estate market may undervalue it.

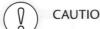

CAUTION

Make sure the extra unit is legal. Especially if an extra living space looks homemade, demand to see necessary permits. If they don't exist, you run the risk that the city or county will close down the unit—or make you fix it—because it doesn't comply with building codes. The neighbors are the most likely ones to file a complaint, particularly if you offer short-term rentals, such as on Airbnb or VRBO. If there are no permits, don't pay any more for the property than you would if the extra unit didn't exist. Also, if you plan to rent out rooms or an entire house via Airbnb or VRBO, make sure your city permits short-term rentals. (Berkeley, for example, doesn't allow rentals shorter than 14 days and places other restrictions on them.) Also check that your insurance company will protect you if short-term renters damage the property or are injured there.

Lease a House You Can't Afford Now With an Option to Buy Later

A lease option is a contract where an owner leases a house (usually from one to three years) to a tenant for a specific monthly rent (which may be scheduled to increase during the contract term) and gives the tenant the right to buy the house for a price established in advance. The tenant pays some money for the option—a lump sum payment at the start of the contract or periodic payments (all nonrefundable). Depending on the contract, the potential buyer normally can exercise the option to purchase at any time during the lease period or at a date specified.

> **EXAMPLE:** Ted and Jane lease Robin's house for $2,700 per month for two years. In addition, they pay Robin $8,000 for the option to purchase the house for $680,000 at any time during the two years. If Ted and Jane decide to buy, the $8,000 will be credited against the purchase price; if not, Robin keeps it.

This example is deliberately made simple to give you the general idea. Most lease option deals are more complicated. For example, the house purchase price might be a fixed dollar amount, plus an amount tied to any increase in the Consumer Price Index. Or, instead of an up-front option fee, the rent might be set at a higher-than-normal amount, with part, or all, of the extra applied to the purchase price if the option to purchase is ever exercised.

 TIP

Get all extra payments credited toward the purchase price. A prospective purchaser who pays a flat fee in exchange for an option to purchase, or agrees to a higher monthly rent to achieve this benefit, makes a good deal only if all money over and above a reasonable rent will be credited toward the purchase price if and when the option is exercised.

A potential buyer who chooses a lease option will get to move into a home without having to come up with a down payment or financing. It also gives the potential buyer time to clean up any credit problems and to see if he or she can handle the house's maintenance and repair costs and other issues. Even better, it allows the luxury of waiting to see whether the value of the house reaches or surpasses the amount of the option price before deciding to purchase. If the value does increase, the house will be easier to finance, as the buyer will already have equity (the difference between the sales price and the then-current market value).

A lease option is often attractive to a seller in a colder market or when the house is a hard one to sell—don't be afraid to ask, especially if the owner:

- is having trouble selling the house at the asking price
- needs to move now, but, for tax reasons, doesn't want the profit on the sale to be taxed in the current fiscal year. Often owners about to retire and enter a lower tax bracket fit this description.
- will, from the initial option fee and/or higher-than-normal rent, gain an excellent short-run return—perhaps filling a house that would have otherwise remained vacant until sold, or
- hopes you won't exercise the option, giving the owner a premium rent (or an up-front option fee payment) while keeping the house.

Lease Option Contract (Renter-Buyer's Perspective)

A lease option contract should address the following:

- **When the option can be exercised.** Avoid lease option contracts that allow you to exercise your option only under very restrictive circumstances —for example, for one week at the end of the second and fourth year.
- **Purchase price if you exercise the option.** It's far better to have it fixed at the start of the lease period, even if an increase for inflation is built in, than to set it by an appraisal at the time you exercise the option to purchase.
- **How much of the rent or up-front option payment will be applied toward the down payment or purchase price if the option is exercised.**
- **Exactly how you can exercise the option.** Written notice sent by certified mail is a good approach.
- **Whether the seller will help you finance the house by taking back a second mortgage.** If so, get the details.
- **Home inspection.** It's best to have the house thoroughly inspected before signing the lease option, to see what repairs are needed.
- **Assignability.** If you choose not to exercise your option, it's nice to be able to sell that right to someone else, if possible, for cash or a share of the house's equity.
- **Any other significant terms of the purchase.**

CAUTION

Beware of termination clauses. Avoid any clause in a lease option contract that ends your option if you fail to perform your duties under the rental agreement in a timely manner. Such a clause could let the owner end the option contract if you're late with the rent, even once. Instead, you want a clause that lets you exercise the option to buy if your rent is paid up at the time you choose to exercise the option.

Have the lease option contract notarized and recorded at the county recorder's office. This way, your right to purchase will appear on any title search, so the owner can't sell the house out from under you.

Finally, unless you're experienced in this field, have the contract drafted or checked by someone who is, such as an attorney.

> ⓘ **CAUTION**
>
> **The seller's loan documents may not allow for a lease option.** The seller will need to make sure the option doesn't trigger a "due on sale" clause (a standard contract clause preventing the mortgage from being transferred to the next owner). An experienced agent or attorney should review the documents.

Buy a Condominium

Many California condos are priced temptingly low when compared to houses. A condominium (condo) owner owns the unit outright plus an undivided share of common areas (halls, parking areas, roof, plumbing, yard, deck, and so on).

To maintain these areas, owners usually must pay monthly fees to a condominium association, in addition to local property taxes assessed on each unit and occasional special assessments. Condos include a number of restrictions on how the property can be used, such as the type of landscaping you can do or the number, weight, or type of pets you can own. (Many condominium associations do not allow dogs at all.) These restrictions are spelled out in a document called the CC&Rs.

Condos come in all shapes and sizes, from duplexes to high-rises, and there can be good reasons for buying one. Many people appreciate the decreased maintenance that comes with owning some areas in common. Particularly if you're considering buying in a city or another area where there's limited land on which to build, a condo may be a fine choice.

Historically, however, condos haven't appreciated in value as fast as single-family homes. And you'll need to carefully check out the overall financial situation before buying. A financially unstable developer, or many owners already in foreclosure, could spell trouble for you, leading to extra fees, reductions in the value of your property, decline of or even failure to build various amenities, and so on.

Also check into whether the condo association has earthquake insurance. Some don't—and even if the one you're looking at does, keep in mind that the owners can vote to cancel the policy in the future.

Buy a Town House

Town houses—usually single-family houses with common walls—have surged in popularity in California because they're relatively inexpensive. And well they should be; they save on land, because common walls and roofs are cheap to build. With most town houses, you hold legal title to your house and the land it's on. You must pay real estate taxes even though you and your neighbors sit on the same piece of land and share common walls.

Town houses may be a better investment than condos. Many are two-story, which means they physically look somewhat like single-family houses; condos, which often contain many units, often physically look more like apartment units. Because many people prefer the size and scale of a house (regardless of form of ownership), town houses are a bit more likely than condos to increase in value.

Does this mean that town houses are as good an investment as small, detached starter houses? Usually not. Most people prefer living in a house that doesn't share walls with its neighbor. Still, if you can't afford a nice starter house in a decent area, an affordable town house may be a better choice than buying a run-down, detached house in a marginal neighborhood.

Buy a Tenant-in-Common (TIC) Interest

Co-author Ira Serkes handled a Berkeley home sale in which the owner continued living in a cottage in the back of the property, while the buyers purchased the house in front. This was arranged by creating a "tenancy in common," or TIC. The buyers obtained a new loan secured by their fractional interest (the house alone, not the entire property). The buyers spent only around two thirds of what they would have for a conventional home in that particular neighborhood (Northbrae).

Buy Into a Cohousing or Cooperative Arrangement

Another way to find an affordable house is to enter into a cooperative arrangement with others. This usually involves finding or building an apartment building or a series of town houses or small units with shared common areas, such as walkways, gardens, or children's play areas. In legal terms, the possible arrangements run the gamut, from condominium-type ownership, in which each buyer purchases his or her own mortgage (cohousing), to cooperatives, in which all share a "blanket" mortgage.

A cohousing community is often conceived of, designed, and developed by the people who will live in it. They are not guaranteed to be low cost. However, their emphasis on compact living units with shared resources, such as common kitchen and dining areas, walkways, gardens, parking areas, and laundry facilities, means that some savings are possible.

For more information on cohousing or similar forms of intentional communities, as well as architects and developers, contact:

- Raines Cohen and Betsy Morris, PhD, the "Cohousing Coaches," at www.cohousingcoaches.com
- Fellowship for Intentional Community, in Rutledge, Missouri, 660-883-5545, www.ic.org. You might enjoy their online *Communities Directory,* which contains descriptions of over 1,200 communities in the United States and abroad.
- CoHousing Solutions, Nevada City, California, www.cohousing solutions.com
- The Cohousing Association of the United States, Bothell, Washington, www.cohousing.org, and
- Northern California Land Trust, in Berkeley, California, www.nclt.org.

Unlike cohousing, housing cooperatives are normally set up as nonprofit or public trust corporations. The nonprofit arrangement is referred to as a "limited equity housing cooperative" or LEHC.

Ken Norwood:
Strawberries, Consensus, and Low Monthly Fees

In the late 1980s, the tenants of our 20-unit property in Berkeley got tired of watching the place go to pot. The tenants decided to organize a cooperative and buy the property. They arranged a private bridge loan for the purchase, which gave them four years to go through the process of organizing as a nonprofit, meet other state requirements, and get long-term financing.

I was interested in cooperative housing and was actually providing architectural services to the group, while renting a room somewhere else. When a unit came open, the group actually loaned me part of the initial purchase price, and I've been happily living here ever since.

Now the property is in great shape—we've just torn up some asphalt to make room for five more fruit trees. We've got four or five green-thumbers, and they voluntarily tend to the strawberries, chard, tomatoes, flowers, and trees around the property. Two common rooms and a roof deck are used for our monthly potluck meetings as well as for parties, exercise (we invested in weight machines), and free laundry. Our monthly meetings are consensus based. We make decisions on how best to improve the property—such as our planned seismic work and attic insulation—and choose new owners. Sellers get a 4% increase over the amount they paid in. And, best of all, our monthly fees are far less than most people in Berkeley pay for rent.

People who want to live in a housing cooperative buy in as shareholders. Shareholders don't own individual units, but their shares entitle them to proprietary leases on specific units. During their ownership, buyers also pay monthly carrying charges to cover the mortgage, insurance, and other expenses. If the cooperative will provide housing for low- and moderate-income people, public subsidies can be obtained to help with these carrying charges.

Limited equity housing cooperatives are highly structured, since they're governed by California law. (Civil Code § 817 and Bus. and

Prof. Code § 11003.4.) To qualify for entry into an LEHC, you'll need to meet eligibility criteria set by the cooperative (which may or may not include proving that you're low income).

You'll also need luck—these cooperatives are developed only as quickly as nonprofit developers can find land or buildings at low cost, which is no simple matter in California. Still, the developers sometimes persuade the previous property owners to sell at a below-market price, which translates into savings for the shareholders.

And there's nothing to stop you from forming your own nonprofit group to create a cooperative—in fact, some disgruntled tenants have used this method to take control of their living space, by getting together and buying out the landlord of their complex.

While limited equity housing cooperatives are affordable to buy into, the law creates a catch when you sell. You'll receive only a little more than your purchase price back, plus interest (a maximum of 10% per year), regardless of the property's current market value. That allows your unit to be resold at an affordable price, but it prevents you from following the traditional path of building equity in a starter home and working your way up as property values increase. Still, if your primary goal is to find a decent place to live, with comparatively low up-front and monthly payments, an LEHC may be a good choice. And if your monthly payments are low enough, you'll have an opportunity to save—and invest—money that you might not have had if you'd been renting.

To find out more about cooperative housing arrangements, contact your city or county building departments or do a Web search for "limited equity housing," "cooperative housing," or "affordable housing."

Buy a House at an Auction

In parts of California where the real estate market has been particularly slow, sellers try to attract buyer interest by auctioning houses. Many auctions are of new houses in situations where developers need to raise quick cash to pay lenders. Foreclosed properties are also sometimes sold at auction.

As a general rule, buying at an auction won't get you a good deal. It should go almost without saying that amateurs (home buyers) rarely beat pros (home sellers familiar with auction procedures and investors who regularly buy at auctions) at their own game. This is especially true when you understand that the seller will take steps to be sure that the house won't sell at a rock-bottom price, including:

- setting a "floor price"—a price below which the house won't be sold
- advertising extensively—to be sure to collect a crowd
- hiring a professional auctioneer skilled at loosening up the crowd and building auction fever, and
- although it's illegal, sometimes planting shills in the audience to bid up the price.

True Story

Anne and Frank: We Bought a Great House at an Auction

We bought a nice house 14 years ago for $400,000 and recently sold it for $900,000. Because we both have fairly good jobs, we thus had the down payment and the income necessary to move up.

We wanted to live in Marin County and heard that some new luxury houses that had originally been listed at $1.8 million had proved unsaleable and were being auctioned with a floor bid requirement of $1.25 million. We were there for the first sale, but didn't bid. The house went for $1.42 million, which we figured was too high. On the second and third house to be auctioned, we noticed that one person (let's call him Ollie) who bid at the first sale was bidding again, but each time dropped out at the last minute.

We smelled a rat (a shill) but didn't say anything. We wanted the fourth house and bid several times, until the price was $1.3 million. Then, when Ollie bid higher, we objected and said we were going to call the District Attorney's Consumer Fraud Unit and the State Real Estate Department and file a complaint. Ollie immediately disappeared, and we got a great house at a good price.

If auctions are held in your area, a better strategy than actually bidding at the auction is to compare the prices for houses sold at auction with those of houses sold in the normal way. (You may need to attend a few auctions to get this information.) Just learning which sellers are motivated to sell is extremely valuable. And if you like what you see at the auction and the seller has other houses to sell (which is common with developers), stop by on a weekday near the end of the month and offer to buy for slightly less than the auction price. Or make a list of sellers with similar properties not being auctioned, and offer to buy for a little less than the auction price.

If despite this advice you decide to bid at auction, follow these basic rules:

- Research how much comparable houses are selling for in the same area—if you don't know the local market well, you're almost sure to get taken. (See Chapter 15 for how to find out comparable sales prices.)
- Attend several auctions without your checkbook (or paying a bidding fee) to get the hang of how they work.
- Research deposit requirements and financing options before you commit yourself to buying.
- Ask for brochures that describe the property, and read all the fine print.
- Check out the house's physical condition before buying. Real estate auction companies must disclose known structural problems and defects of property (except in the case of foreclosure). (See Chapter 19 for details on state disclosure law and inspections.)
- Be sure you're taking clear title to the property. (See Chapter 18 for details.)
- Don't pay more than 10% above the minimum or floor price, or 70%–75% of the original asking price.
- Get help researching.
- Decide in advance how much you'll pay, and don't bid a penny more.
- If there is lots of bidding on a particular house, drop out fast—if you get into a bidding war, you'll surely pay too much.

Raising Money for Your Down Payment

Assisted No and Low Down Payment Plans..72

Five and Ten Percent Down Payment Mortgages.....................................73

Will You Have to Buy Private Mortgage Insurance?................................73

    The Cost of PMI 74

    Impound Accounts...74

How Much Should Your Down Payment Be? 75

Using Equity in an Existing House as a Down Payment on a New One........ 77

Using a Gift to Help With the Down Payment.. 77

Borrowing Down Payment Money From a Relative or Friend 80

Is It a Gift or a Loan? Sometimes It Pays to Be Vague 80

Borrowing From Your 401(k) Plan 81

Tapping Into Your IRA...82

L et's start with the basics. Down payments are usually discussed as a percentage of a house's purchase price, not a specific dollar figure. A 20% down payment on a $300,000 house would be $60,000.

In addition, lenders often use the real estate industry jargon "loan-to-value (LTV) ratio" in referring to the down payment required. A mortgage with an LTV of 90% requires only 10% down, an LTV of 80% requires 20% down, and so on.

Your down payment amount will depend on the interplay of many factors, including:

- your savings from all sources
- your monthly income
- the house's purchase price
- the type of mortgage you choose
- your credit history, and
- the size of the mortgage.

SKIP AHEAD

If you're relatively affluent and will put 20% or more down: You can skip most of this chapter, except for "How Much Should Your Down Payment Be?" It discusses the pros and cons of making a big down payment.

Assisted No and Low Down Payment Plans

The Federal Housing Administration, U.S. Department of Veterans Affairs, California Housing Finance Agency, CalVet programs, and a few California municipalities offer low down payment mortgage plans. Down payment and eligibility rules for these programs are discussed in Chapter 11, Government-Assisted Loans.

Five and Ten Percent Down Payment Mortgages

A few lenders offer mortgages to people who put 5% or 10% down, but only if a buyer has stellar credit and enough income to make the monthly payments within a lender's debt-to-income guidelines.

If you're really strapped for cash, ask your lender about low down payment plans, such as the Fannie Mae HomeReady Program. Some California lenders offer this plan, which features a 3% down payment, competitive interest rates, and flexible qualifying guidelines. The program is, however, limited to home buyers with "low to moderate" income.

 **RESOURCE**

For more information, contact Fannie Mae at 800-7FANNIE or check out www.fanniemae.com.

If you take out a very low down payment loan, be ready to pay a slightly higher interest rate and loan fee (points) and to purchase PMI, discussed below.

Will You Have to Buy Private Mortgage Insurance?

Private mortgage insurance policies are designed to reimburse your mortgage lender up to a certain amount if you default on your loan and the foreclosure sale price is less than the amount you owe the lender (the mortgage and the costs of sale).

Today, most California lenders require PMI on loans where the borrower makes a down payment of less than 20%. PMI typically protects lenders for 20%–25% of the purchase price of the house, offsetting at least some of the loss resulting from foreclosure and resale.

The Cost of PMI

Expect to pay between 0.5% and 1% of your loan amount for your PMI premiums, depending in part on the size of your down payment.

Monthly payments aren't the only possible PMI payment plan. You'll likely be given a choice of whether to pay the full PMI premium amount at closing, split the PMI into a flat fee at closing along with ongoing monthly payments, or simply make monthly payments.

Some lenders offer to pay your PMI, but charge you higher interest in return. This isn't necessarily a worthwhile deal, because you can eventually stop paying PMI when your equity in the house has risen, while you'd be stuck with the higher interest rate for as long as you keep the loan.

> **TIP**
>
> **PMI tax deductible through 2016.** If you meet the income guidelines, PMI is tax deductible for mortgages on a primary residence. Keep your eye on the news and Nolo's online updates for word on whether the deduction will be extended.

Impound Accounts

PMI policies also require that you set up an impound account to pay the lender (or organization that services the loan) the cost of the premium. The lender in turn pays your property taxes and homeowners' insurance. These impound accounts result in your paying for taxes and insurance before you need to, thus losing the interest you'd earn if you kept that money in the bank. Even worse, some lenders require that you pay up to a year's worth of PMI into the impound account when the house purchase closes, thus increasing your up-front costs. And you still pay an amount monthly.

If you're required to set up an impound account, monitor it carefully. In the past, some borrowers have faced significant hassles because the lenders forgot to pay the taxes and insurance, with the buyers unfairly receiving a negative credit rating as a result.

TIP

PMI isn't forever. Federal law requires lenders to automatically cancel PMI once the loan-to-value ratio reaches 78% (whether because the property appreciated in value or because you've paid down the mortgage). The law also allows you to request (in writing) that the lender cancel your PMI when your loan-to-value ratio reaches 80% and your mortgage is in good standing.

How Much Should Your Down Payment Be?

If you can afford to make a large down payment, should you? Consider the following factors in support of it:

- **The larger your down payment, the lower your monthly payments.** It feels good to have adequate money each month for other expenditures.

- **The larger your down payment, the less it will cost you to borrow.** For example, if you put 20% down on a $500,000 house and borrow $400,000 at 4% for 30 years, you'll pay $287,478 in interest over the life of the loan. If, however, you put 40% down and borrow $300,000 at 3.5%, you'll pay $184,968 in interest.

- **Lenders won't require PMI if you make a down payment of 20% or more.** That might save you hundreds or thousands of dollars a year.

- **It's easier to get a good loan.** With a large down payment, the lender knows you're unlikely to default, and, even if you do, the house can almost surely be resold for enough to cover the mortgage.

- **It's easier to find a willing seller.** Whether you're in situation where the seller is choosing between offers, or is worried about finding a buyer who will really be able to get a loan and close the deal, making a large down payment raises you high in the seller's estimation. You may even find the seller willing to make other concessions just to keep you on the hook.

- **A large down payment is like forced savings.** Money tied up in a house can't be spent on frivolous things. But it may be available if you need it in an emergency, by refinancing the house or taking out a home equity loan.

- **A large down payment and a short-term mortgage mean you are likely to own your house before you retire.** Many people sensibly want to pay off their mortgage before they retire (when their income is likely to decrease) or have to pay other family expenses such as college tuition.

But there are also reasons not to make a big down payment, even if you can afford to:

- **You can buy a more expensive house.** (This assumes you qualify for the monthly mortgage payments.)

- **You'll have more cash available.** That will let you spend comfortably on closing costs, loan fees, and "new house" expenses like moving and redecorating.

- **The interest portion of your mortgage is tax deductible.** Unlike other debts, you can deduct the annual interest paid on mortgage loans up to $1 million from your federal and California income tax returns. This figure is for married couples who file a joint income tax return; you can deduct up to $500,000 if you're single. See IRS Publication 936, *Home Mortgage Interest Deduction*, available at www.irs.gov.

- **You can invest the money.** Whether you'll earn more doing this than it costs you to borrow the money with a large mortgage depends on your rate of investment return.

- **You'll have money available for other needs.** If you tie all your money up with a big down payment, you may find yourself having to borrow it back on a home equity loan (usually at a higher interest rate than the first mortgage) if you want to remodel the house, put your kids through college, or whatever else. And interest paid on a home equity loan is deductible on your federal income tax only for loans up to $100,000. If you need to borrow more, there is no deduction.

- **If your house appreciates, you'll receive a higher return on your investment with a lower down payment.** For example, if you put 20% down and took out a loan for the balance at 10% interest, and the house appreciated 8%, your return on your original investment would be 40%. If you put 10% down, by contrast, your return on that same house would be 80%.

- **The appraisal becomes less critical.** For instance, if you offer $1,000,000 with a down payment of $280,000 (28%), the property has to appraise at a mere $900,000 in order for you to get an 80% loan of $720,000.

Using Equity in an Existing House as a Down Payment on a New One

Trading up is an integral part of home buying. You buy a starter house, wait for it to appreciate, sell it, and use the profit for the down payment on a nicer house. It may take two or three sales to get your dream house.

In a rising real estate market, such as is occurring in many parts of California, trading up to raise down payment money works better than saving money or making other investments, because it allows you to maximize your investment leverage. For example, if you put $40,000 down on a $400,000 house (borrowing $360,000) and the house value jumps to $500,000, you've made $100,000 with a $40,000 investment. By contrast, if you deposited the same $40,000 in an unleveraged investment, such as stock or art, and it went up the same 50%, you'd end up with $60,000.

Using a Gift to Help With the Down Payment

If you're fortunate enough to receive a gift of part or all of the money you need for a down payment, you're in great shape—your monthly payments will be lower, and the amount of house you can afford will be higher than if you borrow for the down payment.

However, keep an eye on your lender's rules regarding the source of your down payment. If you get an FHA mortgage, you won't face any restrictions on the amount or percentage of the gift so long as it is a bona fide gift (not a loan) and it comes from a blood relative. If you get a conventional mortgage and put down less than 20% of the purchase price, however, some percentage of the down payment must come from your own funds.

RESOURCE

Giving gifts. For detailed information on estate and gift taxes, see *Plan Your Estate*, by Denis Clifford (Nolo).

Get a Gift Letter

If you're lucky enough to receive gift money well in advance of applying for a loan, and three months of your bank statements reflect this extra money, you're in good shape and don't need to ask what a gift letter is. (The lender views money that has been in your account for three months or more as "seasoned," that is, it's been sitting there long enough to be treated as your own.)

Date _____

To Whom It May Concern:

I/We _____ intend to make a GIFT of $ _____

to (*recipient(s)*) _____ , my/our (*relationship*) _____ ,

to be applied toward the purchase of property located at: _____

_____

There is no repayment expected or implied in this gift, either in the form of cash or by future services, and no lien will be filed by me/us against the property.

The SOURCE of this GIFT is: _____

Signature of Donor(s)

_____

Print or Type Name of Donor(s)

_____

Address of Donor(s): Street, City, and State

_____

Telephone Number of Donor(s)

ATTACHMENTS:

1. Evidence of Donor(s)' ability to provide funds

2. Evidence of receipt of funds by Borrower

Get a Gift Letter (continued)

If, on the other hand, a large deposit shows up in your bank account closer to the time you apply for a loan, the lender is going to question where that money came from. The lender may suspect that the money was meant to be a loan—for example, from a sympathetic friend—rather than an outright gift. You'll need to allay the lender's concerns by providing a written document stating that the money was indeed a gift, with no expectation of reimbursement.

A sample gift letter is above. The letter should specify the amount of the gift and the type of property for which it will be used. Most important, the letter should say that the money need not be repaid. In addition, if money has not yet been transferred, be prepared to document that it's available, by providing the name of the savings or securities institution where it's kept, the account number, and a signed statement giving the mortgage lender authority to verify the information.

Often parents and grandparents will help when it comes to buying a house. Gifts up to $14,000 per year per person (2016 figure—it's indexed to go up with inflation) can be given free of tax. This means, for example, that every year your mother and father can give you and your spouse $56,000 total without having to file a gift tax return.

If a gift will exceed the gift tax exclusion, the gift giver will have to file a gift tax return with the IRS—but, thanks to legislation passed in 2001, there's a good chance he or she won't have to pay gift taxes at all, ever. That's because computing the gift tax debt is now put off until the giver's death—at which time the first $5.45 million of the person's total gifts given will be exempt from tax (for deaths in 2016). The result is that only the wealthiest of people, who give away more than $1 million over their lifetime, will need to give a second thought to gift tax debt.

However, the estate tax is perpetually in flux. For more information, see the "Wills, Trusts & Probate" section of Nolo's website at www.nolo.com.

Borrowing Down Payment Money From a Relative or Friend

Another way to raise money for a down payment is to borrow it from someone you know. While not as advantageous as a gift (since you'll have to pay it back, and it will affect your debt-to-income ratio), it can help if:

- **You're short for the down payment, but have a relatively high monthly income.** If lenders conclude that you have enough income to pay a first mortgage and another loan, they may let you borrow some of the down payment. Most lenders will require that at least 5% of the purchase price come from your own funds.

- **The person lending you money for the down payment will accept no, or very low, payments for several years.** If you don't need to make payments, your debt burden won't increase. Understanding this, a relative or friend may forgive payments for a few years. During that time, the house may rise in value; you can then refinance the mortgage and pay off the down payment loan. (We discuss this strategy in Chapter 12, "Private Mortgages.")

CAUTION

Before arranging for a loan for the down payment, check with your lender or loan broker. There are many ways to structure down payment loans, and you want to be sure that your plan will be approved by the lender. In general, the loan must be at least pegged at "market" interest for a minimum of five years.

Is It a Gift or a Loan? Sometimes It Pays to Be Vague

Some people are tempted to ask a friend or relative for a loan but pretend it's a gift when applying for a mortgage. This scenario may be superficially attractive, but it's technically fraud. While it's unlikely you'd be prosecuted, you'd be taking a big risk.

But, fortunately, you can legally treat money as a gift, as far as a lender is concerned, while reserving the right to repay your benefactor if necessary. For example, if your parents advance you money but worry that circumstances might cause them to need it later, your response might be that you'll do your best to help if they run into problems. As long as there's no written loan agreement and your statement is one of intent (not a promise), the money qualifies as a gift.

Borrowing From Your 401(k) Plan

An excellent source of down payment money if you've got a secure job is a loan against your 401(k) plan. Check with your employer or the plan administrator to see whether your plan allows for loans. If it does, the maximum loan amount under the law is the lesser of one-half of your vested balance in the plan or $50,000 (unless you have less than $20,000 in the account, in which case, you can borrow the amount of your vested balance, but no more than $10,000).

Other conditions—including the maximum term, the minimum loan amount, the interest rate, and applicable loan fees—are set by your employer. Any loan must be repaid, with interest, within a "reasonable amount of time," although the Tax Code doesn't define "reasonable." Ten or 15 years are common loan terms. You may be able to arrange repayment via payroll deductions.

Find out what happens if you are terminated or leave the company before fully repaying a loan from your 401(k) plan. If the loan would become due immediately upon your departure (or, as is common, after 60 days), income tax and penalties may apply to the outstanding balance. But, you may be able to avoid such hassle by repaying the loan before leaving.

Borrowing against your 401(k) plan has several advantages:

- By borrowing against your own plan, you are receiving the interest payments.
- The loan fees are usually lower than a bank would charge.
- It's quick and convenient, with less paperwork than is usually required in getting a bank loan.

Juan and Yolanda: Help From Customers

We immigrated to the U.S. from Mexico years ago and started a landscaping business. In our mid-30s with two kids, we really wanted to buy a small house. Although we'd saved $15,000 for a down payment, we needed another $10,000 to close the deal. With no deep-pocket relatives or friends to call on, we decided to approach our half-dozen best customers to ask if they'd be willing to pay in advance for gardening services for the coming year. Most said yes. We raised the needed money in a few days.

Tapping Into Your IRA

You can withdraw up to $10,000 penalty free from an "individual retirement account" (IRA) for a down payment to purchase your first principal residence. (However, you may have to pay income tax on the withdrawal, and you might have less time than you'd like within which to return it to the IRA if you decide not to use it.) This $10,000 is a lifetime limit—and it must be used within 120 days of the date you receive it.

The law defines a first-time homeowner as someone who hasn't owned a house for the past two years. If a couple is buying a home, both must be first-time homeowners. Ask your tax accountant for more information, or contact the IRS at 800-829-1040 or see its website at www.irs.gov.

Are You Having Too Many Tax Dollars Withheld?

Many people have more of their income tax withheld than is necessary. Some enjoy getting the large refund at the end of the tax year, others want the IRS to protect them from their own spending habits.

If you're having too much of your income withheld, ask your employer to adjust the amount to a more realistic level (by filling out a new W-4 form). That way you'll be able to use the money now, instead of letting the feds play with it until next April.

Working With Real Estate Professionals

Best and Worst Aspects of Working With a Real Estate Professional............ 84

    Great Things About Working With a Real Estate Professional........................ 84

    Cautions When Working With a Real Estate Professional................................87

Who Your Real Estate Agent Really Works For 90

    Buyer's Agent (Your Best Choice) 90

    Dual Agent (Your Second-Best Choice)..92

    Seller's Agent (A Poor Choice) 92

Hiring an Agent by the Hour 93

Finding a Good Agent...93

    What to Look for in a Real Estate Agent... 96

    How to Help a Real Estate Agent Help You...98

How Not to Find an Agent...98

Getting Rid of a Broker or Agent You Don't Like....................................... 100

This chapter focuses on how a California home buyer can work with a real estate agent or broker to find a good house. It also discusses the positive and potentially negative aspects of your relationship with an agent. In hiring a real estate professional, we recommend you:

- Complete your Ideal House Profile in Chapter 1.
- Decide how much you can afford to pay after reading Chapter 2.
- Estimate what it will cost to buy the type of house you want in the area you want, by checking prices of recently sold comparable houses. The information in Chapter 15 will help you do this.
- Decide what legal relationship you want to establish with a real estate professional, after reading this chapter.
- Find a top-notch real estate professional, as discussed in "Finding a Good Agent," below.

Best and Worst Aspects of Working With a Real Estate Professional

Before describing the different ways you can work with a real estate professional, here are some of the pluses and minuses to consider.

Great Things About Working With a Real Estate Professional

Here are some of the helpful things your real estate professional can provide you with.

Access to detailed market information through the MLS and allied computer services. The MLS database lists not only most homes currently on the market, but other details not publicly available concerning the homes' sales histories and transaction status. The agent can also supply a price list of recently sold homes.

Access to a broker's in-house listings. A salesperson employed by a large or well-connected firm will know about houses listed for sale with that firm before they are widely advertised.

Real Estate People Defined

Here are the key players in the California real estate business. Some can fit more than one of these descriptions simultaneously.

Agent or salesperson. One of the foot soldiers of the real estate business who shows houses, holds open houses, and does most of the other nitty-gritty tasks involved in selling real estate. An agent or salesperson (the terms are used interchangeably) must have a license from the state and must be supervised by a licensed real estate broker.

Broker. A broker may legally represent either the seller or buyer. While brokers (except buyer's brokers) almost always receive compensation from sellers, they owe the highest legal duty (fiduciary duty) to whomever they have agreed in writing to represent (seller and/or buyer). A fiduciary duty is one of utmost care, integrity, honesty, and loyalty, like that of a doctor to a patient. A broker can legally supervise one or more agents and must have two years of full-time experience as a real estate agent or salesperson, pass a state licensing exam, and (like a salesperson) complete a continuing education requirement every four years.

Buyer's agent (or broker). An agent (as described above) chosen by the buyer to help find a house. The agent owes a legal duty of trust to the buyer but is typically paid a commission by the seller.

Dual agent (or broker). A dual agent is paid by the seller but represents both buyer and seller. This legal arrangement must be confirmed in writing by the buyer, seller, and agent.

Listing agent. An agent or broker who lists the seller's house for sale and markets it for the seller. Unless the listing agent signs a Dual Agency Agreement, he or she represents only the seller.

Real estate professional. A term used to include either a real estate broker or a real estate salesperson or agent.

Realtor. A real estate broker who belongs to the National Association of Realtors, a business trade group. (An agent or salesperson may also belong.) There are corresponding state associations (California Association of Realtors) and local Boards of Realtors; the latter usually operate MLSs.

Selling agent. The agent who procures the sale of a home. This person may represent the buyer alone or, by agreement, both the buyer and the seller.

Access to off-market listings. A well-connected agent will also learn about homes that the sellers would prefer to sell privately rather than list in the MLS. Ask whether your agent is a member of TAN, or "Top Agent Network," a great source for listing and marketing off-market listings.

Legwork. An energetic salesperson should do lots of house searching for you. This includes going to broker open houses held for real estate professionals on weekdays (and sometimes closed to the public—though you can ask your agent whether it's okay for you to see the home during this broker open house), as well as personally checking out all listed houses that seem to meet your criteria.

Business experience. An outstanding real estate salesperson will have successfully completed many transactions. The experience may be valuable in helping your house purchase run smoothly. The salesperson's negotiating skills and relationships with other agents may also help you get the best price and terms, or to beat out competing offers. A well-respected agent may even be offered a counteroffer when the seller has a better offer on the table, simply because the seller's agent would rather work with that person than with someone he or she doesn't know or doesn't have confidence in.

Knowledge of related professionals. A good salesperson will be one source of referrals to other important professionals like inspectors, title and escrow company representatives, and loan brokers.

Creative ideas. In a challenging market, your agent may figure out unusual approaches to finding you the right home. For instance, coauthor Ira Serkes sent postcards to over 2,000 homeowners in Berkeley's coveted Thousand Oaks and Claremont neighborhoods, saying, "Wonderful buyers of ours need a home!" A response from the neighbor of someone planning to sell led to his client's successfully buying a beautiful house.

No cost to the buyer. Under the typical contractual arrangement, the seller pays the commission, and the services of the real estate salesperson are free to the buyer.

Cautions When Working With a Real Estate Professional

Most real estate professionals are conscientious, honest, and capable of saving you significant time and money. Nevertheless, real estate has its share of people who are incompetent or care only about their own self-interest.

Because real estate is a relatively easy field to enter, it includes a share of bad apples. These bad apples are often late for meetings, are uninterested in showing you houses, take several days to respond to you, and make you wonder why they're in the profession at all.

How Brokers and Agents Are Paid

Real estate agents work on commission and get paid only after your home search is over, the contract negotiated and all its terms fulfilled, the loan funded, and the deed recorded.

Most listing brokers get sellers to pay a commission of 5%–6% of the sales price. "Discount" brokers typically charge 4%. However, some clients successfully argue for lower commissions, pointing out that buyers are doing much of the house-finding legwork—such as scouting out homes using the Internet and visiting them without the agent.

Because most real estate transactions involve two brokers—the one producing the buyer and the one helping the seller—the commission is divided, usually 50-50 between the two brokerage offices. That's $20,000–$24,000 per office on an $800,000 house. Within each office, the salesperson who handled the transaction gets a share, often 50%. And, the salesperson must pay expenses, which include wear and tear on a car, gas, phone, and so on.

Still, great agents go out of their way to make sure you get the house for the best price and terms. They know that if they save you $10,000 on the purchase price, after splitting commissions this way it will only affect the size of their check by a few hundred dollars. Knowing you'll refer others to them, and possibly be a repeat customer, is more important than that little bit of extra cash.

Although your salesperson has a legal duty to fairly represent your interests (unless representing the seller exclusively as a seller's agent), this agent has a more basic conflict of interest. Unless you're paying by the hour, the agent gets nothing until you buy a home, and the amount (based on commission) depends on the price of the house you buy.

A bad apple may therefore try to convince you that a house is worth more than it really is, because if you bid high, you're more likely to get the house and the salesperson will get the commission with little legwork.

A bad apple salesperson may also downplay the shortcomings of a particular home or neighborhood, be it size, commute time, or quality of local schools, in an effort to get you to say yes. Or, the salesperson may show you a long list of unsuitable houses if he or she doesn't know of any houses that meet your specifications at a price you can afford. Rather than admit it, some (especially inexperienced ones) will drag you over half the county muttering something like, "I know this isn't your cup of tea, but I want you to get a feel for the market." The agent is hoping to wear you out so that you'll eventually purchase one of the houses.

The agent may even lack the experience or ethics to best represent the buyer's interest. In unusual situations, the agent may try to pressure you into buying by misrepresenting the facts (for example, implying that you need to offer the full asking price because of competition that doesn't exist) or withholding material information (not telling you the roof leaks). Sometimes these tactics are subtle, such as, "This place is such a bargain; I'd buy it myself if I could."

In the worst case, it may turn out that the salesperson owes a legal duty of trust (fiduciary duty) to the seller and is legally obligated to protect the seller's interest by maximizing the price. This is true if the salesperson is legally a seller's agent rather than a buyer's agent or a dual agent.

Our recommendation: When you evaluate the suitability of a house, don't rely solely on the advice of a person with a major financial stake in your buying it. Take the responsibility to make your own informed choices; among other things, be knowledgeable about the house-buying process, your ideal affordable house and neighborhood, your financing needs and options, your legal rights and the local zoning laws if you're planning to remodel, and how to evaluate comparable prices.

True
Story

Barbara Kate and Ray: Touring with Traci

Tired of paying too much rent for too little space in our San Francisco apartment, we began to ponder buying. We met with Traci, an agent at a large real estate firm. Traci led us to a plush conference room, then through an elaborate list of considerations.

"Naive," proclaimed Traci, scanning our wish list: two bedrooms, good sunlight, lots of closet space, perhaps a little space for a garden. "But I'll see what I can find—in this price range." She added a final admonition: "I only work with people I really, really like."

Apparently, Traci really, really liked us—she phoned at seven the next morning with three houses for us to see that very evening. The space in all three was mostly taken up by the kitchen—the one room we confirmed restaurant-goers hadn't even thought of including on the wish list. None of them had a second bedroom—our number-one priority.

Two nights later, an excited Traci phoned at 11:50 with an exclusive news flash. A nearby two-bedroom owned by her coworker was going on sale the next day. "I've got the keys. I can tour you through right now, before anyone else sees it. I have already prepared the paperwork. I think we can close on this one," whispered Traci. We declined the offer of the midnight ride; the house was still for sale six months later. A week later, Traci had pegged Barbara Kate as the softer sell and suggested that "just the girls" go look at houses. She tracked Barbara Kate down at home, where she was in bed with pneumonia, unwilling and unable to make any girlish outing. But Traci was undaunted. She phoned back that afternoon with a weather report promising a warming of five degrees and "a blanket for you in the trunk."

Two weeks later, Traci called, having found our "dream house": two bedrooms, good sunlight, good neighborhood. She never mentioned it had only one small closet—in the pantry. Outside, post-tour, Traci became adamant. "What can I do to get you to buy that place?" she asked, with a Rumpelstiltskin-like stomp for punctuation.

It was our sixth tour with Traci. It was our last. We're still paying too much rent for too little space. But it beats the alternative.

Who Your Real Estate Agent Really Works For

California law requires salespeople who help buyers find houses to alert them in writing that they have three different options:

- **Buyer's agent.** The salesperson you work with legally represents you exclusively.

- **Dual agent.** The salesperson you work with legally represents both you and the seller.

- **Seller's agent.** The salesperson you work with legally represents the seller exclusively.

These three choices are outlined in the "Disclosure Regarding Real Estate Agency Relationships" form you'll be asked to sign as soon as you start working with an agent. The agent may also have you sign a form called "Confirmation of Real Estate Agency Relationships" at this time. There (in accordance with Cal. Civil Code Section 2079.17), you'll be given three choices as to whom your agent (called the "Selling Agent" in this context) represents, either:

- the buyer exclusively

- the seller exclusively, or

- both the buyer and seller.

In any case, you and the seller will confirm your relationships with your agents in the purchase contract as described in Chapter 16 (Clause 16).

Buyer's Agent (Your Best Choice)

A buyer's agent has "a fiduciary duty of the utmost care, integrity, honesty, and loyalty" to you. Your real estate professional rejects any legal duty of care to the seller (called "subagency" in real estate speak) and represents you exclusively. Can you legally insist on this? You can ask, although the seller and the real estate agent helping you must agree—and must not have already committed to another arrangement.

You don't have to pay a thing in order to have a "buyer's agent" who works only for you. The seller normally pays the entire commission, which is split between the buyer's and seller's broker. (Some buyers have been known to agree to pay their agent's commission in return for extra assurances that the agent works for them alone, but there's really no reason to do this.)

Oversight by California Bureau of Real Estate

Real estate salespeople (agents) and brokers are licensed by the California Bureau of Real Estate (CalBRE). Under Business and Professions Code § 10176 and CalBRE regulations, the CalBRE may suspend or revoke an agent's license for fraudulent or dishonest acts such as:

- making a substantial misrepresentation, such as failing to make a legally required disclosure about a property (see Chapter 19)
- making a false promise that is likely to influence, persuade, or induce
- acting for more than one party to a transaction without the knowledge and consent of all the parties
- commingling money entrusted to the agent with his or her own money
- making a secret profit, or
- acting fraudulently, negligently, or incompetently.

Also, CalBRE § 10177 provides for suspension of a broker who fails to reasonably supervise an agent.

To file a complaint or find out whether action has been taken to restrict, suspend, or revoke a license, contact the nearest CalBRE office. Unfortunately, CalBRE won't mediate complaints or order that money be refunded or unfair contracts be canceled. Also, it won't tell you whether any complaints have been filed against a broker or salesperson, or whether disciplinary action is pending. Despite these shortcomings, it still pays to complain to the CalBRE if you believe you've been treated in an illegal or unethical manner.

You can reach CalBRE via its website at www.dre.ca.gov. This website also includes updated information on real estate laws and regulations, frequently asked real estate questions, and links to other useful real estate sites.

Dual Agent (Your Second-Best Choice)

Here, the real estate professional is paid by the seller but represents both the buyer and seller in a house sale and owes the same legal duty of fair conduct to each. Are you in a good legal situation under dual agency? In theory, it's acceptable: A dual agent cannot disclose to the seller (without your written permission) that you are willing to pay more than the offering price; conversely, a dual agent cannot tell you if the seller is willing to accept less than the asking price.

A dual agency situation can arise if you've entered into an agency relationship with a real estate agent and subsequently look at a house listed with that agent's company—even if the listing agent is not your agent and works in a different branch office of the company. Your agent should disclose immediately if a property you're interested in is listed by his or her company. Dual agency should only be entered into under a written agreement signed by both buyer and seller.

It's still better, however, to work with a real estate professional as a buyer's agent than with a dual agent (often preferred by large brokerage companies that want to sell houses buyers have listed with them and to do so can't solely represent the buyer). Dual agency can mean divided loyalties. For example, a dual agent might not urge you to ask for a lower price, worried that because he knows the seller is desperate, he'd be breaching a duty to the seller.

Seller's Agent (A Poor Choice)

Run, don't walk, from this agency relationship where "your" agent legally represents the seller. This is the way it was in the old days (and still is in many states), and some real estate offices still push it. Perhaps the agent won't explain this adequately, but all should become clear when you look at the legally required Confirmation of Real Estate Agency Relationships form (or corresponding section of the purchase contract). In the unlikely event that your agent has, under "Selling Agent" (the agent who helps the buyer—don't be misled by the name), checked the box saying, "the Seller/ Landlord exclusively," that's a red flag. By signing, you would agree that your agent represents the house seller's interests, not yours. "Your" real estate agent (as the legal "subagent" of the seller) would owe a fiduciary duty of honesty, integrity, and loyalty to the seller, not to you. For instance, if you make a low offer but your agent knows you will go higher or will pay for repair work, the agent would have to tell the seller.

The only time you might have to accept the seller's agent option is if you're buying a new home in a development, where all transactions are handled by the developer's sales force directly or by a broker who represents the developer/seller. Chapter 7 discusses using a real estate agent when purchasing a new home.

Hiring an Agent by the Hour

A few agents market their services directly to potential buyers at an hourly fee. The idea is that you get expert help with no built-in conflict of interest, because the agent has no financial stake in whether or not you buy a house. Rates vary, with a typical house purchaser using between 20 and 50 hours of time.

Most of these arrangements are with licensed real estate brokers, who operate independently of large brokerage companies. A salesperson (agent) can legally provide advice by the hour, but only with the permission of an employing broker.

Few experienced agents go this route, however, because more money can be made on commission, and they don't want to take on any potential liability for their involvement without proportional compensation.

Hiring an agent by the hour is cost-effective only if you do most of the grunt work inherent in finding a house, deciding on the offer amount, and negotiating with the seller yourself.

Finding a Good Agent

As you read this, a veritable herd of real estate agents are trying to find you—the ready, willing, and able buyer. Over 400,000 Californians are licensed real estate salespeople or brokers, and most are underemployed (though the best ones may be quite busy). So the problem isn't finding someone to work with, but finding someone you *want* to work with. The best way to do this is through recommendations from people who've purchased houses in the last few years and whose judgment you trust. (Sellers may give you a good steer, too, but agents who primarily work with sellers have somewhat different skills from those who focus on working with buyers.)

Another possible source for obtaining recommendations is local title companies.

After collecting the names of several agents, arrange to talk to each before making a decision. While you can always get rid of an agent you don't like, it's better to find someone good in the first place.

RESOURCE

Check out websites of individual real estate agents. These give you a good sense of the real estate agent's listings and the services provided, and should include customer testimonials. If you can't find the website of a particular agent, check the National Association of Realtors' site, www.realtor.org; and search for "Find a Realtor." Also check for reviews of the agent on Yelp, Trulia, and Zillow. If an agent in whom you're interested doesn't have any reviews, ask why not.

True Story

Referrals Mean a Lot

Coauthor Ira Serkes, a Berkeley Realtor whose business is over 50% referral, puts it this way:

"Many real estate agents take a long-term approach. We want our buyers to be satisfied customers, so we try to negotiate the best price possible. If we can save the buyer $5,000 we'll do it, even if that means we earn $150 less in commission. We look upon that $150 as our investment in our future. We know that when clients are happy with our service, they will refer friends, family, and neighbors who want to buy or sell a house. The long-term value of a referral business is much more important than receiving a few hundred dollars more on one sale."

Sample Hourly Fee Agreement

This agreement is made between _____ (Buyer) and _____ (Agent) on ___*(date)*___ , concerning the contemplated purchase by Buyer of real property generally described in the Buyer's Ideal House Profile, which is attached. [*You created this Profile in Chapter 1. A copy should be marked Attachment A and stapled to this agreement.*]

1. Buyer agrees to retain Agent as a consultant on an hourly fee basis to assist Buyer in his or her attempt to locate and purchase property described in Buyer's Ideal House Profile. The terms of this agreement shall be as follows:

    A. "Agent" shall mean the licensed real estate broker or agent named above, acting directly as the employing broker of record or through an agent employed under the Broker's license.

    B. Buyer is retaining Agent as an independent contractor and not as an employee.

    C. Agent is a member of a local Multiple Listing Service (MLS); Agent will share with Buyer nonconfidential information from any Multiple Listing Service to which Agent has access as a participating member concerning properties fitting the description in Buyer's Ideal House Profile.

    D. Buyer and Agent agree that Agent shall assist Buyer, to the extent requested by Buyer, in completing offer and counteroffer forms, arranging financing, dealing with escrow procedures, and completing other paperwork pertaining to the real property purchase. This advice shall not include legal or tax advice.

2. Agent shall charge Buyer for consultation services at the rate of $ ____ per hour. Agent's services shall not exceed ____ hours for the contemplated purchase unless the parties mutually agree in writing. Buyer shall pay no commission to Agent; Agent will accept no commission from any Seller from whom Buyer buys.

READ, UNDERSTOOD, AND AGREED TO BY:

Buyer: _____   Date: _____

Buyer: _____   Date: _____

Agent: _____   Date: _____

Supervising Broker: _____   Date: _____

What to Look for in a Real Estate Agent

The agent or broker you choose should (ideally, at least) have the following qualities:

- integrity
- dedication and availability to you
- good rapport with other agents
- experience in the type of services you need
- knowledge of the area you want to live in, and
- sensitivity to your taste and needs.

While the first trait, integrity, needs little elaboration, here are a few words about the other characteristics you should look for.

Dedication and availability to you. Because it's fairly easy to get a real estate license, many dabble in it for a few months or years, often part time, and become discouraged and move on. You don't want to be the guinea pig on which one of these neophytes practices. On the other hand, some agents so overbook themselves with clients that you won't get the time or attention you deserve. Make sure you select an agent with the skills, knowledge, and time necessary to represent you properly. See "Tough Questions to Ask Real Estate Agents and Brokers," below.

Good rapport with other agents. Although you want an experienced agent, you don't want one who's racked up a history of unpleasant dealings with sellers' agents. That can actually lead to your offer being rejected, even if it's better or at a higher price than others. Ask other real estate professionals about a particular agent to see what his or her reputation is.

Experience in the type of services you need. If you're a first-time home buyer you'll probably need more patient guidance, especially with financing issues, than will someone who has owned several houses. If you're looking for a new tract house or a condominium (read Chapter 7 carefully), you may need more specialized help.

Knowledge of the area. Be sure the agent is extremely knowledgeable about the city, county, or, better yet, neighborhood you want to live in.

Sensitivity to your tastes and needs. You and your real estate agent need not agree on everything but it certainly helps if your tastes are compatible.

Tough Questions to Ask Real Estate Agents and Brokers

Here are some questions to ask when interviewing real estate salespeople:

- How long have you been in real estate? How long in this area?
- Are you a licensed real estate broker or an agent?
- Are you full time? If yes, for how long?
- How many buyers have you personally found houses for in the past year? How does this compare with other real estate salespeople in the area?
- Can you give me the names and phone numbers of satisfied customers, or testimonial letters?
- Have you completed any nationally sponsored advanced real estate training programs offering professional designations, such as Graduate Realtor Institute (GRI); Certified Residential Specialist (CRS); Accredited Buyer Representative (ABR); or Certified Luxury Home Marketing Specialist (CLHMS)? (While advanced training doesn't guarantee that an agent will do a good job, typically people who invest time and money in courses take their profession seriously.)
- What systems do you use to make sure all transaction details are completed in a timely manner?
- How will we keep in touch? Will you text or email me home information and updates, preferably daily?
- What other tech tools do you use that will make the process more efficient for me? For instance, can you create a custom map of properties to consider? Can we digitally sign the offer rather than do it by personal meeting or fax? Are you able to review the disclosure package by sharing your screen with us while we're in two different locations? Can you "log" our driving route so I can see how we got to the houses you'll show us? Will you be able to show me which rooms get sun during the winter day?
- Do you keep an up-to-date list of lenders, inspectors, roofers, painters, contractors, and other service providers you have personally used and can recommend?
- Can you provide me with a CMA (comparative market analysis) of each home I'm considering against other similar homes?

How to Help a Real Estate Agent Help You

While you're checking out real estate agents, they'll surely be assessing you. The agent will want to know whether you:

- are highly motivated to buy, or are just a "Looky-Lou" (real estate slang for a person who makes a hobby out of looking at houses and is, essentially, a waste of time)
- can realistically afford to buy a decent house, and
- are reasonably sensible and considerate. An experienced real estate professional knows how miserable it is to work with people who are demanding and rude.

To alleviate an agent's understandable concerns, and show you're really serious about house hunting, here are some tips for your first meeting:

- Give the agent a copy of your Ideal House Profile. (See Chapter 1.)
- Give the agent an idea of your price range and a copy of your financial statement or, even better, a letter from a lender stating that you are preapproved for a mortgage up to a designated amount. (See Chapter 2.)
- Explain why you want to purchase a house in the near future.
- Treat the agent in a businesslike way. This should allay fears that you're demanding, complaining, or neurotic.

How Not to Find an Agent

Here is some advice on how not to find an agent.

Don't be swayed by seeing a lot of the agent's signs on local houses for sale. Although it's a possible sign of popularity, those agents may specialize in representing sellers, not buyers.

Avoid asking an agent near where you live now to make a referral in a faraway area you're moving to (unless the agent actually knows an experienced colleague there). An agent who receives a referral from someone else in the business is expected to compensate the referrer with a percentage of his or her commission. Some salespeople are overanxious to make referrals and may steer you to someone they met once at a real estate conference or otherwise know only casually. Other salespeople are required to go through their agency's relocation department and can't recommend the best agent for you.

Don't choose an agent solely based on affiliation with a nationally advertised chain. Most offices of a nationally advertised chain are individually owned and operated, and pay a franchise fee to the national organization. While the national organization may establish some operational standards and provide a degree of training and support, a local branch is no better than its particular owner and staff.

Don't seek referrals from the Better Business Bureau or local Board of Realtors. They either can't make a referral or will simply send you to the next name on their list.

True Story

Amy and Bruce: Other People's Agents

We found our real estate agent, Kate, through the grapevine of friends and coworkers. We were happy with the choice; she was knowledgeable, efficient, and cooperative, never pushy. We felt comfortable knowing she was looking out for our interests.

We came to feel very differently about the seller's agent, Bob. The annoyances were minor at first. He was always late for meetings. The papers he prepared were sloppy and full of mistakes. He didn't tell our agent that another prospective buyer was making a bid the same day we did, then claimed he'd left a phone message. (Kate rechecked her voicemail; he hadn't.) The last straw was when Bob's failure to relay messages about key points to the sellers nearly made the deal fall through.

By this time, the sellers weren't happy with Bob, either, but they didn't fire him, and we couldn't. Luckily, we could go around him. We went to the broker Bob worked for and told her that from then on, we would either speak to the sellers directly or communicate through her, not Bob. From that point on, we got reliable information—and soon we got the house.

Don't work with someone you meet at an open house, unless and until you thoroughly check the person out. Some real estate salespeople offer to keep houses open for other agents precisely because they're short of business and looking for clients. While you may meet a wonderful agent this way, you can usually do better by getting recommendations from people you trust.

Don't work with someone just because he or she is your first contact when you phone or visit a real estate office. Many real estate offices have "client protection" policies, meaning that you "belong" to the first agent you happened to talk to or who showed you a house. Obviously, the agent is the only person protected by this sort of arrangement, so if you're treated as if you were the property of someone you don't even know, leave.

CAUTION

Check real estate licenses. Make sure your real estate agent's license has not been suspended or revoked—and that the agent actually has a license in the first place! We've heard stories of people who pose as agents, hoping to make quick money from unwitting buyers. Call the nearest office of the California Bureau of Real Estate or check the CalBRE website, www.dre.ca.gov.

Getting Rid of a Broker or Agent You Don't Like

Suppose you realize that your relationship with a real estate professional isn't working. Perhaps the agent repeatedly shows you houses you hate or doesn't show you enough houses. Or maybe you discover that the agent isn't as ethical or careful as you'd like—he or she dismisses your legitimate concerns about the physical condition of the property or pushes you toward a particular lender even though you suspect there are cheaper alternatives. Even if the agent simply doesn't return your phone calls promptly, you may want to work with someone else.

If you're not satisfied with your agent, don't hesitate to switch. Your agent is a business colleague, not a personal friend. To keep things simple, just make sure you end the relationship before the agent starts negotiating a purchase for you.

Here is how to legally end the relationship:

- If you're working with an agent in a relationship where the seller pays the commission, you need only notify the agent that you no longer want to work together. This is true whether you've signed a Disclosure Regarding Real Estate Agency Relationships form or not. That's it.

- If you've hired an agent by the hour, pay for the services you've used and end the relationship. If you committed to a set number of hours and haven't used them, pay only for what you've used. The agent may demand payment for the rest. If so, point out that the agent has a legal duty to try to earn other income in the remaining hours and to subtract that income from what you owe (this is called "mitigating damages"). You may eventually decide to make a small settlement, but don't be in a hurry or pay for time you haven't used.

- If you've hired a buyer's agent to whom you've agreed to pay a commission, there are three ways to end the relationship:

  - If you're unhappy with the agent before you locate a house, simply write a letter terminating the relationship, and don't look at any other houses the agent tries to show you. Even if the contract states that you're bound to work with the agent for a longer period, the letter may serve to resolve the issue.

  - If you've found a house you want to buy with the help of the agent, you're legally (and ethically) bound to honor the terms of the contract. In short, pay the agent the commission; he or she has earned it.

  - If you locate a house on your own but it's during the term of an exclusive buyer-broker contract that calls for the agent to get a commission on any house you buy (a rare situation), and you haven't written the agent to terminate the contract, you technically may owe the agent a fee. Should you grit your teeth and pay it? Consider the fairness of the situation. If the agent did a lot of work for you but didn't happen to locate the house you bought, you owe the money and should pay it if that's what the contract says. But don't pay a large chunk of money to someone who has done nothing to earn it. If you refuse to pay because you received no services, the agent must sue you to collect. This costs time, money, and goodwill. Few agents want it known publicly that they sued a buyer because the agent didn't do his or her job. Also, before you're actually sued, you'll probably have a chance to settle the dispute for a smaller amount. If you do, get a release of all claims when you make your payment. (See *101 Law Forms for Personal Use,* by the Editors of Nolo (Nolo), for forms.)

When You're Really Thrilled With Your Agent

Buyers often wonder if it's okay to "do something" for their agents. The best thing to do is refer the agent to your friends, coworkers, and relatives. In addition, consider buying the agent a gift. Some people we know bought their agent the finest bottle of Napa wine they could afford. Another couple we know gave their agent some books on topics of interest to him. Another gave a $500 cash bonus. (The deal was a mess—the agent was a savior.)

Use your imagination.

How to Find a House

The Best Time to Look for Houses 104

Organizing Your House Search 104

Where to Look for Houses 105

Find Homes on the Internet 106

Check the Classified Ads... 108

Visit Sunday Open Houses 109

Take Advantage of Your Agent's Access
to the Multiple Listing Service... 110

Use an Agent With Good Technical Skills 110

Enlist the Help of Personal Contacts 111

Do Your Own House Scouting... 112

Find Foreclosures, Probate Sales, and Lease Option Properties 114

Finding a House When You're New to an Area 114

Finding a Newly Built House.. 116

n Chapter 1, you did an important part of identifying what you want by creating your Ideal House Profile. Now you need to devise a plan to find a house that matches it as closely as possible.

Pay close attention to your time and financial constraints. For example, the house search of a well-paid executive with money in the bank, who needs to relocate over the summer so her kids' schooling won't be interrupted, differs tremendously from that of a sporadically employed foreign language translator who likes his apartment but eventually wants to buy a modest place with a small down payment.

The Best Time to Look for Houses

When you look at houses may be out of your control. A major event in your life such as a new job or need to move your children before the start of school will mean you must find a new house quickly. If you have the luxury of timing your purchase, however, here are a few hints:

- House prices often jump in the spring, absent some major external factor, such as a recession.
- Historically, mid-November through the end of February is a slow time for the housing market.
- Bad news, such as job layoffs, can temporarily depress a local real estate market.
- When interest rates are low, there's often more competition for housing.

Organizing Your House Search

Set up a file folder on each interesting house. Include a completed House Priorities Worksheet; the information sheet from the open house; the MLS information; ads; and your notes. This may seem like overkill, but the more houses you look at, the harder it will become to keep track of details.

Set up a simple spreadsheet for each house, with columns for the street address and city, price, number of bedrooms and baths, date, comments, or whatever else is important to you. Here's an example:

Address	6938 San Lorenzo	411 Solano Avenue	169 Colusa Avenue
City	Berkeley	Albany	Kensington
Price	$975,000	$850,000	$1.1 million
Bedrooms	3	2	3
Bathrooms	1	1	2
Date seen	2/14/xx	2/21/xx	1/22/xx
Comments	Nice home with lots of light	Some deferred maintenance, but big yard	$14,000 termite report!

Ira Serkes adds, "I like to map the homes using batchgeo.com. You simply put the address, city, state, and anything else you want to map into separate columns on an *Excel* spreadsheet. Copy and paste the contents into the box above the green "map now" button. It will map the addresses for you, which you can organize by bedrooms, price, city, square footage, and so forth."

Where to Look for Houses

There are lots of places you may find your new home. Below are some of the best places to get started.

CAUTION

Don't knock on sellers' doors or directly contact sellers' agents. If you see an interesting listing, either visit the open house or ask your agent (if you have one) to arrange an appointment. If you contact the seller's agent directly, or ask him or her to show you the place, you may inadvertently create a situation where that agent claims to have represented you and expects part of your agent's commission. (Of course, it's a different matter if you see a "For Sale by Owner" or "FSBO" listing—a FSBO owner might even welcome a knock on the door, though it makes more sense to call or email first.)

Find Homes on the Internet

Most home buyers start their search online. Many sites display photos or virtual tours, which may be all you need to determine whether the house is worth a visit.

Here are the best sites for house listings on the Internet.

Zillow and Trulia. These two portals to real estate listings (which have actually merged, but retain separate identities) are the first stop for many house hunters. They shouldn't be your last or only stop, however. Critics charge that their data is not as accurate or up to date as you'll find on a Realtor-run Multiple Listing Service site.

Real estate sections of local newspapers. If you live in a major metropolitan area, such as San Francisco or San Diego, online newspaper classifieds are a good bet. Go to the website of your local paper and see if it has a similar section—most large metropolitan papers do, and even smaller communities may too.

The California Living Network (CLN), at ca.realtor.com. The CLN provides real estate listing information from nearly every MLS in California, sponsored by the California Association of Realtors. The CLN also has a Spanish-language equivalent, at www.sucasa.net.

Realtor.com. Operated by Move, Inc. for the National Association of Realtors (NAR), this pulls together home listings based on NAR's relationships with nationwide MLS services. Be sure to check out www. realtor.com/newhomes if you're looking for new construction.

The Owners' Network at www.owners.com. This site lists homes for sale without a broker. Also try www.forsalebyowner.com.

Craigslist.org. This is an excellent source for homes listed by real estate professionals or owners. Listings are broken down by major metropolitan area.

Websites sponsored by local real estate brokers. Some of the best include detailed photographs and downloadable flyers with more extensive information on the property for sale and its surrounding neighborhood than you'll find on an MLS site. Coauthor Ira Serkes's website, for example, at www.berkeleyhomes.com, offers a direct link to the MLS where you can search for San Francisco or East Bay homes.

Once you identify a house that looks interesting, give your real estate agent the MLS number or property address. Your agent can send you any additional information that's available and schedule appointments to visit in person. If you're not working with an agent, you can call the listing agent directly (or the owner, if it's FSBO).

House Hunting Tips

Here's advice from seasoned house hunters:

- Bring measurements of your largest pieces of furniture and musical instruments.
- Pace yourself; don't try to see more than six to nine houses in a day. Try to visit a few in the evening after work.
- Visit a site like www.mapquest.com and plot the open house locations to save driving time. Or try www.batchgeo.com, where you can create your own map.
- Come equipped with a method for taking notes, a calculator, tape measure, graph paper, your House Priorities Worksheet (Chapter 1), and a digital camera or video recorder. (But ask the agent or house owner for permission before using it.)
- If you're interested in the house, fill out the worksheet carefully. Take notes on the layout, condition of major appliances and fixtures, and problems such as stains on the ceiling or cracks in the basement. Use the tape measure to check that the room's dimensions are the same as on the listing sheet and big enough for your needs.
- Don't let the current decor influence you. Remember, the uglier it is, the more likely you are to buy for a reasonable price. Think creatively about what can be changed.
- Take notes on the things you'd like to find out more about. Don't, however, pepper the seller's agent with questions. It's safer to let your agent ask the questions.

How to Translate Real Estate Ads

Ready to translate the exaggerated language of classified ads? Here's a humorous glossary of the most common euphemisms.

Convenient to shopping. For a month before Christmas, your front lawn will become a parking lot.

Cozy. Rooms are the size of closets; closets don't exist.

Fixer-upper or handyman special. Nothing that an experienced four-person construction crew couldn't fix in nine months.

Fruit trees. Impossible to say anything better.

Half-bath. A small closet contains a 60-year-old toilet located three inches from a basin half the size of a teacup.

Low-maintenance yard. Half-dead Bermuda grass interspersed by an occasional patch of pastel-colored gravel.

Modern kitchen. The rest of the house looks like the birthplace of Abe Lincoln.

Needs tender loving care. Last owner was a recluse with a dozen incontinent dogs.

Not a drive-by. So ugly you have to be dragged in by the ear.

Off the beaten path. A bloodhound couldn't find it.

Priced to sell. No one was interested at a higher price.

Quaint. Need you ask?

Starter house. If your alternative is to live in a city shelter, it will look good; otherwise, keep looking.

Check the Classified Ads

Many California newspapers publish real estate classifieds, usually on Sundays. Reading them will help you learn the real estate market, and spot new listings and price reductions. However, their online listings often draw on another home listing service, such as HomeFinder.com.

Visit Sunday Open Houses

To really get the feel of the market, visit some open houses. Don't be terribly selective at first; your goal is to broadly orient yourself as to general market conditions and current price levels, not to buy the first or second house you see.

Don't Be a Victim of Illegal Discrimination

Illegal discrimination is the refusal to show property to someone, allow them to make an offer to purchase, or accept an offer from them on the basis of characteristics such as age (except in qualifying for senior citizen housing), ancestry, color, creed, gender, having children, marital status, national origin, physical or mental disability, medical condition, genetic information, race, religion, or sexual orientation.

If you believe you've been discriminated against, file a complaint with the California Department of Fair Employment and Housing within 60 days. (Check the government pages of your phone book for the nearest office, call 800-884-1684, or go to www.dfeh.ca.gov.) You may also want to see a lawyer who handles this type of work.

If you prove the discrimination and the property is still available, you're entitled to buy it for the fair market value and you're eligible to receive substantial damages under California Civil Code § 52. If it's not still for sale, the seller must pay you damages.

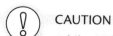

CAUTION

While you're looking at open houses, real estate agents are looking at you. Agents view open houses as a way to find more clients, not just to sell property. Be prepared for agents to ask your name and phone number so they can contact you later. Just say no, unless you really do like the person and will take the time to check him or her out. While it's possible to connect with a good agent at an open house, there are better ways, discussed in Chapter 5.

TIP

The sellers may also be looking you over. Open houses are an opportunity for you to make a good impression on the seller—which may tip the balance your way in a bidding situation. Not all sellers attend, but they could be there incognito. Dress respectably, and if you're with someone, keep your comments about the house positive. (You can sneer at their choice of linoleum when you're back in your car.) If there are any tenants who will be staying, try to chat them up—tenants have been known to lobby sellers in favor of a particular future landlord.

Take Advantage of Your Agent's Access to the Multiple Listing Service

Local Boards of Realtors for most areas of California maintain a database called the MLS, which lists most houses for sale. Listings usually include the price, the address, and a photo of the house; the number and type of rooms; the size of the lot; and other features included, such as the kitchen appliances.

Real estate agents also track comparable sales data, including most houses sold through the MLS during the previous three months, arranged by city or neighborhood, each with the original asking price and the selling price.

Until recently, real estate professionals associated with a local Board of Realtors had a monopoly on MLS and comparable sales information. While most MLS information is now available online, as described above, the "real" MLS still contains more information than is publicly available, which your agent can look up for you.

Use an Agent With Good Technical Skills

If you work with an agent, find one with good computer and related skills who will check new listings several times a day and text or email you new information as soon as it comes out. Some real estate professionals, such as coauthor Ira Serkes, create customized websites allowing clients to view detailed information on their latest house prospects.

In addition to providing up-to-date sales listings, real estate agents can access a wealth of other data for their clients, such as:

- the date a particular property was last bought and for what price, plus property taxes, legal information, and details on the neighborhood
- comparable sales data in bar chart form, with each property's address, asking price, and final selling price
- information on properties that never sold and were taken off the market (in which case you might approach the owners with a new offer), and
- loan origination and mortgage rate comparison programs to speed up loan qualification.

Real estate agents and brokers also normally have access to houses before they're opened to the public.

Enlist the Help of Personal Contacts

If you know people who live or work near where you want to buy, ask them to become house scouts. When people plan to move, friends, neighbors, and business associates almost always know about it before a house is put on the market.

Approach your friends and acquaintances in a formal, structured way. You want them to understand that you're seriously requesting their assistance, not just fantasizing about owning a new home. Here is how to do it:

- Prepare a cover letter or email containing a brief—perhaps humorous—description of exactly what you want your scouts to do. Generally, this should encourage your scouts to spread the word about your needs and, of course, to call you immediately if they spot a likely house, especially if they hear about it before it goes on the market. Attach your Ideal House Profile.
- Send your letter and worksheet to friends and fairly close acquaintances. Include local businesspeople with whom you have a friendly relationship. Doctors, lawyers, dentists, and insurance brokers may also be good sources of information. They routinely have advance information about impending moves.

- If your house search turns out to be prolonged, contact your scouts with periodic progress reports and reminders that you still need help.

Do Your Own House Scouting

In addition to enlisting the help of friends, you can do much looking on your own.

Canvass Neighborhoods

While it may be a little aggressive for some tastes, we know people who have found houses simply by notifying every owner in the area of their interest in their neighborhood. If you're part of that neighborhood's listserv, or know of someone who is, that's an easy way to reach a lot of people. Or, if you have the time, you might hand carry a flyer door to door and hang signs on notice boards in laundromats and grocery stores.

Another possibility is to mail a friendly letter containing your house specifications to everyone in a particular area after getting the names and addresses from a "reverse directory," available at the public library or at www.whitepages.com. (Click the "Address" tab. You'll need at least one address from that neighborhood with which to get started.)

Look for Houses That May Soon Be on the Market

Driving around neighborhoods and looking for run-down houses (peeling paint or weeds in the front yard, no curtains in the window) is one way to find houses that may soon be for sale. For many reasons (impending foreclosure, ill health, divorce), run-down properties, especially rentals, are often available for purchase, even though they aren't formally listed.

If you locate a likely house, ask neighbors if they know whether the house is for sale and the name and phone number of the owner. You can also find the owner's name at the county assessor's or recorder's office, from a local title or escrow company, or using the online reverse phone directory described above or such sites as PropertyShark.com.

Sample House Scout Letter

Dear Friends:

We are facing a challenge and need your help!

We've been house hunting for months, but without much luck. We're looking for a 3- or 4-bedroom home in Piedmont or the Montclair district of Oakland. Our lender tells us we can pay up to $1.65 million.

It's important that the house be light and airy, with a private backyard that is (or can be) closed in for our old hound, Faithful Fred. We've attached a sheet listing the most important attributes of our ideal house.

Do you know of anyone thinking of selling? Can you help in one or more of the following ways?

- Keep your eyes open for suitable houses already on the market.

- Look for houses that are for sale by owner we might otherwise miss. (These don't appear in real estate listings and are often hard to find.)

- Tell your friends, neighbors, and business associates—they'll probably hear about a house from someone moving long before it's listed with a broker.

- Ask your doctors, dentists, lawyers, and other service providers, who are often the first to know when people plan to move.

If you hear about or spot a house that seems even remotely likely, give us a call pronto, at 555-4377.

Thanks for your help.

Dennis and Ellen Olson

P.S. As soon as we move in, we plan to throw the best dance party you've ever been to for all our house scouts. And whoever tips us off about the house we buy will be promptly invited to dinner for four at your choice of Chez Panisse in Berkeley or Masa's in San Francisco.

How to Approach an Owner You Don't Know

The reason you want to know about houses that may soon be for sale is to contact the owner and potentially make an offer before it's listed. This is often easier said than done. Many people, especially those moving because of health, financial, or marital problems, aren't likely to appreciate an aggressive buyer.

It's best to approach a potential seller as politely and nonaggressively as possible. If you have a mutual friend, ask that person to introduce you. If this isn't possible, write the owner a friendly note (use a nice card), saying you've heard he or she might be moving and, if so, would he or she be willing to show you the house. Follow up with a phone call a few days later. If you meet with resistance, back off.

If you get to see a house, and you like it, you'll naturally want to know how much the seller wants. It's fine to ask, but don't be pushy. The seller may not have thought about it, and if he or she thinks you're trying to "steal" the home, you'll probably never hear from him or her again. Do mention that if a sale can be conducted without brokers (or with one broker who gets a 2%–3% commission instead of the customary 5%–7%, or who works by the hour), the seller will save a good bit of money, plus the hassles of readying the house for showings.

Find Foreclosures, Probate Sales, and Lease Option Properties

In Chapter 3, we discuss finding properties subject to foreclosure and probate sale, and houses you may be able to lease with an option to buy.

Finding a House When You're New to an Area

If you're completely unfamiliar with the area you're moving to, you're at an obvious, and serious, disadvantage—you don't have the basic information normally considered essential to locating a good house, in a congenial location, at a fair price. While a good salesperson can show you the best homes in your price range in different neighborhoods, it will take some time to figure out which communities you'll feel most comfortable in. Getting a real sense of what houses are worth may also be difficult, but a good market analysis can help. Chapter 15 explains how to find the prices of comparable houses.

Some brokers train their agents to be "relocation specialists." While they can't know your personal desires, they have thorough knowledge of schools, community services, and neighborhood features, and if you're clear about what you want, they should be able to answer your questions.

If you're in a hurry, a sensible alternative to trying to find a house right away is to leave your furniture in storage and rent a furnished place until you have a sense of your new turf. Sure, this means moving twice, but it's better than paying too much for a house in an undesirable area that you may have difficulty reselling when you want to move, which is likely to be soon.

Talk to friends, coworkers, shopkeepers, homeowners, and anyone else familiar with where you're moving to before settling on a geographic area. Emphasize the personal by telling them who you are and what you like. You want to know the specific towns and neighborhoods where you'd fit in. In our view, it's more important to live in such an area than in the perfect house.

RESOURCE

Looking for city, community, and neighborhood information? Check out schools, housing costs, demographics, crime rates, and jobs via the California state Web page (www.state.ca.us) and Sperling's Best Places (www.bestplaces.net). HomeFair, www.homefair.com, also has useful links to help you decide where to live based on home prices, schools, crime, salaries, transportation, demographics, and community services. Realtor.com can help you identify communities that meet your preferences as to house type, size, age, and price range, as well as neighborhood demographics and schools.

Paul and Barbara: Our House Scouts Came Through!

After the birth of our second child, we searched for a bigger house in our general area for almost a year, to no avail. Finally, we started telling as many people as possible about our search. One day, a friend went for her teeth cleaning, and her dentist mentioned that he was retiring in about six months and moving. Our scout asked if he and his wife planned to sell their home. They did! She mentioned us to the dentist and then relayed his invitation for us to call. We looked at his house, and loved it.

We suggested to the dentist and his wife that if we could agree on the price, we could jointly handle the entire sale without real estate agents.

They named a moderately high, but fair, price, and we said yes. It turned out, however, that they had promised to list the house with a real estate broker friend. To honor that promise, they paid her a 3% commission in exchange for helping with the contract, inspections, and closing.

We not only got a great house, we got a great deal. If we hadn't heard about the house and it was put on the market months later, the combination of fast-rising local prices and the need to pay an additional $15,000 in real estate commissions would have increased the price by $50,000 or more, effectively putting it out of our price range.

Finding a Newly Built House

We discuss new houses in Chapter 7. One point worthy of mention here is that to get a good deal on a new house, you need to understand and follow the market for some time. New housing developments, and new sections of old developments, are continually coming on the market. The best tend to sell quickly; the worst hang on for months.

It's extremely difficult to accurately judge the new house market in a weekend, or even a week. The best approach is to follow it for some time, making a careful list of all new projects in the geographical area that interests you.

New Houses, Developments, and Condominiums

Pitfalls and Pluses of Buying a New House 118

Choose the Developer, Then the House 121

Using a Real Estate Agent or Broker 123

Financing a New House 124

    Help Arranging a Loan 124

    Government Housing Programs 125

    Buydowns and Other Direct Financing Subsidies 125

Optional Add-Ons and Upgrades 126

Choosing Your Lot 132

Restrictions on the Use of Your Property: CC&Rs 134

    Role of Homeowners' Associations 135

    How to Check Out a Development or Condo 137

Dealing With Delays 139

Inspect the House Before Closing 142

Guarantees and Warranties 143

f a newly constructed house is definitely not for you, skip this chapter. But if you're open to buying a new house, read on for pros and cons and for suggestions on ways you can save time, aggravation, and money.

Also, while much of this chapter focuses on new houses, there's lots of useful advice for people buying an existing condominium or a property governed by a homeowners' association and CC&Rs.

Pitfalls and Pluses of Buying a New House

Buying a newly built house in California usually means purchasing in a tract development. There are some disadvantages to this, including:

- **Your choice is limited to relatively few models.** Most developers have a few floor plans to choose from, and while you can usually customize features like cabinets or light fixtures, you'll be limited to the available configurations.

- **You may have to deal with a slick sales rep.** Home developers tend to have commissioned sales representatives trained in carefully orchestrated techniques designed to make as much money as possible. (We use the terms seller, builder, and developer interchangeably in this chapter to refer to the person, or company representative, who is building the houses and trying to sell you one.)

- **You'll be lured to the development based on a seemingly impossible low price.** Then you'll be shown model houses that are typically loaded with expensive extras.

- **Many developers make their profit by selling add-ons and upgrades.** These are commonly overpriced; other developers price their houses high to start with and will resist calling in their workers to install anything extra.

- **You'll get discount financing and extra features only if houses are selling slowly.** But you may get low-quality construction, too. Meanwhile, the seller will charge you top dollar, with no extras, if sales are hot.

New House Contracts: Special Considerations

As we mention in Chapter 16, you can use the standard California contract when buying a new house. You will want to complete the developer's contract very carefully, to allow for homeowners' association membership, optional add-ons, and warranties. You may also want to obtain and review copies of documents relating to the construction of the house. Other clauses unique to new houses relate to developer delays, deposits on optional items, and development and improvement plans in undeveloped areas.

- **You'll be asked to sign a contract written primarily to benefit the seller.** It will likely be handed to you on a take-it-or-leave-it basis, with little opportunity to negotiate over most terms.

- **Once you place your order, you have little control over when your house is delivered.** The exception, of course, is if you buy a model already in inventory.

- **Lemons happen.** The fact that a home is new doesn't mean it was properly built. In fact, complaints about the quality of new home construction are quite common. For example, Ira Serkes helped a buyer place an offer on a two-year old, $1,500,000 home in the Oakland Hills. When the inspector turned on the bathroom shower, the water flowed down the floor and into the house. The inspector also discovered that half the windows were failing because they'd been improperly installed.

- **If the house turns out to be a lemon, getting problems fixed is extremely difficult.** Getting your money back is next to impossible.

- **The price is seldom negotiable.** The sellers usually adopt a "take it or leave it" approach. This doesn't mean you shouldn't attempt negotiation, especially if the home seems overpriced —but your most likely bargain is to get the seller to include additional amenities at the same price.

Does this mean you should forget about buying a new house? No. New houses often have many advantages over comparable older houses, such as:

- **Price.** Many developments are built on large chunks of land, meaning a low per-house land cost. In addition, because many houses are built at once, building supplies are purchased in bulk, bringing construction costs down. And, when new houses don't sell, developers are often pressured by their lenders to raise money quickly, sometimes by slashing prices.

- **Amenities.** Many new house developments include plans for pools, tennis courts, golf courses, and meeting rooms. This is great, as long as the developer has the financial capacity to follow through and actually build them—sometimes a problem. You'll also need to make sure that any user fees are reasonable.

True Story

Marcia and Drew: Boy, Were We Naive

We visited a model home; we liked it and the financing the builder offered. We told the salesperson we had some design changes in mind and were assured that the developer was fair and flexible and would work everything out as we went along. We took him at his word and signed on the dotted line. Within a few days, problems began. For one, we wanted to eliminate some completely nonfunctional pillars in the living room. The builder said "no way." We then asked for different bathroom countertops and offered to pay the extra. Again, we got no cooperation and had to hire an outside contractor to remove the countertop and install the one we wanted. Whatever we requested turned out to be either impossible or prohibitively expensive. When we asked to see the original salesperson who had promised us "total cooperation," we learned that he was now working as a scuba diving instructor in Hawaii.

I guess you can say we learned the hard way. Next time, we'll be better prepared.

- **Designed for modern tastes and needs.** New-home builders keep a sharp eye on the latest trends, and will make sure that if buyers currently favor open floor plans, guest suites, and LED lighting, that's what their homes will contain.

- **Less immediate maintenance and fix-up work.** Since everything is new, you should spend less time and money on repairs or improvements, at least in the early years if the construction was properly done.

- **Lower utility bills.** New homes are usually more energy efficient than older homes, (but, ask the builder to estimate the gas and electric bills).

- **Rules governing your neighbors.** CC&Rs regulate many aspects of community life, especially the look of yards, driveways, and exteriors. If you appreciate order, this will be an advantage.

Choose the Developer, Then the House

The most important factor in buying a new house is not what you buy (that is, the particular model), but rather whom you buy from. You want a solid house, delivered on time, from a quality, financially stable builder who stands behind his or her work.

Usually a few developers build in a particular locale, and their reputations are well known. To check out a particular builder, talk to:

- **Existing owners in the development you're considering (or in a recently completed development by the same builder).** If they like or hate the developer, you probably will, too. The homeowners' associations will be an especially good source of information because they often hear about, and sometimes coordinate, complaints from buyers. Also check out postings on homeowner-run websites such as www.hadd.com (Homeowners Against Deficient Dwellings) or www.hobb.org (HomeOwners for Better Building).

- **An experienced contractor.** Have your contractor look at other houses the developer is building. It's hard to assess the quality of construction techniques on a finished model; it's much easier if someone with experience can get access to a house as it's being built.

- **County planning or building office staff who deal with local developers.** For the best results, ask your questions positively. "Do Brady and Jones finish their projects on time, with few complaints?" will probably be answered candidly, while "Is it true Brady and Jones is a real schlock outfit?" might not be.

- **Real estate agents who've worked in the area for some time.** While agents won't usually deal directly with new house sales, they will likely have handled the resale of other houses built by the same developer and will thus know developers' reputations.

- **The Contractors State License Board (CSLB) for any complaints filed against the developer.** You can reach the CSLB at 800-321-CSLB, or see www.cslb.ca.gov. The CSLB will tell you only about complaints that have been fully investigated and referred for legal action. Remember, however, that the lack of complaints doesn't necessarily say anything positive about the builder.

TIP

Looking for a green builder? If you're looking for a house that was built without excessive waste, is energy efficient (perhaps even solar powered), and uses less water than the typical home, then look for a builder certified by an independent organization such as Building It Green (www.builditgreen.org).

RESOURCE

Look for new houses online. For details on new home developments throughout California, check out specialized new-home websites, such as www.newhomeguide.com. Of course, don't forget to check other online sources of homes for sale, as discussed in Chapter 6.

Using a Real Estate Agent or Broker

Chapter 5 discusses the legal and practical issues of working with a real estate broker or salesperson. Unfortunately, those rules don't always apply when purchasing a new house:

- Developers don't want to pay a commission to a real estate salesperson, so they hire their own sales staff (who only represent them). Not surprisingly, local real estate people, knowing they won't earn a commission, won't show these houses and may even bad-mouth an entire development in an effort to divert you to houses where commissions are being paid.

- Developers with slow-selling projects may cooperate with local real estate salespeople. This can extend to offering prizes and other come-ons to the salesperson who brings in the most potential buyers. Thus, you may be dragged to completely unsuitable developments for the sole (but unstated) purpose of qualifying the salesperson for a drawing for a trip to Mexico.

Find Out How Many Houses or Condos Are Owner Occupied

If considering a house in a new development or a condominium, find out early on what percentage of the units are owner occupied. The higher the percentage, the better maintained the development is likely to be. Owners have more at stake (resale value) than do renters.

This information may also affect your ability to get a competitive loan from a conventional lender. If you are buying in a new development, lenders often require at least 50% owner occupancy before granting a loan. In a condominium building, many lenders make loans only where two-thirds or more of the owners occupy their units. If you don't qualify for a loan as a result of low owner occupancy in a new development, you may need to arrange financing with a developer, perhaps on less-favorable terms. In a condo, you may still be able to borrow from a conventional lender, but you may have to put down 20%–30%.

- Some developers cooperate with agents under their own (often unusual and not widely published) rules. For example, a developer might not pay a commission if you first visit without your agent, even if your agent is involved in every subsequent step of the purchase; but the developer would pay one if your agent was with you when you first registered. Knowing this, the agent with whom you are working is economically motivated to steer you away from any such tracts you've visited on your own and toward one with rules that will result in a commission if you buy.

If you want professional help negotiating the purchase of a new house, hire an agent familiar with the local new housing scene for a fee before you sign a contract.

If the developer won't pay the commission, ask for a break in the sales price, or upgrades, such as higher quality countertops.

Financing a New House

The discussions on how to determine how much house you can afford (Chapter 2) and the various ways to finance your purchase (Chapters 8 through 13) apply to buying new, as well as existing, houses. A few noteworthy differences, however, exist.

Help Arranging a Loan

Often, developers of new housing will help you locate financing by referring you to a local bank or savings and loan that has already appraised the property, or to a loan broker. As discussed in Chapter 13, a lender will check your creditworthiness and appraise the house to see if it's worth what you agree to pay. For new houses, however, a lender often does a blanket appraisal of all development houses and agrees to approve loans for creditworthy borrowers up to a set amount. If you borrow from one of these lenders, no new appraisal will be necessary.

A developer cannot, however, insist that you accept financing through this network. This is important to remember if the developer pressures you to use its lender or offers incentives to accept a loan with a higher-than-normal interest rate or fees. Such practices have been the subject of consumer complaints, including cases in which the developer secretly offset the supposed discount incentives by raising the house's base price. To get the best deal on a loan, be sure to comparison shop.

Government Housing Programs

Some builders may have their developments qualified for special government loan programs, such as the California Housing Financing Agency. For more on this, see Chapter 11, "Government-Assisted Loans."

Buydowns and Other Direct Financing Subsidies

If sales are slow, developers may increase buyer affordability through a "buydown" of the mortgage. This means the developer pays a part of your monthly mortgage for a set period of time. For example, if you find a house with $1,200 in monthly carrying costs, and you have $300 a month of other debts, normally you'd need a family income of at least $4,550 per month to qualify. But if the builder pays $150 a month toward your mortgage for five years, you'd need a gross income of only $4,100 a month to qualify. (This assumes a debt-to-income ratio of 33%. Most lenders want this ratio to be between 28% and 36%.)

More commonly, the builder will buy down your mortgage by subsidizing the interest rate you pay. One way is through the 3/2/1 subsidy, where the developer subsidizes part of your mortgage for three years, decreasing the subsidy each year. The table below shows how a buydown for a $100,000, 30-year loan at a fixed rate of 5% might work.

Why would a developer buy down your mortgage? When sales are slow, unsold inventory accumulates. Developers must continue to pay interest on the money borrowed to finance construction. Selling a house, even if it means helping pay your mortgage to do it, reduces this burden. Sure, it reduces the developer's profit as compared to selling all houses with no subsidy, but when this isn't possible, profits (albeit lower ones) depend on selling homes.

How a Builder Buydown Works			
	Your Interest Rate	Your Monthly Payment Monthly	Mortgage Subsidy From Full 5% Fixed Rate
Year 1	2%	$370	31%
Year 2	3%	$422	21%
Year 3	4%	$478	11%
Years 4–30	5%	$537	(none)

If you do not need the lower payment that a buydown would give you, consider bargaining for something else instead. For example, you might try to purchase for a lower price, thereby lowering the down payment, or ask for extra features such as a deck or better-quality light fixtures at no extra cost. In short, the buydown is a tip-off that you have room to bargain for a better deal.

Another reason for substituting a lower price for the buydown is that many buydowns take back many of the benefits they claim to provide—they give you a mortgage that has a higher-than-market interest rate after the buydown period is exhausted.

If you can choose between a buydown of your mortgage and a significantly lower price, a reduced price (resulting in a smaller mortgage) will normally save you more if you plan to own the house for a long time. If you intend to own the house for only a few years, however, a short-term mortgage buydown is probably better, as you'll pay less during this period. (To help with the calculations, use an online mortgage calculator.)

Optional Add-Ons and Upgrades

Many developers advertise their houses at comparatively low prices to get you to come out and have a look. The moment you become seriously interested, the price goes up as the developer tries to sell you high-profit extras (such as an extra fireplace, a personal spa, or a home office), upgrades (replace sliding doors with French doors, or tile countertops with granite), or design changes (greenhouse windows or security and alarm systems).

Buying extras and upgrades may enable you to semi-custom-design your home at a reasonable price. Many buyers appreciate a wide choice of kitchen cabinets, floor coverings, air conditioning systems, windows, skylights, and sprinkler systems. You may even be able to add on a room or two at a reasonable cost. But before you get too carried away, pull out your Ideal House Profile (Chapter 1). What do you really need to add to meet your needs, and how much will it cost? Use this figure to compare one new house to the next.

Be sure you investigate all payment options. Typically, some upgrades must be paid for up front, while others can be added to the price of the house and paid for over time—obviously a much more affordable option if you're on a budget. If you do agree to pay a substantial amount of extra cash, make sure the funds are deposited in an escrow account, to be released only when the work is done.

True Story

Helen: How I Got the Carpet I Wanted

I bought a new house in El Sobrante that came with low-quality carpeting. The developer offered two better grades, but I didn't like either—they were overpriced and still not really top grade. Thus, my offer to purchase was contingent on the developer's installing the carpeting of my choice, at no charge. He balked, but I pointed out that he was planning to install carpet anyway, so what was the difference? He finally agreed and also agreed to give me the carpeting that came with the house. (Why I had to bargain for this is a real mystery, as, of course, I'd paid for it.) At any rate, I purchased my own carpet at a local warehouse for $3,800 and had it delivered. The developer installed it. I then sold the original carpet through a classified ad for $1,500. Not only did I save several hundred dollars over the cost of upgrading to the developer's supposedly top-quality carpet, I also got the carpet I wanted.

Clues to Good Construction and Amenities

The more you pay for a newly built house, the more—and better-quality—amenities you should expect. Here are some things to examine.

Air conditioning. If you live in a hot area, be sure the central air conditioning is adequate. In many tracts in the Central Valley, air conditioning units that supposedly meet minimum standards don't do the job.

Building site. Review a copy of the soils and engineering report, which the builder should have available, and the Transfer Disclosure Statement and the Natural Hazard Disclosure Statement. (See Chapter 19.) You are obviously not interested in buying a house that is likely to flood or slide off a hill, or that is built in immediate proximity to an earthquake fault. Also check U.S. Geological Survey maps for soil stability and earthquake and flood zones.

Carpets and drapes. Poor-quality carpets and drapes are often an indication that the house itself is poorly built.

Electrical outlets and jacks. You'll want sufficient outlets per room, with plenty of hookups for phone, cable, Internet, and computer.

Energy efficiency. Insulation is measured by an "R" factor. In cool areas of California, look for a development that exceeds R19. Good insulation now will save you enormous heating bills later. Make sure the air conditioning, heating systems, and other appliances are the most efficient.

Entryways. Are the front and back porches covered? Stepping directly into the rain is a nuisance, but eliminating porches saves developers a few dollars.

Floors. The best, but most expensive, floors are hardwood or ceramic tile. Make sure any plywood floor has two layers.

Foundation. Poured concrete is superior to concrete block.

Inside doors. It's usually worth paying extra for solid core doors if they don't come with the house.

Kitchen cabinets. If you're paying top dollar, you want hardwood cabinets, not plywood. Again, this is a good tip-off as to whether you're dealing with a quality developer.

Clues to Good Construction and Amenities (continued)

Soundproofing. Make sure you won't hear neighbors or highway noise. In developments where houses are only a few feet apart, or if you're on a busy street, this is particularly important. If some houses in the development are already occupied, check this out with the occupants.

Yard. An underground watering system is a good sign that the builder is committed to quality. Given a choice, it's more efficient and convenient, and it's often less expensive, to install an underground watering system before the yard is graded.

CAUTION

Negotiate refunds on optional items. If you cancel your contract, some builders will not refund the deposits you paid for optional items. If you plan lots of expensive upgrades, try to negotiate the right to a full (or at least partial) refund if the options (for example, a new security system) haven't been bought or installed. Or negotiate the right to keep any optional items that you've paid for and that haven't been permanently installed.

Upgrades can add 5%–20% or more to the cost of a new home. To get the most for your money, follow these steps:

1. **Make sure prices are fair.** Steer clear of developers who deliberately use poor-quality materials in highly visible spots in their models, almost forcing you to upgrade to overpriced substitutes. Always confirm, in writing, what you are getting at what price, and whether the developer will allow you to make changes on your own and give you an allowance for materials and labor not used (kitchen cabinets, floor coverings). This can commonly be an issue if you don't like the developer's standard kitchen cabinets, floor coverings, or bathroom fixtures, or the optional upgrades the developer offers, and want to separately purchase and install these items yourself.

To double-check the prices of extras, visit consumer-oriented showrooms, do-it-yourself home stores, and home improvement shops.

2. **Negotiate the cost of extras.** Consider asking for one free extra for every two you buy. For example, if you pay top dollar for a stainless steel refrigerator and glass tile, ask the developer to install a better stove at no charge. This is particularly reasonable if the developer does not credit you with the cost of the original item when you upgrade. Also, as mentioned above, don't be afraid to ask for the right to purchase and install extras or upgrades on your own. If you're considering adding an expensive option such as an oak staircase, built-in window seats, or a deck, you may get a better deal from an outside contractor.

3. **Inspect model houses carefully.** Be sure that the linoleum, tile, rugs, and kitchen cabinets are of good quality, and that they're the ones you'll get if you buy a house. Many new house contracts contain a clause saying that the model's features are not necessarily the features you'll receive—you are guaranteed only the functional equivalent of what you see, which will almost always be different and will cost the builder far less. If you suspect this problem, shop elsewhere, or make a list of the precise features you're concerned about (include makes and models) and include it in your contract.

CAUTION

Know what you're buying. Model homes will almost always feature the best of everything, including large mirrors to make the rooms seem larger. Don't be fooled into expecting that your home will have the same details. If in doubt, get your understanding in writing or included as a contingency in your purchase contract. And be sure to look at an "unfinished" model, to see exactly what you're buying.

Sample Supplementary Agreement

February 1, 20xx

On January 12, 20xx, Alex Stevens, Sales Manager for ABC HomeCrafters, presented me with a contract to purchase the house at 8 Warden Crescent. After a discussion, I agreed to sign this contract with the following conditions:

- ABC HomeCrafters agrees to install a drainage system along the rear property line, according to the specifications set out in Attachment A to this agreement, and a redwood deck with railing behind the kitchen, according to the specifications set out in Attachment B. In exchange, I agree to pay $11,000 above the amount agreed to in the purchase contract dated January 17, 20xx. Payment will be made by March 10, 20xx.
- Work on the drainage system and deck, plus all landscaping called for in the purchase contract, will be completed on or before November 1, 20xx. If any work is not completed by this date, we agree that the money to cover the cost will remain in escrow until the work is completed.

2/1/xx	*Patricia Nelson*
Date	Patricia Nelson
2/1/xx	*Alex Stevens*
Date	Alex Stevens, for ABC HomeCrafters

4. **Take care of the essentials before negotiating the flashy add-ons.** Investing in essentials (a fenced yard, wiring for your tech needs, or extra office space) tends to add more to the resale value of a home than other add-ons (a hot tub, wine cellar, or home theater). Whatever you do, don't buy the builder's model with all the upgrades unless you get it at a huge discount. Recouping the cost of all the extras at resale is likely to be impossible—resale buyers tend to be far less excited than original owners about add-ons.

5. **Get it in writing.** When dealing with a developer's sales representative, get all promises as to what will be done, and when, in writing. If you haven't yet signed the purchase contract, make sure it includes all agreed-upon changes. If the developer's contract allows installing appliances or using materials different from those in the model, establish exactly what you will get and when. If you've already signed the contract, and you later negotiate for changes, write them down in a separate document.

Developers often resist writing things down, wanting you to rely on oral promises. ("Sure, the deck will be built by March 1.") Oral commitments are notoriously unreliable and, in practice, almost impossible to enforce.

See our sample above of what a supplementary written agreement should cover.

Choosing Your Lot

In some new developments, you will need to select a lot before your house is built. Sometimes you must choose before any house has been built. This can be tricky, as many builders won't even allow buyers on site, for insurance reasons. And even if they will, it can be hard to know what the area will ultimately look like, especially if it's full of earthmovers and construction equipment. Still, if you take your time and really study the developer's maps, you should get a pretty good picture of what a particular house will be like. Here are some things to consider:

• **Privacy.** Study the elevation of the lot. Will passersby on the street, or neighbors, be able to look into your windows? If so, will they be viewing rooms where you want privacy?

• **Driveway.** Will you have a clear view down the street? It's dangerous to pull out into the middle of a blind curve.

• **Noise.** A lot at the end of a cul-de-sac will be quieter than one on a main access road, especially if you're on a hill or a corner. Also look at how close you'll be to the house next door. Many developments jam numerous houses so close together you can hear the neighbors' TV.

- **Flooding.** Lots on the tops and sides of hills are usually dry. Lots at the bottom are often prone to flooding, especially if they're near a stream.

- **Geology.** It is impossible to see below the surface of a lot, and most geologic testing is prohibitively expensive. But in a new development, you can ask to see geologic reports that were done to obtain building permits.

Getting a good lot at a good price is often a matter of timing. The best locations in each price range usually go first. Most developers offer waiting lists for popular locations where houses are under construction. In deciding whether to take an okay lot in a section now being built or to wait and hope for a better location in the next section, consider the following:

- Salespeople who receive a full commission if you buy now—as opposed to a small cut if you put down a deposit on a house that won't be built for a while—will sometimes overpraise existing lots and emphasize possible difficulties and delays in connection with sections where future building will occur. If, however, you state that you'll buy in the yet-unbuilt area or not at all, these difficulties are likely to quickly evaporate.

- Developers often, but not always, build the more desirable sections of a tract first. This excites buyers' interest and moves in many people quickly, creating a positive atmosphere for later sales.

- In large developments where new sections open periodically, the longer you wait, the more choice you'll have. This strategy may cost you dearly, however, if the development is popular, because the developer may then mark up prices for newly built houses, and the resale price of existing houses will likely also increase.

- Sales in yet-to-be-completed sections of developments often fall through, and good houses may reappear on sales lists, sometimes just before closing. So, if you can commit quickly, you may save time and money by staying in touch with a developer and being ready to move fast when a good deal presents itself.

If you're buying a lot in an undeveloped area, be sure you get the developer's written confirmation of promised improvements, such as sidewalks and parks. If choosing between developments, favor the ones where the amenities have already been built.

Restrictions on the Use of Your Property: CC&Rs

Many new house developments and community associations, such as condominiums, include, as part of the deed to a property, a number of restrictions on how the property can be used and the responsibilities of the homeowners. These CC&Rs commonly limit things like the color or colors you can paint your house (often brown or gray), the color of the curtains or blinds visible from the street (usually white), whether you can rent the place out if you move, and even the type of front yard landscaping you can do.

With some CC&Rs, you don't have the right to cut your lawn, plant a tree, or tend flowers; instead, you pay a monthly fee to a gardening company that does the work. Typical CC&Rs in condos have additional restrictions, such as limits on the placement of television satellite dishes and the banning of some home-based businesses.

CC&Rs in California may not, however, prohibit owners from keeping at least one pet—unless the homeowners' association's bylaws were adopted before this law took effect in 2001. That leaves plenty of developments that prohibit pets or limit their number and poundage.

Getting relief from overly restrictive CC&Rs after you move in isn't usually easy. You'll likely have to submit an application (with fee) for a variance, get your neighbors' permission, and possibly go through a formal hearing at which you may not succeed. And if you want to make a structural change, such as enlarging a window, building a fence, or adding a room, you'll likely need formal permission from the association in addition to complying with city zoning rules.

Avoiding Disputes With the Homeowners' Association

California has seen its share of foreclosure actions by homeowners' associations against individual homeowners—the ultimate sign that their relationship has collapsed. Worse yet, the amounts foreclosed over tend to be relatively minor—under $5,000. These aren't cases where the homeowners have failed to pay the mortgage, but more often where they've failed or refused to make assessment payments and perhaps been punished with additional fines or collection costs.

Many disputes will simmer along without getting to a foreclosure action, and in many cases, it's the homeowner who sues the association. To minimize lawsuits, state law requires homeowners' associations and their members to attempt arbitration or mediation when there is a dispute over who should do what according to the CC&Rs. (Civil Code § 1354.)

Role of Homeowners' Associations

Some CC&Rs—especially with condos—put costly decision-making rights in the hands of a homeowners' association. These associations assess mandatory monthly fees for common property maintenance, which can get expensive in older housing developments requiring upkeep, or in upscale areas with a pool, golf course, or other recreational facilities. Many associations in housing developments let their boards raise regular assessments up to 20% per year and levy additional special assessments, for a new roof or other capital improvement, with no membership vote. Ask how much these assessments have been raised in recent years and whether any large new ones are being discussed. Fees of several hundred dollars a month are typical.

In some housing developments, homeowners' associations are well run. The residents, especially those who buy in an effort to build equity and move on, appreciate the fact that their associations are sensitive to making decisions that will enhance the value of the properties.

Steve and Catherine: Study Your CC&Rs

After burning out looking at overpriced quaint old houses, we decided to check out new ones. We found the ideal house in a beautiful development in Sonoma County. And the price was right, too. "What's wrong?" we asked ourselves.

We didn't have to wait long for the answer. "Here are your CC&Rs," the sales agent said as she handed us a package about an inch thick. Arrgg. No way will I live in a place governed by dozens of rules and a homeowners' association. Case closed.

But wait. Why did we like this house? It was near a school, and our son had about five years to go before he graduated from high school. Then we could move to our dream rural hilltop. In truth, we were very interested in enhancing short-term property values. Suddenly, the CC&Rs looked quite different. By preserving the attractive character of the development, the CC&Rs might be our friend, not our enemy.

So, with some trepidation, we bought. Surprise! Over four years later, we're still happy with how the CC&Rs work. They provide a framework for resolving minor neighbor disputes and have set maintenance standards that keep our community looking spiffy. So far, we've not been set upon by power-hungry CC&R enforcers. And as we hoped, property values have done comparatively well.

Unfortunately, some associations are poorly run. Often the majority of residents aren't interested in management details, which can mean a small group of activists gains control and imposes restrictive and sometimes expensive rules and policies. These can lead to bitter squabbles, where neighbors fight each other, using the association as their arena, and splinter groups war with boards of directors. A mismanaged or underfinanced association can go bankrupt and lose assets such as cash reserves.

Does the Association Have Adequate Reserves?

In condominiums, the money in reserve must cover repairs to all common spaces: roof, garage, and so on. While a $50 or $500 per month homeowner's fee may seem steep when added to your mortgage, insurance, and taxes, you are better off with a fee that's too high, not too low.

Low fees often equal inadequate reserves. When something needs repair, and the reserves are too low, the owners must pay. Usually the association authorizes the repair and bills the owners through a special assessment. If your co-owner(s) don't have the money, you may have to pay their share or face a lawsuit or other collection efforts by whoever did the repairs.

How to Check Out a Development or Condo

While development or condo living is not for everyone, many people like the idea that rules govern the conduct of their neighbors, and are happy to obey the rules themselves. If you now live in an area where people fix their cars in the driveway until midnight, and the house on one side of you hasn't been painted in 15 years and the one on the other side is bright purple, a little order may be welcome. To investigate further:

- **Get a copy of the CC&Rs and relevant documents.** Many listing agents selling condos will not give out CC&Rs until you have submitted an offer—which should include a contingency that the CC&Rs are okay with you, of course. But CC&Rs are public documents, which you can get by visiting the county recorder's office. It is harder to get bylaws and minutes of association meetings before making an offer. But after the offer is accepted, you should firmly ask for them, or ask to attend a board meeting. If anyone hesitates to hand them over, be worried.

- **Read the CC&Rs carefully and decide whether the rules are compatible with your lifestyle.** Perhaps, for example, you can live with the prohibition on brightly painted houses, but can't live without your beloved dog.

- **Knock on a few doors.** If you find a friendly neighbor, politely ask what he or she likes the most and least about the community. Ask how long he or she has lived there, and whether there have been any arguments between the owners and the association during that time.

- **Check the membership fees and assessments and how easy it is for the board to increase these amounts.** Review past budgets and the history and amount of fee and assessment increases. Also, find out how much money is in the reserve account. If you know the roof needs to be replaced in one year for $500,000 and the association has only $100,000 in reserve, you could be facing a shocking special assessment soon after you buy. But the association must, by law, disclose to you before you buy whether there are plans for special assessments or whether they are contemplating any legal actions. Also, California law prohibits association boards from levying any regular assessment over 20% greater than the previous year's, or any special assessments totaling more than 5% of budgeted gross expenses—unless, that is, they get the owners' approval. (Cal. Civil Code § 1366.)

- **Ask about the parking situation.** Find out how much parking is available, whether there's an extra charge, and where and how parking spaces are assigned.

- **Make sure the association has adequate liability and property insurance.** Your mortgage lender or insurance agent may be willing to review the policy for you.

- **Find out whether the development is involved in litigation.** If the association is suing the developer, for example, you may have difficulty getting a loan. California law compels sellers to inform buyers if the association is fighting a builder to make repairs and to provide a list of the association's demands. (Civil Code § 1368.)

- **Sniff out any financial or legal trouble.** Seek as much information as possible concerning the physical condition of the entire development and the financial position of the homeowners' association. State law requires associations and developments to give homeowners access to information about unpaid fees and assessments, defects, and a timeline for repairs. (Civil Code §§ 1375, 1375.1.) Also ask to see any community newsletters, which will contain clues to any trouble. You should have a good general contractor (or an accountant, depending on the situation) review all disclosures. California requires that even small condo associations have financial reviews every few years, so be sure the condo association has complied with this law.

- **Think like a landlord.** If you ever plan to rent your house or condo, even if it's only a short-term rental, such as on Airbnb or VRBO, pay close attention to rental restrictions and rules affecting tenants and your liability for their actions.

(See our offer form in Chapter 16, which includes a requirement that you review and approve items such as CC&Rs and homeowners' association budgets.)

RESOURCE

CC&Rs and homeowners' associations. Many homeowners' associations belong to organizations that publish a wide variety of useful materials. These include:

- **Executive Council of Home Owners (ECHO)**, www.echo-ca.org, and
- **Community Associations Institute (CAI)**, www.caionline.org.

CC&Rs and bylaws must conform to the California Corporations Code, §§ 5000 through 10014.

Dealing With Delays

If you agree to buy a house that isn't finished (or even started), you'll be asked to sign a very one-sided contract. You'll be given numerous deadlines (to make deposits, agree to design changes, get loan approval, and more), while the developer will have great leeway—even up to a year from the target date—to deliver the house.

Do what you can to change this. Most importantly, you want to establish some reasonable date at which you can cancel the contract and get all of your money back if the developer doesn't deliver your house. At some point, you should be entitled to walk away or assign your contract to another buyer. Again, get it in writing.

Developer delays can cause serious problems, especially with your mortgage loan. As discussed in Chapter 13, "Obtaining a Mortgage," lenders normally won't lock in (guarantee) a particular interest rate for more than about 30 days, although you can sometimes get an extension if you pay a higher fee up front. Thus, if the closing on your new house is delayed several months at a time when interest rates are rising, you'll end up paying a higher rate and, in a volatile economy, may no longer be eligible for the loan.

If you have to cancel your contract because interest rates have jumped so much that you can't afford the house, you'll most likely have to forfeit your deposits to the builder. In this situation, try (in writing) to have the deposits returned to you. Or insist that your contract with the developer contain a financial penalty if the house isn't ready in time.

If you're a current homeowner, you also face the problem of selling your existing house so you can move into your new one when it's ready. When you aren't sure exactly when a new house will be ready, your best bet is to sell the old one with a contingency that allows you to either delay the closing on your old house or to continue to live in it (and pay rent) for as long as possible.

If you have a choice, it's possibly better to delay the closing, because mortgage interest is deductible but rent is not. Also, you will be paying rent based on the purchaser's monthly carrying costs, which will almost always be higher than yours.

The buyer of your old house will probably want some limitation (say 60, 90, or 120 days) on your right to remain living there. You may find yourself living in a motel if completion of your new house is seriously delayed.

If you rent, especially if you have a month-to-month tenancy, you're in a better position. When your new house is ready, give your landlord

30 days' written notice of when you plan to move out. Even if you have a lease of a year or more, you're probably in pretty good shape. Although you're liable to pay the rent for the entire lease, your landlord is legally responsible to try to rerent your place and to subtract the new tenant's rent from what you owe. See *California Tenants' Rights,* by Janet Portman and David Brown (Nolo), for steps to take to ensure that your landlord rerents a place promptly.

Most Common New Home Defects

Buying a new home may help you avoid termites, corroded wiring, and other defects that aging homes commonly develop. However, new homes can present their own array of problems—some of them quite serious. Careless and hurried work, particularly by unskilled laborers, is often the cause. Here are the areas to make particularly sure your inspector checks on:

- **Foundation and drainage.** Some builders skimp on materials, fail to install drains, or don't let the concrete dry enough before continuing with construction. The result can be cracks that allow water into your basement or crawl space. The grading of the surface around your home is also critical to the health of the foundation.

- **Paint.** Some builders save money by thinning the paint or by not applying enough coats. Add to that the streaks and splatters that can result from hurried work, and you've got a potential problem worth examining.

- **Framing.** The bones of a house are its wood framing. The inspector will need to check not only that all the beams and joists are in the right places, but that the initial drying and settling of the wood hasn't caused cracks in the gypsum or plaster drywall or sagging floors.

- **Leakage.** Around the roof and windows, faulty flashing (gutter protection) or improper installation of or badly placed shingles can leave cracks for rainwater to enter, causing mold, rot, and insect infestation. Inside the walls, pipes can leak if they're not joined correctly or have been damaged during construction.

Inspect the House Before Closing

The biggest complaint of people who live in newly built developments involves the developer's failure to do all the things promised in the purchase contract in a timely fashion—such as installing small items like shower heads, cabinet hardware, and closet fixtures; repairing or replacing malfunctioning appliances, heaters, or air conditioners; or completing promised landscaping. Sometimes more serious problems occur, such as shoddy construction or the omission of a room in the plan.

The best way to protect yourself is to include a contingency in your contract allowing you to conduct inspections during specific phases of construction as well as before escrow closes. (See our offer form in Chapter 16.) You can then refuse to close escrow until everything is complete and to your satisfaction. Otherwise, once escrow closes and you take occupancy, the developer pockets the money and has little incentive to finish anything quickly or correctly.

To make sure you're getting the best-quality construction, it's worth hiring professionals experienced in checking out new homes to inspect the site at key points in the building process, such as during the framing of walls, doors, and floors. You'll also want to hire a professional home inspector during the entire construction process and definitely before closing.

Also do your own final inspection. Bring a tape measure, and be ready to take notes. Be as methodical as you can—open every cupboard door and window, turn on every faucet, and test every appliance.

Resist promises that if you'll close and move in now, the developer will fix all problems promptly. ("We'll install the washroom sinks the day they arrive, and start the landscaping as soon as the rain ends.") It's amazing how quickly "impossible to get" parts can appear if you refuse to close until everything is done.

But what if you're living in a motel (or will be soon) if you don't move in? If significant and costly work remains, insist that the necessary funds be placed in a trust account after escrow closes. Then ask for a written agreement providing that if the work is performed on time, the money will be released to the developer; but if it isn't, the funds go to you to hire someone else to do the work.

If the developer refuses, at the least make a list of what needs to be done, assign a new completion date to each, and have it signed by the developer (see the sample, below).

Guarantees and Warranties

You've probably heard horror stories about new houses that began to disintegrate the day the buyer moved in. This shouldn't be a problem if you buy from a reputable developer. To protect yourself further, ask whether the developer provides any guarantees. Even better is a new-house warranty provided by a third-party insurer.

Sample Agreement to Complete Work

Date: December 1, 2017

To: John Addison, Acme Development
From: Abigail Williams
Re: 11 Tulip Drive

On December 17, 2017, escrow is scheduled to close on the house I am planning to buy at 11 Tulip Drive. The price I am paying includes a high-quality sod lawn. In exchange for my promise to go ahead with the closing, Acme Development agrees to complete all yard grading and drainage work, and to install this lawn by March 15, 2018.

I'm sending you two signed copies of this memo. Please sign one on the "Agreed to by" line and return it to me by December 10, 2017.

Sincerely,

Abigail Williams

Abigail Williams

Agreed to by: _____
John Addison, Sales Manager
Acme Development

Developer guarantees. Most developers give a one-year guarantee on new houses. The better guarantees include all workmanship and materials.

In addition, appliances will be new and will come with their own warranties. Get all model and serial numbers and a copy of each appliance warranty.

One problem with developer guarantees is that you have only the developer's promise that a problem will be fixed. If the developer goes out of business, as many do, you're out of luck. Also, most developer guarantees are worded vaguely, guaranteeing "acceptable standards of workmanship and material." This is hard to enforce if a developer doesn't voluntarily stand behind his or her work.

Independent company warranties. Some developers purchase new-home warranty policies from independent companies, which are far better than developer guarantees. Typical policies cover workmanship and materials for one year; plumbing, electrical, heating, and air conditioning systems for two years. Less typically, but worth looking for, are policies that cover major structural defects for ten years.

Definitions of defects in material and workmanship, and your rights, are spelled out in much more detail than in developer guarantees. And most third-party policies contain fair dispute resolution procedures if you're dissatisfied with the response to a claim.

If your developer doesn't—or won't—offer third-party warranty coverage, you can purchase your own house warranty. Be sure you're aware of all restrictions, deductible dollar limits of coverage, and dispute resolution procedures. (See Chapter 19 for more on home warranties.) ●

Financing Your House: An Overview

How Mortgage Lenders Think 146

Who Lends Mortgage Money? 147

Standardized Loans: Fannie Mae, Freddie Mac,
    and the Secondary Mortgage Market 147

Mortgage Types 148

Comparing Fixed Rate and Adjustable Rate Mortgages 149

The Cost of Getting a Loan 150

Which Mortgage Is Best for You? 152

    How Much House Can You Afford? 152

    Is Your Income Likely to Increase Soon? 152

    How Much Down Payment Can You Make? 152

    How Long Do You Plan to Own Your Home? 153

SKIP AHEAD

Already arranged to finance your house? Skip to Chapter 14.

Arranging to finance a house can be disheartening. To qualify, you must normally come up with a good-sized chunk of cash for the down payment. Then you need to borrow a huge sum of money and make monthly payments for what seems like the rest of your life. And, if you don't want to end up with a lousy deal, you must understand seemingly endless details about the variety of mortgages with different interest rates, up-front costs, and fine-print terms.

Chapters 8 through 13 provide the basic information necessary to sensibly finance the purchase of a house. If you carefully read all our material before making important decisions, you'll be equipped to obtain a good mortgage at a competitive price.

How Mortgage Lenders Think

The more money you have for a down payment and the higher your credit score, the better deal you're likely to get. You'll be a likely candidate for a favorable mortgage loan if:

- **You make a large down payment.** People rarely default on their loans when they have a large personal stake in the property—at least 20%.

- **You have an excellent credit history.** People who have paid their bills on time for many years are likely to continue to do so. The reverse is also true.

- **The property is worth more than the loan amount.** The lender feels secure that if you default, the property can be sold for more than enough to repay the loan. Again, the reverse is also true.

Unfortunately, the less money you have to put down, the lower your income, and the greater your debts, the more likely you are to be stuck accepting a mortgage (if you can get one at all) that takes even more money out of your pocket, as you have to pay a high interest rate, many "points" (up-front units of cash), or for private mortgage insurance.

Who Lends Mortgage Money?

Many entities, including banks, mortgage banks, mortgage brokers, and credit unions, make home loans. Large lenders tend to work statewide, while smaller ones specialize in narrower geographical areas, types of housing, or types of mortgages. Fortunately, because mortgage rates are widely published and available online (see Chapter 13), and many types of loans are standardized no matter who the lender is, comparison shopping is not difficult. Government-guaranteed loans (see Chapter 11) offered by the Federal Housing Administration (FHA) and the U.S. Department of Veterans Affairs (VA) are also options.

As you sift through all the financing possibilities, remember: There's no one universally desirable mortgage, only one that will help you buy the house you want with maximum efficiency at a minimum cost.

TIP

Don't overlook private financing. To bypass lender rules and restrictions, some home buyers borrow some or all mortgage money privately, that is, from parents, other relatives, and friends. (Chapter 12 covers private mortgages.)

Standardized Loans: Fannie Mae, Freddie Mac, and the Secondary Mortgage Market

Most financial institutions that lend money don't keep all the loans they make in their portfolio, but rather sell most of them to investors on the "secondary mortgage market." Several large institutions, including the Federal National Mortgage Association (FNMA or Fannie Mae) and Federal Home Loan Mortgage Corporation (FHLMC or Freddie Mac), buy a large portion of these mortgages.

But the secondary mortgage market buys only mortgages that conform to their financial qualification standards and rules regarding maximum loan size. The result is that most lenders follow these rules, and many mortgages are remarkably similar. For example, Fannie Mae and Freddie Mac buy loans in two different-sized tiers: $417,000 and less, and $417,001 to $625,500. That second tier is called the "high-balance conforming loan amount." The exact amount varies by county. These limits change annually.

If you need a mortgage larger than the limit where you're buying you probably need what's called a "jumbo" loan, which typically has a slightly higher interest rate than Fannie Mae or Freddie Mac loans. These loans are more difficult to get and have more stringent lending guidelines. If you need a loan for more than the conforming loan or high-balance conforming loan limit where you live, you'll almost certainly want to work with a mortgage broker, who can help you figure out the best option.

RESOURCE

Online mortgage resources. For information on Fannie Mae and Freddie Mac loan limits and programs, check their websites at www.fanniemae. com (click "Homeowners & Communities") and www.freddiemac.com (click "My Home by Freddie Mac®").

Mortgage Types

There are two basic types of mortgages, and a few permutations of these types.

Fixed Rate Mortgage. The interest rate and the amount you pay each month remain the same over the entire mortgage term. Variations are available, as explained in Chapter 9.

Adjustable Rate Mortgage (ARM). With an ARM, the interest rate is set for a fixed period, and then adjusts.

The most popular type of ARM is known as a hybrid ARM, which starts out as a fixed loan for a certain period of time—usually three, five, seven, or ten years. At the end of the fixed period, the loan begins to adjust, either biannually (every six months) or annually.

Interest-only ARM. This operates similarly to a hybrid ARM, in that it starts with a fixed period of three, five, seven, or ten years. During that initial fixed period, however, you'll be making payments of interest alone, without paying down the principal. These mortgages are priced slightly higher than traditional amortizing ARMs, but they satisfy buyers who need a better cash flow. Also, if you later make a large payment to the lender in order to reduce your principal balance, the amount of your required payments will immediately reflect that, being calculated based on the new, current principal balance. By contrast, when you make a principal reduction on a fully amortized mortgage product, your regular payments will stay the same; you will just pay off your mortgage sooner.

Comparing Fixed Rate and Adjustable Rate Mortgages

Before shopping for a mortgage, you'll probably want to decide whether a fixed rate or an adjustable rate mortgage (ARM) is a better fit for you.

With a fixed rate mortgage, your interest rate is fixed for the life of the loan. That means your monthly payment is always the same, which can be good for home buyers who want to minimize their financial risk and are happy with the current interest rate. Check with your mortgage originator about the availability of 2-1 buydowns in your marketplace. This means you will (by paying points) bring your interest rate down to 2% under the posted rate in Year One and by 1% in Year Two. After that, you'll be charged the posted interest rate for the remaining life of the loan. The downside is that you're paying a premium for that certainty. Fixed-rate loans usually have higher interest rates than the starter rates for ARMs. (The lenders build in a cushion against the possibility of interest rates increasing while they're stuck with charging you the same old rate.)

The classic ARM is attractive to people who need the initially low rate to afford a house and are prepared for the possibility of later rises in the interest rates. If interest rates drop, you may be able to obtain a no-cost refinance, and thus improve your interest rate and cash flow—whether you're currently in an ARM product or a fixed product.

The Cost of Getting a Loan

Every mortgage comes with several fees. Here are the common ones:

- **General fees.** Banks (but not other types of lenders) typically charge loan application fees (anywhere from $1–$1,600) to cover the cost of processing, underwriting, administering, and drawing up documents for your loan. You will also need to pay fees to various third parties—including the appraiser who confirms the value of your house, the escrow company that acts as middleperson in the transaction, the title insurance company that figures out whether the seller has the right to sell you the property free and clear, credit reporting companies, and so on.

    These closing costs typically add up to 2% of your purchase price. The fees are added to your down payment money and paid at closing.

- **Points.** Many lenders also offer loans that come with a fee in the form of points. Each point is 1% of the loan principal. Points, too, can add up fast—1% of $100,000 is already $1,000.

    Not all mortgages come with points. But by choosing to pay a point or more up front, you can usually "buy down" your interest rate, for an overall savings in the long term. For example, you might be offered a 30-year fixed rate loan of $500,000 with two points ($10,000) at 4.75% interest, or the same loan with no points at 5.25%. Let's run some numbers to see when paying points on this loan will start to save you money:

No-points loan	5.25%	$2,993.52 monthly payment
Two-points loan	4.75%	$2,840.74 monthly payment
Loan comparison		$152.78 monthly difference

As you can see, the loan at two points allows you to pay $152.78 less every month at mortgage payment time. To find out how long it will take you to recoup your $10,000 investment, simply divide it by $152.78. You'll see that it will take approximately 65 months (five-plus years) until you've saved enough to equal your investment. After the 65 months, you're looking at pure savings.

So before comparing points or discount to interest, factor in how long you plan to own your house. The longer you live in your house (or pay on the mortgage), the better off you'll be paying points up front in return for a lower interest rate.

TIP

When choosing a mortgage, remember that you're not likely to keep it for long. According to Rainey Gray-Gross, a senior mortgage consultant in Danville, California, "A lot of my buyers come in thinking they want a 30-year fixed mortgage because Mom and Dad had one. Their parents may even be offering financial help with the transaction, and encouraging them to opt for this supposed security. But consider that, on average, people in the U.S. keep their 30-year fixed mortgage for only seven to ten years. After that, they refinance, sell the house, or come into money and pay the loan off. The statistics in California are even more striking, with a five-to-seven-year average on how long people keep their mortgage. With that in mind, it makes good sense to at least look at your other options."

Tax Deductibility of Points or Loan Discount

Points on a mortgage are tax deductible. The IRS allows buyers to deduct points paid for them by the home sellers—in addition to points buyers themselves pay for a mortgage.

For more information on the tax deductibility of points, call the IRS at 800-TAX-FORM or go to www.irs.gov.

RESOURCE

For calculators to help make decisions on paying points or refinancing, see Nolo's website at www.nolo.com/legal-calculators.

Which Mortgage Is Best for You?

As California mortgage broker Kathy Fuller advises, you'll want to "Consider your own financial situation and timeline before choosing the best mortgage product for you." In choosing a mortgage, it helps to ask yourself the following four questions.

How Much House Can You Afford?

Deciding how much house you can afford is directly related to choosing a mortgage. The more easily you can afford a particular purchase (that is, the lower your debt-to-income ratio), the more likely you can qualify for a good mortgage at a competitive interest rate. Chapter 2 gives detailed instructions on determining the maximum amount a lender will let you borrow to purchase a house, based on your income, down payment, and other factors. If you haven't yet done so, read Chapter 2 and complete the calculations.

Is Your Income Likely to Increase Soon?

If your income is modest now but likely to go up soon, you may be able to get a mortgage with smaller initial payments that will increase in the future. This will allow you to buy a more expensive house.

One option is an ARM that is fixed for the first three, five, or seven years. This gives you short-term security and usually a lower interest rate, hopefully until your income increases. The downside is that if interest rates go way up later, when the loan becomes adjustable, your monthly payments could go higher than you had foreseen.

How Much Down Payment Can You Make?

The reality is that the less money you put down, the fewer lenders and loans you'll have to choose from, and the higher your mortgage payments will be. A few lenders will require as little as a 3% down payment. FHA requires a 3.5% down payment.

While lenders want to lend no more than 80% of the home's total value, you can arrange to make a 10% down payment in one of two ways: either by buying PMI in order to protect the lender from the possibility that you default, or by structuring your financing in the form of two loans: 80% on a first mortgage and 10% on a second, with no PMI.

How Long Do You Plan to Own Your Home?

The length of time you plan to own your house is very relevant to choosing a mortgage. For example, if you intend to keep your home for five years, why not choose an ARM that is fixed for five years? That will give you a lower interest rate than a 30-year fixed rate loan, but you will still have the security of knowing exactly how much your payments will be for the next five years.

If inflation becomes more of a danger, however, interest rates are likely to increase. In this situation, ARM interest rates will surely go higher, perhaps much higher, than those for fixed rate mortgages.

Refinancing: The Effect on Points and Interest Rates

Whether to opt for a loan with more points and a lower interest rate doesn't only depend on how long you'll have the house, but on how long you'll own the loan. Refinancing to get a better interest rate has the same effect as selling the house and buying another.

If interest rates are fairly high when you look for your initial loan, and you expect them to drop before long, you're a candidate to refinance soon. You'll want to shop for a loan with the fewest points, even if this means paying slightly higher interest.

Many borrowers today opt for zero-cost refinance loans. This allows them to follow the market down until it reaches a point where they feel they've gotten the lowest interest rate possible, after which they can focus on reducing their principal balance.

RESOURCE

Several useful websites cover market trends and forecasts on mortgage interest rates. One especially good one is sponsored by HSH Associates at www.hsh.com. Also see www.bankrate.com.

Fixed Rate Mortgages

Should You Choose a Fixed Rate Mortgage If You Can Afford One?........... 156

**Not All Fixed Rate Mortgages Are the Same: Points, Interest Rates,
  and Other Variables**.. 157

Mortgages Lengths and Payment Schedules... 158

  Short-Term Fixed Rate Mortgages Versus Prepaying Your Mortgage......... 158

Back in the 1970s and 1980s, mortgage rules were simple—interest rates were always fixed in advance and repayable in equal monthly installments over a term of 15 to 30 years. The mortgage lender, usually a bank on a downtown corner, required the purchaser to make a down payment of 20% or more and have steady income and a good credit rating. The fixed rate mortgage is the one that most closely resembles this old system.

Today, new mortgage options come and go, including more affordable types of fixed rate mortgages.

Should You Choose a Fixed Rate Mortgage If You Can Afford One?

Many people ask whether they should get a fixed rate mortgage if they can afford one. The answer is different for every borrower. A fixed rate mortgage offers two main advantages:

- **The amount you must pay is established in advance and does not increase.**
- **You may save on interest costs.** Even though many adjustable rate mortgages (ARMs) offer a lower initial interest rate, the total interest paid on a fixed rate mortgage may be less than on an ARM if interest rates go up substantially and stay up for an extended period. This is because the interest rate on ARMs increases over a few years' time to a current market rate. If market rates go up, so do the interest rates on ARMs.

You may want to forgo a fixed rate mortgage, however, if:

- **You'll be moving to another house or refinancing within three to four years.** If you're not planning on keeping your mortgage for a long time, you can probably find an ARM that will cost less in the short term. For example, if you plan to move within five years, a five-year hybrid ARM will have a low interest rate for five years, then adjust to a higher rate after that. You'll theoretically never pay the higher rate, as long as you move or refinance before it kicks in.

- **You believe that interest rates are likely to fall substantially (unlikely in the current market).** In this case, ARM rates will stay close to their initial level, or perhaps even drop. By contrast, if you have a fixed rate mortgage, you'll have to refinance to take advantage of lower rates.

Monthly Payments for a $100,000 Fixed Rate Mortgage

This chart shows the variation among monthly payments for a 30-year, $100,000 fixed rate mortgage at different interest rates.

Interest Rate	Monthly Payment	Interest Rate	Monthly Payment
3.5%	$449	6.5%	$632
4.0%	$477	7.0%	$665
4.5%	$507	7.5%	$699
5.0%	$537	8.0%	$734
5.5%	$568	8.5%	$769
6.0%	$600	9.0%	$805

Not All Fixed Rate Mortgages Are the Same: Points, Interest Rates, and Other Variables

Purchasing a good fixed rate mortgage involves comparing several features. In addition to interest rates, you need to consider:

- **Private mortgage insurance premiums.** Buyers are commonly required to purchase PMI when the lender supplies more than 80% of the financing (that is, you put less than 20% down). PMI protects the lender if you fail to make your mortgage payments. The cost of the insurance usually gets added to your monthly mortgage payment. We discuss PMI at greater length in Chapter 4.

- **Discount or points and interest rates.** Points are up-front charges made by a lender as a condition of lending money at a particular rate. One point equals 1% of a loan. In Chapter 8, we discuss the relationship of points to interest rates and show you how to determine how many points, if any, you should pay.

Mortgages Lengths and Payment Schedules

Not all mortgages last for 30 years; 15-year terms are also available. (Ten- and 20-year loans are also available but less commonly used.)

Additionally, when refinancing, you can customize the loan term to accommodate the remaining years on your existing mortgage.

Short-Term Fixed Rate Mortgages Versus Prepaying Your Mortgage

Lenders commonly offer 15-year mortgages at more favorable interest rates than 30-year mortgages. That's because the faster the loan is paid off, the lower their risk of interest rates jumping (and eating up their profits) or buyers defaulting.

Even if the interest rate is low and you'll save money in the long run, the relatively large monthly payments of a shorter term mortgage may decrease your ability to take out other loans (for home improvements, a new car, and the like) or make other investments. You'll also be committed to high monthly payments, which may take quite a bite out of your income.

However, you will save significant interest over the long term. For example, with a $100,000 fixed rate loan at 5%, you'd have a higher monthly payment but pay nearly $51,000 less in interest with a 15-year mortgage. And that doesn't even account for the lower interest rate you're likely to pay.

But you can achieve similar savings and benefits by voluntarily paying more principal each month on a longer-term loan. The advantage of prepaying a long-term mortgage is its flexibility—you don't legally obligate yourself to the higher payment, so you can change your mind and pay less if need be.

Even prepaying a small amount per month makes a large difference in your total payments. For example, by paying an extra $75 per month on a 30-year, 4.5% fixed rate $400,000 mortgage, you'd repay the loan in 28 (not 30) years and save over $27,000 in interest. If you don't want to pay a little extra each month, consider making a yearly lump sum payment—perhaps when you receive your tax refund.

CAUTION

If you plan to prepay a mortgage, remember this rule: No matter how much extra you pay in one month, you still must make at least the regular payment the next month.

RESOURCE

How to calculate savings from prepaying your mortgage. Go to Nolo's website at www.nolo.com/legal-calculators and choose "How much will I save by increasing my mortgage payments?"

Most Fixed Rate Loans Aren't Assumable

Fixed rate loans in California (except government-guaranteed loans) are generally not assumable by a buyer. If you get a fixed rate loan and later sell your house, you must either pay it off and have the buyer take out a new loan or get the lender's permission for the buyer to assume yours. The latter rarely occurs, for obvious reasons: The buyer won't want the loan if it's above the current market rate, and the lender won't allow it to be assumed if it's below.

Adjustable Rate Mortgages

When Should You Finance With an ARM?.. 162

Loan and Payment Caps.. 163

ARM Indices and Margins... 163

Assumability... 165

Hybrid Adjustable Rate Mortgage... 165

Summing Up—What Good ARMs Look Like 166

While adjustable rate mortgages, or ARMs may be a fine way to finance a home, especially if you're on a tight budget, they can be dangerous if you don't know exactly what you're getting. Fortunately, once ARM language is deciphered, obtaining a good one isn't too difficult. We'll show you how in this chapter, and in Chapter 13 we'll explain how to measure the true cost of a mortgage, adjusting for interest, margins, index, and finance charges.

When Should You Finance With an ARM?

Initial ARM interest rates are lower than those for fixed rate mortgages. However, the rate can change on a predetermined schedule such as monthly, semiannually, or annually. When it does, the new interest rate is tied to a current market rate (called an "index") plus the lender's profit (called a "margin"). If market rates have increased since you first took out the loan, your loan payment will increase, too.

ARMs can be a good choice in either of the following cases:

- You need money for other purposes—say to start a small business— so having a lower initial monthly payment makes sense.

- You plan to move or refinance in the next three to five years. Because your initial ARM interest rate is lower than a fixed rate, an ARM is cheaper than a fixed rate loan for the first few years.

Don't Believe All the Ads

Many lenders heavily advertise low initial ARM rates—but before you get drawn in, realize that:

- The advertised start rates don't last long (usually six months).

- Discounted rates don't necessarily help with loan qualification, because your ability to handle the loan is usually analyzed using the first-year rate, not the discounted rate.

- The lender will probably get its money back by including less attractive ARM features in the fine print, such as higher periodic interest rate caps.

Loan and Payment Caps

The term "cap" sounds simple. If you have a 5% ARM with a 5% life-of-the-loan cap and a 2% one-year periodic cap, your mortgage can't go above 10% and can't increase to more than 7% after one year.

But be aware that the "5% life-of-the-loan cap" refers to five percentage points, not a 5% increase. Five percentage points raise an interest rate of 5% to 10% during the life of a loan, a 100% increase.

Most ARMs also cap the maximum amount your interest rate can go up in a particular adjustment period (periodic caps) between one and two percentage points per year, often adjusted every six months. For a loan with an initial rate of 5%, a one percentage annual point cap means the rate can rise to 6% in one year.

ARM Indexes and Margins

By now you understand that when interest rates go up, so do ARM payments. Different ARMs, however, are tied to different financial indexes, some of which fluctuate up or down more quickly than others.

Indexes that lenders often use include those tied to the rates paid on six-month or one-year U.S. Treasury Bills (called "T-bills"). Other common indexes use the rate at which U.S. T-bills are sold in Europe (LIBOR) the 11th Federal Home Loan Bank District.

Lenders don't simply lend you money at the interest rate of the index, which is only slightly above what they pay their own CD depositors. Instead, lenders tack on two to three interest points (called a margin) to cover their costs and to make a profit.

So your payments don't jump too quickly, you want an ARM tied to a financial index that is likely to fluctuate slowly. Look for a loan where the lender computes interest rates based on an average of the index calculated over a number of weeks, because it will take a while before a quick spike in interest rates moves the average significantly higher. The most volatile indexes (and therefore the worst if interest rates spike) are computed on a daily or weekly "spot basis." Sure, they can go down fast, too, but if you can't afford a big increase, they're not worth the risk.

ARM Terms Defined

Before getting an ARM, review the following mortgage terminology.

Adjustment period. The time that goes by before the interest rate or payment amount changes. Most loans have monthly, semiannual, or annual adjustment periods. Annual or semiannual are preferred; try to avoid monthly adjustment periods, if possible.

Caps. How much your interest rate can go up or down over the term of your mortgage (life-of-the-loan cap). Also, how much it can go up or down at each adjustment period.

Life-of-the-loan cap (or overall cap). This is the maximum (usually five to six percentage points) that the interest rate can increase or decrease over the life of the loan. For example, if the interest rate starts at 4%, and the life-of-the-loan cap is six percentage points, your interest rate can never exceed 10%. (Although arithmetic dictates that your loan could decrease to –2%, ARM loans always include a floor provision, usually of 1%.)

Periodic cap. This limits the amount the interest rate of an ARM can change at each adjustment period. With a periodic cap, your interest rate might go up by as much as 1% every six months or 2% annually— with your payments increasing accordingly.

Index. A market-sensitive financial yardstick to which ARM interest rates are linked. An index computed by averaging rates over a fairly long term (such as 26 or 52 weeks) will move up or down more slowly than one tied to daily or weekly rates.

Margin. The factor or percentage a lender adds to your index interest rate to arrive at the interest rate you pay. Most initial interest rates are set at, or below, the index interest rate (with no margin added). This means that, subject to the periodic or payment caps, ARM interest rates will automatically rise in the first several years to reach the market rate, unless the index interest rate falls substantially during this period.

Fully indexed rate. An ARM's true base interest rate after all initial discounts are filtered out. The fully indexed rate is calculated by adding the margin to the index. If your loan is based on the LIBOR index with a 2.5% margin, your fully indexed rate is 4.03% when the LIBOR is 1.53%.

Don't get so caught up in the index that you forget to look at the margin, the number added to the index to arrive at the interest rate you are charged. In the current market, we believe that a fair margin is 2.25% to 2.5%. This is because a small difference in the margin can translate into substantially higher loan costs. On a 30-year, $130,000 loan with a 2.5% margin and a 5% index, your interest rate will be 7.5% and your payments $909. With a 3% margin, your interest rate will be 8% and your payments $45 more per month and $19,440 more over the life of the loan.

Assumability

A few ARMs—mostly the government-backed ones, from the FHA or VA—are written to allow creditworthy purchasers to assume them from the seller. After the interest rate discounts offered in the first few years are eliminated, ARMs track current interest rates, and lenders have nothing to lose by someone's assuming your loan.

Should you, for the sake of making your home's resale value look hard for an assumable loan? Probably not. Many purchasers will want a fixed rate loan and won't want to assume an ARM. And even if they want an ARM, they'll normally be able to get a new one at an initial rate lower than your current one. Only if interest rates skyrocket, as they did in the early 1980s, and you have an ARM with a tight life-of-the-loan cap, will a subsequent purchaser want to assume it. This, of course, is because your ARM will then be cheaper than a new loan.

Hybrid Adjustable Rate Mortgage

Some lenders offer a hybrid mortgage that features an initial fixed rate (often for three, five, seven, or ten years) that later converts to an ARM. You get the security of fixed rate payments in the early years and risk paying more later, when, hopefully, you'll have more income or can refinance.

This mortgage is especially popular with people who don't expect to own their houses beyond the point when the conversion to an ARM occurs. Because of life's unexpected happenings, however, look carefully to see that once the loan turns into an ARM, it's a good-quality one. Specifically, check the caps, the index, and the margin used.

Summing Up—What Good ARMs Look Like

When it comes to ARMs, we recommend that you get the best margin and index you can, and be skeptical about initial discounted rates. Look for an ARM that conforms to these guidelines:

- a margin that is as low as possible, such as 2.5% for a hybrid ARM (fixed for three, five, or seven years)
- a periodic cap that limits interest rate increases to no more than two interest rate percentage points per year, and
- a life-of-the-loan cap of 5% to 6% over the start rate.

What to Ask When Choosing an ARM

If you're considering an ARM, here are the basic things you'll want to know before you commit:

- **Initial rate (start rate).** How long is your initial interest rate fixed for? For example, it may last one month, six months, one year, three years, five years, seven years, or ten years.
- **Index.** What index is your ARM's interest rate based on (for example, the LIBOR or the T-bill index)?
- **Margin.** What's the bank's profit margin—in other words, what percentage will your lender add to bring your interest rate above the index rate?
- **Periodic caps.** By how much could your interest rate go up or down, and how often does it adjust? (For example, it might change by 1%, 2%, or 5%, and this could happen every month, six months, or 12 months.)
- **Lifetime cap.** What is the lifetime maximum interest rate of your loan?

Government-Assisted Loans

Veterans Affairs Loans.. 168

    New Houses and VA Loans.. 170

Federal Housing Administration Financing... 170

California Housing Finance Agency Programs.. 172

CalVet Loans... 172

Down Payment Assistance (DAP) Programs.. 173

F our government-assisted mortgage programs (and some local financing programs) are available to help Californians buy homes. These are:

- U.S. Department of Veterans Affairs (VA)
- Federal Housing Administration (FHA)
- California Housing Finance Agency (CalHFA), and
- California Department of Veterans Affairs (CalVet).

Veterans Affairs Loans

So-called "VA loans" are available to men and women who are now in the service and to veterans with an other-than-dishonorable discharge who meet specific eligibility rules, most of which relate to length of service. You must submit VA Form 26-1880, *Request For A Certificate of Eligibility*, available on the VA website, www.va.gov.

However, the VA doesn't actually make mortgage loans, but guarantees part of the house loan you get from a bank, savings and loan, or other private lender. If you default, the VA pays the lender the amount guaranteed, and you in turn will owe the VA. The idea of VA loans is to give veterans home-financing opportunities with favorable loan terms and competitive interest rates, which may be lower than conventional Fannie Mae or Freddie Mac loans.

The VA itself doesn't set a maximum loan amount, but limits the amount of your loan that it will repay. (In some instances, a VA loan amount can be as high as $1 million.) Through 2016, at least, that amount was 25% of loans up to $417,000 in most California counties (the Freddie Mac conforming limit, just in case the loan is sold on the secondary market). The amount is even higher for many California metro areas, such as Alpine, Los Angeles, Marin, Monterey, Mono, Napa, Orange, San Benito, San Diego, San Francisco, San Jose, San Luis Obispo, San Mateo, Santa Barbara, Santa Clara, Santa Cruz, Sonoma, and Ventura.

Also, the loan amount may not exceed the VA's Certificate of Reasonable Value (CRV), based on the VA's appraisal of the property.

RESOURCE

To find out more, visit the VA website at www.benefits.va.gov/ homeloans.

In the following situations, the purchaser will need to come up with a cash down payment, in addition to the VA loan guarantee:

- The loan exceeds the guaranteed loan limit.
- The sales price of the house exceeds the VA's CRV. All VA purchase contracts give the buyer the right to cancel the deal if the contract price exceeds the CRV.

The VA's guarantee effectively replaces the down payment. The guarantee protects the lender against loss and makes it easier for veterans to get favorable loan terms. You still must repay the whole loan, but you won't have to pay PMI.

Eligible VA borrowers must apply directly to a lender for a VA-backed loan, and meet the lender's qualification standards regarding income and credit. And, they must show that they plan to live in the house themselves (not rent it out, for example).

As a general rule, most mortgage companies make VA loans, but some banks don't. Contact a regional office of the VA for a list of lenders active in the program.

You must pay the VA an administrative fee for the loan, ranging from around 1% to 5% of the total borrowed, depending upon the amount of the down payment; members of the Reserves and National Guard pay the highest fees. The interest rate is often slightly below the market rate. If the borrower is disabled, the VA funding fee will be waived. Also, under VA guidelines, the borrowing vet cannot pay certain of the closing fees.

CAUTION

Don't procrastinate in applying. The VA warns that you should expect to wait four to six weeks for a decision on your application.

These loan benefits are reusable You can also refinance a VA loan with a new loan.

New Houses and VA Loans

For most loans for new houses, the VA inspects construction at various stages to ensure compliance with the approved plans. The builder must provide a one-year warranty that the house is built in conformity with the approved plans and specifications. If the builder provides an acceptable ten-year warranty, the VA may only require a final inspection. (See Chapter 7 for more on inspections of new houses.)

Federal Housing Administration Financing

The Federal Housing Administration (an agency of the Department of Housing and Urban Development) insures loans made to U.S. citizens, permanent residents, and other noncitizens who have Social Security numbers and permission to work in the United States. You must meet financial qualification rules. Under its most popular program, if the buyer defaults and the lender forecloses, the FHA pays 100% of the amount insured.

This loan insurance lets qualified people buy affordable houses. You can use it for both fixed and adjustable rate loans. The major attraction of an FHA-insured loan is that it requires a low down payment, usually about 3.5%. This money can come from family members or other sources. (Conventional lenders require a minimum 5% down payment from the borrower's own funds.) The FHA also counts nontraditional sources of income when assessing your ability to make your monthly payments or down payment, including seasonal pay, regular overtime and bonus income, and money from a community savings club (a popular way of saving money in many minority communities).

The FHA loan limits vary by county and can go as high as $625,500 in some high-cost areas, such as San Francisco, Oakland, and Los Angeles. Check with a regional FHA office or on the HUD website at www.hud.gov to find current rates in your area.

Like most government benefits, FHA loans have downsides:

- **Upfront mortgage insurance premium.** This can be as much as 1.75% of the loan amount.

- **Monthly mortgage insurance.** If you'll be making a down payment of less than 20%, you'll be required to pay for mortgage insurance. This is similar to, but not exactly the same as PMI and often more expensive than PMI.

- **Condition of the property.** Fixer-uppers and properties needing significant repair won't qualify for the standard FHA loan program. If you want to buy a house in need of repair, any work recommended by FHA appraisers or by a licensed pest control inspector must be done before the sale closes. Fixer-uppers might, however, qualify for the FHA's Rehabilitation Loan Program (Section 203(k)). The details of this program are beyond the scope of this book. Contact the FHA for more information.

- **Appraisals.** An FHA-approved appraiser must establish a fair market value for a house. FHA appraisers also have specific requirements. If the appraisal is less than what you pay for the house, the difference must be made up in cash, not by the FHA loan. A clause must be inserted in all sales contracts giving the buyer the right to cancel if the appraisal value is lower than the agreed-upon sales price.

- **General red tape.** It is often said that FHA loans are subject to inordinate bureaucratic snags and delays. But this isn't always true. In the hands of an experienced mortgage broker or other FHA loan originator, FHA loans can be processed in about the same time as conventional loans.

RESOURCE
You can also get information on FHA loans, or find a regional HUD office, by calling the FHA Resource Center at 800-CALL-FHA or by checking the FHA website at portal.hud.gov.

California Housing Finance Agency Programs

The California Housing Finance Agency (CalHFA) provides down payment assistance to first-time home buyers or people who haven't owned a home in three years. You must meet certain credit and income requirements.

The assistance takes the form of a loan, up to 3% of the sales price or appraised value of the property, whichever is less. The money can be applied toward the down payment or closing costs for eligible fixed-rate mortgage loans.

The property price itself must not exceed certain limits, which vary by county and also depend on whether the home is new construction or a resale of an existing property.

Unlike the VA and FHA programs, CalHFA will help only if your income doesn't exceed certain limits established for the county where the house you want to buy is located. Check with CalHFA, as the limits change fairly often. Income limits vary based on the number of people per household.

CalHFA recommends that you contact an approved CalHFA lender for an analysis of your personal situation.

 RESOURCE

For up-to-date information about the CalHFA program and a list of approved lenders, call 877-922-5432, or check the CalHFA website at www. calhfa.ca.gov.

CalVet Loans

The California Department of Veterans Affairs, through the CalVet Loans Program, provides loans to qualified veterans who purchase homes within the state. CalVet home loans are direct loans funded from the sale of tax-exempt bonds. No taxpayer revenue is used to fund this program.

CalVet loans work a little differently from ordinary mortgage loans: CalVet buys the property you select, then immediately sells it to you using a contract of sale. You make monthly payments directly to the department. It is set up as a 30-year loan, though you can pay it off sooner with no penalty. The department holds title to the property until you have paid in full.

 RESOURCE
If you are a veteran and would like to know whether your military service qualifies you for a CalVet loan, visit the CalVet website at www.calvet.ca.gov.

Many borrowers can qualify for a no-down-payment loan. Other CalVet home loan programs offer down payment options as low as 3% of the purchase price.

Single-family homes, condominiums, and manufactured homes on private land are currently eligible for loans.

The interest rate on CalVet home loans is based on the continuing cost of bonds sold to fund the program. The interest rates are variable, not fixed. However, the initial interest rate is set at the time you submit your application, and subsequent rate increases are limited to 0.5% over the life of the loan. Your initial interest rate will depend on the particular funding source.

You will also be charged loan origination and funding fees, which depend on the loan amount and on the size of your down payment.

What if the house you wish to buy costs more than the maximum CalVet home loan (even after your down payment)? You are free to seek a second mortgage from another lender to close the gap.

Down Payment Assistance (DAP) Programs

Several California cities and counties offer various forms of financial assistance with down payments, primarily to first-time home buyers who are buying modestly priced properties. Often, these are the result of the city or county selling bonds for low "municipal rates" and passing the savings on to local purchasers. Call your city or county housing or planning office and inquire about any programs in your area. Programs come and go fairly quickly, because below-market-rate mortgage money tends to get committed very quickly.

RESOURCE

Looking for more information? The federal Housing and Urban Development office maintains a Web list of California cities offering first-time homebuyer assistance programs. See www.hud.gov (search for "Homeownership Assistance: California").

Private Mortgages

Advantages of Private Mortgages 176

Getting a Loan From Friends or Relatives 177

　Approaching Friends, Relatives, and Other Private Lenders........................... 178

　Making an Effective Loan Presentation 179

　Responding to a Proposed Lender's Questions and Concerns....................... 181

　Finalizing the Loan 182

Shared Equity Transactions.. 182

Second Mortgages—Financing by Sellers.. 182

**Second Mortgages—Financing by Private Parties
　Other Than the Seller**.. 184

Financial institutions and government programs are not the only sources for mortgage loans. A great deal of mortgage money is supplied by private sources—parents, other relatives, friends. Borrowing money privately is usually the most cost-efficient mortgage of all.

The three broad approaches to borrowing all or most of the money necessary to buy a house privately are:

- Borrow from friends or relatives.
- Borrow from the seller.
- Borrow from a noninstitutional private lender.

Advantages of Private Mortgages

The principal advantages of a private mortgage are:

- **Low interest.** Friends and relatives often charge far less than conventional lenders.

- **Flexible repayment structures.** Private lenders may let you pay interest only, or less, for a few years, or otherwise customize your payment schedule.

- **No points or loan fees.** Institutional lenders normally charge thousands of dollars in up-front points and fees. You avoid these costs by borrowing money privately.

- **Easier qualifying.** Private lenders don't insist on a great credit score.

- **Saving on private mortgage insurance.** By borrowing privately, you avoid paying PMI, which institutional lenders require if you borrow 80% or more of the purchase price.

- **Minimal red tape.** To borrow from an institutional lender, you must fill out an application form, provide verifying documentation, and wait for approval. The process is much simpler when you borrow privately.

- **No lender-required approval of house's physical condition.** Private lenders don't usually require that a house's major defects be repaired before closing, as institutional lenders may.

Getting a Loan From Friends or Relatives

To consider whether private financing, either in whole or part, will work for you, ask yourself two questions:

- Can a parent, grandparent, other relative, close friend, or business acquaintance afford to lend the money?
- Does that person trust you?

If the answer to both of these is "yes," follow up with two more:

- Of those people who can help, who is most likely to do so?
- Of those who can help, who tends to make reasonably conservative investments, such as bank CDs and money market funds, not speculative investments, such as stocks, commodities, or commercial real estate?

This last question is important, because people who invest conservatively are more likely to be interested in lending mortgage money at an interest rate higher than they get now. By contrast, people who invest aggressively in an effort to achieve larger returns won't be as impressed by the prospect of getting an interest rate a little better than a bank would pay (though they may lend anyway, for personal reasons).

The hardest part about borrowing money is convincing the lender that the investment is safe.

CAUTION

Beware of imputed interest. The IRS assumes that mortgage lenders receive reasonable interest on every loan and assesses taxes accordingly. This is true even if the lender charges no interest or low interest to a family member or friend. The "imputed" interest rate charged for loans of more than $10,000 changes, but generally is between 3% and 9%. (See the IRS's "Index of Applicable Federal Rates (AFR) Rulings" at www.irs.gov.) So even if your generous friend or relative charges you less, the IRS requires him or her to report interest income at that rate. If your friend doesn't and is audited, the IRS may readjust his or her income using the imputed interest rate and charge the tax owed on the readjusted income plus a penalty.

Approaching Friends, Relatives, and Other Private Lenders

Start with the idea that you're not asking for charity. You're offering a business proposition: a loan at a fair rate of interest, secured by a first mortgage.

If your relative or friend has the money to lend and knows you're trustworthy, chances are he or she will make a loan. If your relative or friend doesn't trust you—you've racked up large credit card bills, bounced checks, or even forgotten to return a lawn mower—he or she will probably back off quickly.

True Story

Mort: My Good Friend Helped Me

Several years ago, Mort found a house he wanted to buy. Although he had enough money to make a good-sized down payment, he needed more to finance the entire purchase. Upon hearing about the new house plan, Babette, his good friend, volunteered to lend Mort $200,000, to be repaid over 20 years, at a very competitive interest rate, secured by a first mortgage.

Why would Babette make this generous, unsolicited offer? Certainly, the trust and good regard accumulated over a long friendship was important. Financial factors were also important. Babette had just retired and was living off the interest from her investments, and she wanted a higher rate of return on her money than she currently received from CDs.

They quickly struck a bargain. Mort got a fixed rate, 20-year loan at 6.5% (about 1.5% points lower than the going rate at the time) and saved close to $10,000 on the fees, and $170,435 in interest over the life of the loan (assuming he would have taken out a 30-year fixed rate loan). He also saved the hassle and time of filling out a loan application.

But what was in it for Babette? She got a 6.5% interest rate on her money at a time when CDs were paying 5%. She also got a first mortgage on the house. Should Mort default, Babette could foreclose, have the house sold, and recover the balance of her loan, plus the costs of sale.

So, are potential lenders likely to trust you? If you can unequivocally say "yes," terrific. If it's "no," or "maybe, with coaxing," consider what you can do to improve their view of your reliability. If you currently owe money to a relative or friend, pay it back in full before proposing a new loan. If you were wild in your younger years but are now staid and responsible, make sure your parents spread the word to wealthy Uncle Harry before you show up on his doorstep asking to borrow $380,000.

Once you decide whom to ask, think carefully about how to raise the subject. Never surprise a potential lender by blurting out a request at a social event or other inappropriate occasion. Make an appointment, even if you see the person regularly and the formality seems odd. Give the person a general idea of what you want to talk about, but save the details. For example, you might say, "Grandpa, I'm trying to buy a house and I'm reviewing a number of ways to finance it. Can we sit down and talk soon?" If Grandpa never seems to find the time, you have your answer. If he says "How about Tuesday?" be on time and prepared to make an effective presentation.

Making an Effective Loan Presentation

Before approaching anyone for a loan, put together a businesslike proposal explaining:

- **How much you wish to borrow.** Be as specific as you can if you don't have a particular house in mind yet.

- **The interest rate you propose to pay.** It should normally be higher than what financial institutions currently pay their investors, and lower than what you'd pay an institutional lender. Find out what CDs pay and what fixed rate mortgages cost. Propose paying around half the difference. For example, if fixed rate mortgages cost 4% and banks pay 2% on CDs, you might propose paying 3%.

- **The loan terms you propose.** This should include the length of the mortgage and the amount of the monthly payments. Use the amortization table in Chapter 2 or an online mortgage calculator to come up with exact figures.

How a Large Down Payment Minimizes the Lender's Risk

If you miss payments, the mortgage holder or lender has the legal right to have the property sold through foreclosure. Proceeds (after the costs of sale are subtracted) go to the first mortgage holder. If you have more than one mortgage, the mortgages are numbered in the order in which they were recorded at the county recorder's office. The lower the number (first being the lowest), the more likely the mortgage holder will be paid if you default.

If the sale price doesn't cover the mortgage debt, the mortgage holder doesn't get all that is owed. For this reason, lenders want the house to be worth considerably more than what they lend. Even allowing for the fact that houses usually sell for relatively low prices at foreclosure sales, most lenders feel safe in lending 80% of appraised value, with the buyer making a 20% down payment.

- **A copy of the family financial statement you prepared in Chapter 2.** This lists your sources of income, existing debts, and other financial information.

- **A copy of a recent credit report from a credit reporting agency.** Get a free one at www.annualcreditreports.com.

- **An estimate of the purchase price of the house you want to buy.** This won't be exact unless you've already made an offer and had it accepted, but do your homework. Be ready to show the potential lender your Ideal House Profile from Chapter 1 and a fairly tight estimate for such a house. If the potential lender wants to make sure the house you find will be worth what you want to pay, offer to get it appraised prior to purchase.

- **How much you have available for a down payment.** If it's 20% or more, point out that you're investing more than enough of your own money to guarantee that the lender will have little risk of loss, even if you default.

- **Your debt-to-income ratio.** As discussed in Chapter 2, financial institutions have found that it's safest to lend to people whose monthly carrying costs don't exceed 28%–36% of their monthly income. Even though a friend or relative probably won't insist on rigid qualification rules, it can be important to demonstrate that you'll have enough income to comfortably make the payments.

When you meet with the potential lender, present your proposal in general terms first. Be prepared to provide copies of all documents. This gives the other person a chance to back off gracefully, if desired. If you sense this happening, say, "Thanks for listening," and change the subject. People have many reasons for not lending money—don't take "no" as a personal rejection.

If the person shows interest, present the details. Allow ample time for questions, and don't expect a decision on the spot.

Responding to a Proposed Lender's Questions and Concerns

First, and most important, if you plan to approach a relative who doesn't have much business savvy, consider whether the loan makes sense for that person. For example, if Aunt Muriel's health is such that she may need most of her money in the next few years, don't borrow from her, even if she'll lend it. She's better off having access to her money, even at a lower interest rate.

Often, friends or relatives will be concerned about what happens to their investment should you become ill or disabled and unable to pay them back, or if you (or another breadwinner) die. The lender fears being caught needing the mortgage repaid and having to foreclose on a distressed family member or friend to get it.

One way to deal with this concern is to purchase both life and disability insurance on yourself and any other cobuyer, and to keep the insurance in force until the loan is repaid. Term life insurance for younger people, particularly, will cost little. (With a life insurance policy, you'd make the friend or relative the beneficiary.)

A good disability policy is expensive, but worth it. Make sure your policy pays at least 60% (more is better) of what you would have received had you been able to work.

Finalizing the Loan

If your presentation is successful, and your friend or relative agrees to lend you the needed money, you need to prepare the paperwork. Given what's at stake, this wouldn't be a bad time to hire an attorney. Here's what's needed:

- A promissory note for the amount of the loan, including the rate of interest and repayment and other terms. Nolo offers electronic promissory notes at www.nolo.com.

- A mortgage or, to use the technically correct term, a deed of trust. As part of the closing process on the house you buy, simply pay the title (or escrow) company a modest fee to prepare and record a deed for you.

CAUTION

A promissory note is not enough. Some people skip the preparation and recording of a deed of trust, reasoning that a promissory note is enough. It isn't. The lender isn't fully protected—from either subsequent lenders or purchasers—unless a formal notice of the loan is publicly recorded.

Shared Equity Transactions

If you're considering borrowing privately, you may also be open to purchasing a house with an investor. In this scenario, you ask a private investor to contribute toward the purchase and share equity in the house as a co-owner. When the house is ultimately sold, the investor will make a profit on his or her portion. For more information, see Chapter 3.

Second Mortgages—Financing by Sellers

In theory, if a seller has no immediate need for money, he or she can transfer the house to you and receive nothing in return but your promise to pay in the future, secured by a mortgage. In practice, however, because most sellers have no personal reason to help you, they will insist that your down payment and amount borrowed add up to the sales price.

Still, some sellers will finance at least a portion of your purchase price themselves. In this situation, a conventional lender has usually agreed to lend you a substantial portion, and the seller provides a much smaller portion, say 10%, of the total secured by a second mortgage.

Here are some of the reasons a seller may provide a second mortgage:

- **To sell a house that has been on the market for a long time.** Taking back a second mortgage makes a house easier for a buyer to finance and, therefore, for the seller to sell.

- **For tax reasons.** If the seller doesn't qualify for the exclusion of capital gains, he or she will owe taxes for the year of sale. (See Chapter 14 for more on tax laws.) The seller may benefit by receiving a portion of these profits in future years, particularly if he or she is retiring and expects an income drop to a lower tax bracket.

- **For investment.** Because second mortgages are riskier than firsts, it's sometimes considered reasonable for the buyer to pay a fairly high rate of interest. A seller may take back a second mortgage if you'll pay a higher rate of interest than banks do on CDs, short-term U.S. government securities, or money market funds.

Second Mortgages: A Buyer's Wish List

- A reasonable interest rate
- Low initial payments so as to not jeopardize first mortgage financing
- No prepayment penalty
- No balloon payment for at least five years, and the automatic right to extend the loan if it's impossible to refinance to pay the balloon in full on the due date, and
- The right to have a subsequent creditworthy buyer assume the second mortgage.

Seller financing can be as flexible as the buyer and seller agree, with variable payment structures or interest rates. You can, for example, have low interest rates in the first year or two, with increases later. Or you can provide for fixed monthly payments with a floating interest rate.

To allow for the possibility that your income and the house's value may decrease or increase more slowly than expected, institutional lenders usually require that at least five years of interest-only payments pass before the balloon payment is due on the second mortgage. You should also insist on an option to extend if you can't refinance the first mortgage.

> ⚠ **CAUTION**
>
> **Don't overextend yourself.** The need to arrange a second mortgage with a large balloon payment tells you that you're stretching your finances close to the breaking point and betting heavily on future property value appreciation to pull you through. Also, be aware that interest rates may increase substantially by the time the balloon payment is due and you need to refinance. Consider whether you're in danger of purchasing more house than you can reasonably afford.

Second Mortgages—Financing by Private Parties Other Than the Seller

Sellers aren't the only people who can provide second mortgages. Relatives and friends can make second loans, and some private investors will as well. Loan brokers can bring prospective borrowers and prospective second mortgage lenders together for a fee. Finally, many commercial lenders make second mortgage loans.

Preparing a Second Mortgage

Step 1: Determine the terms of the second, including the dollar amount, length of the loan, interest rate, and repayment terms. Make sure the second mortgage doesn't include a prepayment penalty.

Step 2: Be sure the lending institution that will provide the first mortgage knows and approves of the terms and conditions of the second.

Step 3: Prepare the necessary paperwork—the buyer's promissory note for the amount of the second mortgage, containing all mortgage terms. Relatively straightforward arrangements can be handled by the title or escrow company that is doing the closing. For more complicated mortgages, including one with an adjustable interest rate, you may need the help of an experienced real estate lawyer. In addition, the title or escrow company should prepare and record a second mortgage (a deed of trust) at the county recorder's office.

Step 4: Make sure your purchase contract contains all the terms and conditions of the second mortgage (required by Civil Code §§ 2956 through 2967).

Obtaining a Mortgage

Gather Information on Mortgage Rates and Fees..188

Researching Mortgages Online..188

Work With a Mortgage Broker...189

Interview Lenders...191

Credit and Income Preapproval..192

    Tips for Speeding Up Loan Approval...192

    Getting the Lender's Commitment 193

    Locking In Interest Rates 193

Get the House Appraised 194

The previous chapters described the kinds of mortgages available, and their pros and cons. You should have a good idea as to the type you want and can afford. Now it's time to actually get a mortgage, either on your own or with the help of a broker.

Assuming you're in decent financial shape (if you're not sure, refer back to Chapter 2), real money can be saved if you carefully shop for a mortgage. Everything else being equal, even a one-quarter percentage point difference in interest rates can mean savings of thousands of dollars over the life of a mortgage. To help you shop, this chapter will cover:

- where to get the latest information on mortgage rates and fees
- where to find useful information online
- how a good loan broker can help you
- how to work directly with mortgage lenders
- how to complete the loan application and get a speedy approval, and
- what to expect from the lender's home appraisal.

Gather Information on Mortgage Rates and Fees

Interest rates and mortgages change frequently—and sometimes dramatically—so you need to be up-to-date. Fortunately, mortgage interest tables are readily available online.

Advertisements for mortgage loans will give you a feel for the market, but take them with a grain of salt. They always presume "best-case scenarios" to arrive at the lowest possible rate. Also, remember that interest rates change daily, sometimes even twice or more a day. By the time you see an interest rate advertised, it may already be history.

Researching Mortgages Online

Many online services provide mortgage rate information. While these sites don't list all the loans available, they offer a great way to get a sense of market rates and terms.

Individual lenders provide mortgage rate information online as well as all kinds of advice for buying a home—from choosing a mortgage to negotiating closing costs. Simply search for the name of a specific financial institution. However, realize that many of them present only their standard mortgage plans and deliberately provide only enough information to get you to personally contact the lender.

Sites such as HSH Associates, at www.hsh.com, publish mortgage and consumer loan information but do not make loans. The "Find Our Best Mortgage Rates" area of hsh.com allows you to compare mortgage rates from financial institutions in a specific area, and gives market forecasts and the latest ARM indexes.

Several websites have gone beyond providing basic mortgage rate information and actually allow you to compare rates from dozens of lenders, based on the amount, type, and length of mortgage you want. You can even prequalify and apply online.

Other Internet mortgage loan sites include:
- www.bankrate.com
- www.quickenloans.com
- www.interest.com, and
- www.lendingtree.com.

Work With a Mortgage Broker

Another approach to looking for a loan (after doing your own preliminary work) is to hire a mortgage broker, a person who specializes in matching house buyers and appropriate mortgage lenders. Assuming you qualify financially, a savvy broker can find you a competitively priced mortgage that meets your needs.

Mortgage brokers must have a real estate broker's license (although someone who works for a broker needs only a salesperson's license). They usually receive two types of compensation:
- a commission from the lender that is a portion of the points you pay on your loan; if there are no points, the lender pays the broker and recoups this payment by charging you a higher interest rate.

- a processing fee, ranging from $500 to $800; brokers may charge this fee up front or at the close of escrow.

The broker is legally required to tell you both the amount and source of his or her compensation. Look for this information on the Loan Estimate.

Benefits. Working with a loan broker can make it much easier to find the cheapest rates. If you are a first-time home buyer or simply don't have the time to shop for mortgages, you'll appreciate the help a good loan broker can provide, such as:

- reviewing your financial profile and, if necessary, counseling you on steps to improve it before applying for a loan

- providing information about types of mortgages that meet your needs, comparing different mortgages, and translating difficult loan language

- identifying the financial institutions that offer the type of mortgage you want and are likely to qualify for

- helping you prepare the papers needed to apply for a loan (if you don't use a loan broker, you'll do this directly with the financial institution)

- acting as a buffer between you and the lender, clearing up problems such as a supporting document that's inappropriate, before the lender ever sees them, and

- talking to lenders on your behalf, to anticipate and solve any problems.

California has thousands of loan brokers; some work alone, others in fair-sized companies. To find a good one, ask friends, relatives, acquaintances, and your real estate agent for a recommendation. Then make a few phone calls and check out the referrals.

If you have a problem with a loan broker or a bank loan department, you can file a complaint with the Bureau of Real Estate (www.dre.ca.gov).

Mortgage brokers are required by law to publish their Bureau of Real Estate (BRE) and Nationwide Mortgage Licensing System (NMLS) license numbers and a telephone number where you can verify their license status. (California Business and Professions Code §§ 10235.5, 10236.4, and 10236.5.)

Interview Lenders

An alternative to working with a loan broker is to comparison shop for a loan on your own. Even if you plan to work with a loan broker, doing your own research helps you get the best deal and educates you about market conditions so you can work more efficiently with the broker.

One good way to mortgage shop is to interview several lenders. Start by identifying lenders offering loans appropriate for you, based on their ads or recommendations from your real estate agent or friend, relative, or employer. If you regularly do business with a bank, credit union, or other financial institution, it makes sense to check whether it offers reasonably competitive loans.

To the extent possible, gather all information on the same day, so you can do an accurate comparison.

After reviewing the lenders' written material, make an appointment to meet a residential real estate loan officer or to speak with one by phone. If you, or a relative or close friend, own a business and have an ongoing relationship with a bank, ask for an introduction to a real estate loan officer. You may get some extra personal time and attention this way.

When you call to schedule an appointment or obtain information, be sure to verify that the lender offers the type of loan you want, in terms of rates, fees, and points.

When you visit or speak to a lender, your goals are to review the following materials with the loan officer:

- The various mortgage plans available, including the required down payment, APR, interest rate, points, loan origination fees, credit check charges, and appraisal fees. If you've read the written material, what the loan officer tells you should come as little surprise.

- The family financial statement you prepared in Chapter 2. Based on this or an online mortgage calculator, the loan officer should be able to give you a good idea of the type of mortgage you qualify for.

- All details important to you. For example, if you plan to make a low down payment, find out whether PMI is required. If you're considering an ARM loan, ask about periodic caps, life-of-the-loan caps, and so forth.

Credit and Income Preapproval

We recommend that you apply for preapproval before you make an offer on a house. If you don't, any offer you make on a house will not be considered competitive. To get preapproved for a loan, you'll have to fill out an application form and pull together basic supporting documentation, such as W-2s, tax returns, pay stubs, bank statements, retirement statements, and the like. After you are in contract to buy a house, the lender will additionally require:

- A copy of the purchase contract for the house you are buying. (Your real estate agent will give this directly to the mortgage broker or lender.)
- Preliminary title report. (The title company will ordinarily give this to the broker or lender.)
- Property appraisal report (ordered by the broker or lender).
- If you are also selling a house, the listing agreement or sales contract or the Final Settlement Statement if your house is already sold. Final Settlement Statements are prepared by the escrow company handling the sales transaction.
- The original, signed copy of your gift letter, if applicable.

Despite the ads that tout "overnight approval," you should allow a reasonable period for full loan approval (or denial) after you complete a loan application. Before final loan approval (called funding the loan), the lender must verify all your financial, employment, and credit information; arrange an appraisal of the property; and prepare the necessary paperwork.

Tips for Speeding Up Loan Approval

Here are some tips for faster loan approval.

Don't wait until the last minute to collect financial and other documents. Particularly if you haven't yet been preapproved, you don't want the process to be held up while you sift through piles of paperwork. As soon as you can, get your financial files in order, and save every pay stub or bank statement as it comes in.

Neatly complete every section of the application. Your broker may help you with this form. Don't leave any blanks! If some item doesn't apply, write "not applicable" or "N/A."

Tell the truth. Don't exaggerate your earnings or hide negative credit information—the lender will find out anyway. Any misrepresentation (or fraud) may automatically cancel your loan application.

Show you're creditworthy. If you're concerned that something on your application may work against you—for example, you have a job gap— write a simple letter of explanation.

Monitor the process. If you're under time pressure to close by a certain date, or have a limited time when interest rates are locked in, keep close tabs on the process. Make sure your loan officer has all the information needed to process your loan application. Keep in regular touch and document all phone and written communications with the lender.

Getting the Lender's Commitment

If a lender says that you qualify for a loan, ask for a "commitment" or "loan qualification" letter, stating the size and type of the loan and the interest rate you qualify for. The commitment letter will likely specify that certain conditions must be met before final loan approval—for example, that you pay off a long-term debt or that the house appraises for at least the loan amount.

As a precaution, don't remove financing contingencies from your offer (see Chapter 16) until these conditions have been met.

Locking In Interest Rates

It's important to understand that even a commitment letter isn't the same thing as a guarantee to borrow at a particular interest rate or particular terms. If interest rates go up, the lender will demand that you pay the higher amount, unless you've received a "lock-in" or "rate lock." If you haven't, and interest rates rise significantly, the lender could recalculate your debt-to-income ratio to see if you still qualify at the higher interest rate.

A rate lock is a guarantee by a lender to make a loan at a particular interest rate, even if the market changes. Most rate locks are good for about 30, 45, or 60 days and apply to a specific house.

Get the House Appraised

After you apply for a loan, the lender will arrange for an appraisal of the property, to make sure it's worth at least the amount you want to borrow. The fee for the appraisal, around $500 or more, will likely be added to your closing costs, depending upon the size and price of the house and property. Larger houses and multi-unit investment properties all tend to cost more to appraise. Some government loan programs, such as the FHA, set their own appraisal procedures. (See Chapter 11.)

The appraiser will physically inspect the property inside and out. He or she will estimate the value based on recent documented prices of comparable sales within a few blocks of the house, adjusting for differences in size and features among the properties.

Your real estate agent should provide the appraiser with relevant comparable sales data, in order to support the house's market value. Remember this rule: Lenders will set their loan amount based on the home's sale price or appraised value, whichever is LESS. Talk with your mortgage broker and real estate agent about what happens if the house you're in contract to buy appraises for less than you've agreed to pay for it.

RESOURCE

Where to complain about problems with a loan application. If you have a problem with how your loan application was handled and can't work things out with the lender, document your concerns and be prepared to file a complaint with a regulatory agency. Where you complain depends upon the type of financial institution—for example, whether it's a state-chartered bank or a savings and loan. To find out where to complain, start with the Bureau of Real Estate (www.dre. ca.gov). Also, contact the Department of Consumer Affairs (www.dca.ca.gov). If you feel the lender discriminated against you in the loan application process, contact the Department of Fair Employment and Housing (www.dfeh.ca.gov).

Buying a House When You Already Own One

Check the Housing Market Carefully 197

    Strategies in a Hot, Seller's Market 198

    Strategies in a Cold, Buyer's Market 199

How to Briefly Own Two Houses 200

Tax Breaks for Selling Your Home 203

f you already own a home and plan to sell it before buying another, questions of timing inevitably arise. Is it better to sell your old house before buying a new one? Or vice versa?

If you sell first, you'll be under time pressure to find another house quickly. This is stressful, leaves you with limited choices when inventory is low, and may cause you to overpay in an anxious effort not to lose out to another purchaser.

But buying a new house first and then scrambling to sell your old one has its own disadvantages—especially if you're trading up substantially and need to sell your old house for top dollar to make the down payment on the new one. Being under time constraints to close on the new house, you may accept a lower-than-optimum price on your old house to make a quick sale. (There are, nevertheless, significant advantages to buying first, then selling your home after moving to your new one. You'll be able to take your time finding the right home and moving into it. The key is to then quickly prepare your current home for sale. But homes do sell faster, and for the highest price, when they're vacant and prepared for sale with updating and staging.)

This chapter gives you constructive steps to minimize the psychological and financial downsides of selling one house while buying another.

SKIP AHEAD

If you are a first-time buyer or can afford to own two houses at once (even if for just a short period) you can skip this chapter.

RESOURCE

Information for home sellers. *Selling Your House: Nolo's Essential Guide*, by Ilona Bray, J.D., provides the legal, financial, and real estate knowledge needed to sell your house.

Mary Advises: Listen to Grandpa

In selling my house and buying another, I remembered my grandfather saying always, "Buy low and sell high." To accomplish this, he explained, you must get time on your side. People pay top dollar when they're pressed for time and get a bargain when they can be patient.

So the question became, how could I apply Grandpa's advice to my situation? To avoid selling my house in a hurry in order to pay for a new one, I called my dad and asked for a short-term loan. He helped some. Next I called my uncles and a college roommate who has a knack with money. Together, they agreed to advance me the rest of what I needed for a few months. Combined with my own savings, this let me make a very chunky down payment (55% of the purchase price) on a new house without the need to sell the old one. I then listed my existing house for sale at an aggressive price, perfectly prepared to have to wait for a while, and maybe even to take less. Instead, I immediately got a full price offer. I was so surprised, I almost forgot to say "yes." By preparing to be patient, I sold for about $25,000 more and bought for about $35,000 less than if I'd been in a hurry.

Check the Housing Market Carefully

Before you put your house on the market or commit to buying a new one, carefully investigate the sales prices of houses in the markets where you'll be selling and buying. Focus on whether the local market is "hot" (favors sellers) or "cold" (favors buyers).

Judging the relative temperature of the market is important to buyers and sellers and is crucial for people who are both. Your dual position lets you adopt a strategy of protecting yourself in your weaker role while letting your stronger role take care of itself.

CAUTION

Market conditions in California change frequently and vary by neighborhood. One neighborhood may feature depressed prices and foreclosures, while another, just a few miles away, may be typified by multiple offers and rising prices. Don't assume you know how to price your house, even if you bought it just last year or have been reading the real estate news.

Strategies in a Hot, Seller's Market

If sellers have the advantage in the communities where you both now own and plan to buy, selling your current house will likely be easier than buying a new one. Thus, you want to compete aggressively in purchasing a new house, while creating maximum flexibility as to the date you move out of your present house.

One possibility—which involves cutting the timing rather close—is to shop for and ultimately enter into a contract to buy a new home, but for safety's sake, wait to put your current home on the market until after you've removed all contingencies (inspection, loan, appraisal, title, homeowners' insurance) on the new home. It can be hard to get your home ready for sale when you're living there, however. Or, you can guarantee yourself the needed leeway by stipulating to buyers that the sale of your current house be contingent upon your finding and closing on a new one. When a buyer makes an offer on your house, include in your written counteroffer a provision spelling this out. Although few buyers will agree to an open-ended period, some will be so anxious to buy your house that they'll agree to delay the closing until you close on a new house or until a certain number of days pass, whichever comes first.

In hot markets, buyers may let the seller live in the home for an extra two to four weeks—by paying rent (called a "rent-back"), or even for free. Ira Serkes observes, "A buyer paying all cash will likely be flexible on your possession date. If the buyer is obtaining a loan, however, the lender will want the buyer to take possession within 30 days after closing."

Just in case the timing doesn't work out, it might be worth lining up a six- to 12-month rental, so you have a place to move to temporarily.

Is the Market Hot or Cold?

Here's how to take the temperature of a particular housing market (see Chapter 15 for more details):

- If many more people want to buy than to sell, it's a hot, seller's market. Prices tend to rise (often quickly), and buyers must bid competitively (read: high) and have their financing lined up (and be preapproved) in advance.
- If sellers outnumber buyers the market is cold and favors buyers. Sellers often must court buyers by lowering prices and offering innovative financing packages. (See Chapter 12.) In new housing developments, sellers often offer to pay a portion of the buyer's monthly mortgage. (See Chapter 7.)

Because markets can change quickly, it's crucial to have current information.

Strategies in a Cold, Buyer's Market

In a buyer's market, with lots of sellers or unsold homes, your position as a buyer is the stronger one. Consider protecting yourself by making your offer to buy contingent upon your selling your current house. A seller having a hard time finding a buyer is likely to accept this contingency, even though it means waiting.

Be ready for the seller to counter with a "wipe-out" or release clause. This lets the seller accept your offer, but keeps the house on the market, with the requirement that the seller give you written notice if he or she receives another offer and wants to accept it. Then, within 72 hours (or whatever length of time your agreement says), you must satisfy all contingencies and proceed with the purchase, or your offer is wiped out, and the seller can proceed with other offers.

In this situation, a wipe-out clause is not unreasonable, as the seller needs some way to get out of a deal if you never sell your house. We discuss wipe-out clauses in more detail in Chapter 18, "After the Contract Is Signed."

You'll probaby also want to make your offer contingent upon arranging financing. This can have the same practical effect as making your offer contingent on selling your present house, because a lender won't normally approve financing on a new purchase until the sale of the old house is made and the down payment money is in hand; or at least until the lender is confident that your present house will sell soon. But you can't milk this forever. The California home purchase contract puts a deadline on when you must successfully arrange for financing in order for the deal to go forward. You'll therefore need to propose a reasonable date in your contract and abide by it. In any case, you'll want to start talking to prospective lenders early about how much you will qualify to borrow.

Save Money on Real Estate Commissions

If you're selling and buying in the same area, consider using the same real estate agent for both transactions. The agent may be willing to lower the typical 5%–7% commission sellers pay the listing agent. Remember, even a 1% or 2% savings is a lot of money.

How to Briefly Own Two Houses

No matter how carefully you time things, you may not perfectly dovetail the sale of one house with the purchase of another. You may own no houses, in which case you'll have money in the bank and will need a temporary place to live, or you may own two houses at once. The following suggestions should help you pull this off:

- **Raise as much money as possible for the down payment on a new house.** If your savings, without the sale, put the second house within reach, maximize your cash, perhaps by charging living expenses, taking out a loan secured by stocks and bonds, or getting an advance from your employer. Although the interest on credit cards is high, you'll be able to pay bills off promptly when your existing house sells.

Renting Your Own House

When you sell your house contingent upon moving into a new one, you have three options if you need more time to move.

Becoming a tenant. One option is to become a tenant in your old house. Here are a few hints on how to handle this:

- You and the new owner should sign a written rental agreement. Nolo.com offers a lease form, with you as the "tenant" and the new owner as the "landlord" that will work for this purpose—search for "California Residential Lease." Choose a month-to-month rental term but require only seven days' written notice to move, rather than the normal 30 days.

- Your daily rent should be the buyer's daily carrying costs (mortgage principal and interest, taxes, and insurance). This will be considerably higher than what you paid to live in that house (your old mortgage), but the interest you earn on the cash proceeds of the sale will offset this to a degree. In addition, it will probably be less than if you had to move to a temporary place, and it saves you the trouble of moving twice.

- Make sure that both the house and your possessions are insured. The buyer's new homeowners' policy should come with a 30-day allowance for the house to be occupied by its previous owners (that being you). However, if you're planning to stay on longer, the buyers will need to ask their insurance company about either creating an exception within the policy, or arranging for a landlord's policy that converts to a homeowners' policy. You, in the meantime, should arrange for renter's insurance for your possessions. As Adrianne Peixotto of ProInsurance in Novato, California, explains, "I know of cases where burglars broke in soon after the closing, and the buyers had no insurance for their stolen goods. There was one where the burglars broke a sliding glass door and stole a computer, flat-screen TV, jewelry, and more. The buyers' homeowner policy covered the physical damage to the door and walls. But because the stolen possessions weren't the property of the buyer/policyholder, and the sellers doing the rent-back hadn't obtained their own, renter's coverage, they couldn't make a claim for their lost items."

Renting Your Own House (continued)

Delaying the closing. Another possible option is to put off the closing. As long as you are confident the buyer won't try to back out, this can make sense for two reasons. As an owner, you can deduct mortgage interest and property taxes; as a tenant, you can't. As a tenant, your rent will be figured at the new owner's higher costs. Of course, you will have a pile of money in the bank from the sale, but its true value won't equal your higher costs as a tenant.

Renting out your old house. Finally, if you're having a difficult time selling your house—and you must move into your new home right away—consider finding a tenant to rent your old house. Use the rent payments to cover your old mortgage and make your new purchase financially feasible. Try to make the rental temporary, and keep trying to sell your old house—assuming you anticipate a profit. Consult your tax adviser; there can be significant advantages to converting from owner-occupied to rental property. For advice on being a landlord, see *The California Landlord's Law Book: Rights & Responsibilities*, by David Brown, Ralph Warner, and Janet Portman (Nolo).

- **Borrow down payment money from family or friends.** Point out that you need help for only a short period, and offer a competitive interest rate. (In Chapters 4, "Raising Money for Your Down Payment," and 12, "Private Mortgages," we discuss borrowing from private sources.)

- **Get an equity line of credit in advance.** For a small application fee and annual fee, you may be able to arrange a line of credit to be ready if you need to draw on it. Home equity lines of credit are far less available than they used to be, but still possible for borrowers with excellent credit.

- **Seek a bridge loan from a financial institution.** Unfortunately, borrowing money from a financial institution to "bridge" the period between when you close on your new house and when you get your money from the sale of your old one has become impossible. (And even when they were available, bridge loans were expensive, with a host of up-front points or fees for credit checks, appraisals, loan originations, and physical inspections.) But you might be able to structure your home purchase with two loans; and pay off the second loan once you've sold your home.

True Story

Jenny and Gregg: We Had to Act Fast

We found the house to buy so fast, we were late getting in gear to sell our existing house. We knew the sellers of the house we planned to buy wanted a quick, easy sale, and we would look good to them only as long as we appeared ready to close. If we tried to make the purchase contingent on our selling our existing house, they'd lose interest.

Instead, we agonized for a bit and said "yes." Immediately, we put our existing house on the market. Unfortunately, it was harder than we expected to sell at the high price we wanted. We faced the possibility of owning two houses at once. Rather than panic and sell our existing house cheap, we lined up a bridge loan from a bank but held off making the final commitment, which would have cost a lot in fees. We then lowered our asking price slightly, to awaken buyer interest. It worked. The house sold at a still-very-good price, in time for us to make the closings simultaneous. We may have done better if we took the bridge loan and held out for a higher price, but with two kids and two jobs, the last thing we wanted to worry about was owning two houses.

Tax Breaks for Selling Your Home

If you sell your home, you may exclude up to $250,000 of your capital gain from tax. Joint owners may divide their gain and exclude up to $250,000 per person. For married couples filing jointly, the exclusion is $500,000.

Prop 13 and California Property Tax Relief

As a result of the California initiative of the mid-1970s, Proposition 13, property taxes are levied on the assessed value as of March 1, 1975, or the purchase price at any later transfer date, with exceptions for certain intrafamily transfers—for example, between spouses or between parents and children. For people who've owned homes for many years, their values are comparatively low. When they sell that house and purchase another, however, they pay property taxes on the price of the house being bought, which is likely to be higher than the one being sold.

To help older and disabled people deal with this, California law (Propositions 60 and 90) lets owners over age 55 (only one spouse of a married couple need qualify), or owners who are severely or permanently disabled, who sell one house and purchase another within two years in the same county, transfer their old tax assessment rate to the new house. (Revenue and Tax Code § 69.5.) Transferring the tax assessment intercounty is possible if you move to a county that participates in the statewide transfer system. The county tax assessor can tell you whether or not your county participates.

To qualify for this one-time tax break, the new house must in most situations be of equal or lesser value than the old house, though this depends in part on the timing of your purchase and sale (namely, which came first, and how long you wait to purchase your next home). Check with your county tax assessor to see whether the law applies when you contemplate your transaction and consult a tax adviser with regard to strategy. Coauthor Ira Serkes notes, "In the past, some buyers kept within the price limits by paying expenses typically paid by sellers. Counties began recognizing this strategy, however, and now ask about it on the preliminary change of ownership form."

For information on state taxes, contact the Franchise Tax Board at 800-852-5711, or check its website at www.ftb.ca.gov.

The law (I.R.C. (Title 26) § 121) applies to sales after May 6, 1997. To claim the whole exclusion, you must have owned and lived in your residence an aggregate of at least two out of five years before the sale, and it must be your main home, not a vacation or second home (this rule is called the "ownership and use" test). You can claim the exclusion once every two years.

Even if you haven't lived in your home a total of two years out of the last five, you are still eligible for a partial exclusion of capital gains if you sold because of a change in employment or health, or unforeseen circumstances. You get a portion of the exclusion, based on the portion of the two-year period you lived there. To calculate it, take the number of months you lived in the house before the sale and divide it by 24.

 RESOURCE

More information on tax laws involving real estate transactions. Contact the IRS at 800-829-1040; or visit www.irs.gov. See IRS Publication 523, *Selling Your Home.*

What Will You Offer?

How a Contract Is Formed 208

Decide What You Will Offer 208

What Is the Advertised Price? 209

How Much Can You Afford? 211

What Are Prices of Comparable Houses? 211

    Realtors' Comp Information 212

    Comparable Sales Prices Available Online 212

Is the Local Real Estate Market Hot or Cold? 213

Is the House Itself Hot or Cold? 214

What Are the Seller's Needs? 215

Is the House Uniquely Valuable to You? 216

How Much Are You Willing to Pay? 216

Making the Final Price Decision 217

Other Ways to Make Your Offer Attractive 217

This chapter assumes that you've found a house you like and have the financial resources to buy it. Now you must decide how much to offer and what other terms to include in your offer.

How a Contract Is Formed

A contract to transfer ownership requires that one party make a specific, written, legal offer to buy or sell a particular piece of property and the other person legally accept it in writing.

The first legally binding offer in a California real estate sale is usually made in writing by the prospective buyer. Legally binding means that the offer is specific (lays out the price and other terms) and the seller has the opportunity to accept it in writing before it is either withdrawn or the time period for its acceptance runs out.

The seller isn't obligated to accept, even if the offer is for the full asking price, as long as the refusal isn't motivated by an intent to discriminate. (He or she may be under pressure to sell with a full price offer, however, because the contract with the broker probably guarantees the broker a commission if the seller gets such an offer.)

Decide What You Will Offer

In putting together your actual offer and deciding on your offer price, consider:
- the advertised price of the house
- what you can afford
- prices for comparable houses
- whether the local real estate market is hot or cold
- whether the house itself is hot or cold
- the seller's needs
- whether the house is uniquely valuable to you, and
- how much you're willing to pay.

We'll also look at nonmonetary ways of making your offer attractive.

What Is the Advertised Price?

A seller's advertised price should be treated as only a rough estimate of what the seller would like to receive. To find out whether there's a typical differential in the area where you're looking, ask your agent to show you the sales/list price ratio for local homes like the ones you're considering. Sellers' personalities can also play into the setting of the list price. Some unrealistic sellers overprice, others ask for pretty close to what they expect to get, and some underprice their houses in the hope of attracting a wide pool of visitors or creating a situation where potential buyers compete and overbid.

Here are a few of the more common seller profiles.

Optimistic Charlie. He tends to believe (perhaps arrogantly) that his house is especially valuable and is likely to price it way above what comparable houses are selling for—as much as 30%–40% more, although 10%–25% is more typical. Unfortunately, some Optimistic Charlies are encouraged by brokers or agents so anxious to get the listings that they "romance" the Charlies into believing that the houses will fetch inflated prices. But FSBO (for sale by owner) sellers are also notoriously prone to this.

Stuck-in-the-past Suzy. Having bought her house at an all-time market peak, Suzy doesn't want to believe that it's now worth a dollar less than what she paid for it. In fact, she'd like to also like to recoup the $45,000 she spent on a bathroom remodel and roof repair. Unfortunately, prices haven't fully recovered from past drops in Suzy's area. Nevertheless, it may take many weeks of low or no offers for her to accept that she's not going to get her entire investment out of this house.

Straightforward William. William prices his house at exactly what he believes it's worth, not a dollar more, nor a dollar less. William may be stubborn if offered less than the asking price, but he may accommodate a buyer on other terms of the deal. For example, if a physical inspection turns up structural problems, William might agree to pay for $10,000 of needed work in the form of a credit in escrow if the buyer pays the asking price, rather than lower his asking price by $5,000. (Then again, if William is thinking clearly, he'll realize that lowering the house price will also lower the commission he owes to the agents.)

Canny Cynthia. Cynthia deliberately underprices her house. Her plan is to excite a feeding frenzy among bargain hunters, who'll bid against each other so furiously that the winner will pay more than the house is worth. This strategy works best in hot real estate markets when competition is fierce. (See "Is the Local Real Estate Market Hot or Cold?" below.)

Is Underpricing Ethical?

Why would a home seller (or a real estate agent) ask less for a home than it's really worth? To attract more lookers, create excitement, and generate a bidding war, of course.

Frustrated would-be buyers sometimes consult lawyers, hoping to find that sellers are obligated to accept the first offer at the full asking price. They're not.

The present consensus within the real estate community seems to be that pricing a tad under the market to attract a slightly larger pool of buyers is not a big deal; it's when a home is deliberately listed significantly below its true market value (say, a $900,000 home is listed at $799,000) that something is not right.

We believe that it's unethical for sellers to put a house on the market at a price they'd never accept. (These sellers can often be identified by the listing comment "Seller reserves the right to refuse all offers.") Your best recourse, however, is to know the market and not waste your time bidding list price for a deliberately underpriced house.

TIP

Don't be suckered by too low a price. It's tough not to get excited when a house comes on the market with a "too good to be true" price. But loads of other aspiring purchasers will spot the same bargain. Competition may soon drive that price up—perhaps to the point where it's the opposite of a bargain.

What should your approach be to the prospect of a bidding war? Coauthor Ira Serkes notes, "Some buyers feel that they should never make an offer in a situation where other buyers are bidding, and will never pay more than the asking price. In practice, that ends up limiting their home inventory to properties that are priced too high."

In a hot market, or hot neighborhood, you may simply need to get used to the idea of facing competitive bids. Just be sure not to lose your head in figuring out the most you're willing to bid.

How Much Can You Afford?

Chapter 2 focuses on how to determine how much house you can afford, based on your income, savings, and nonhousing long-term debts. Once you know your maximum, lower the number a little, to allow for the following additional expenses:

Closing costs. Your share will be about 2%–5% of the purchase price. (See Chapter 18 for details.)

Moving expenses. The amount depends on how much stuff you have to move, how far you're moving it, and how much you'll do yourself. If you plan on hiring a mover, get an estimate and add about 25%.

Buying furnishings and redecorating. Particularly if you're moving to a larger space, you'll need some money set aside for making it livable

Two months' mortgage payments. The lender will probably want to see that you have two or three months of mortgage payments in the bank, as a cushion in case anything goes wrong like you losing your job.

What Are Prices of Comparable Houses?

Before making an offer, you should know the recent selling prices of comparable houses. If you've been looking for only a short time, or in other areas, you have some research to do. If you're working with an experienced agent, he or she should be able to provide you with the information, preferably laid out in a handy spreadsheet.

Real estate appraisers have developed the following sensible guidelines to distinguish comparable houses from others:

- A comparable sale should have occurred within the last three to six months (the more recent, the better). If prices are fluctuating quickly, comps should be on sales within the last 30 to 60 days. In extremely volatile markets, ask your agent to research prices of houses where sales are still pending. (You won't find this information on public websites.)

- A comparable sale should be for a house quite similar to the one you're interested in. Look for houses of similar age, in comparable locations, and with a similar number of rooms and square footage, and similar yard size. In the real world, however, comparisons often must be made between houses that are somewhat different. A physically comparable house a few blocks away might be in a better school district or have a great view, which will raise the property's value. The more difference between houses, the less informative the comparison.

- A comparable sale should be within six to ten blocks of the house you want to buy. The boundaries should be adjusted if the neighborhood changes significantly in a shorter radius, for example, if a major road or freeway marks a border between two different residential areas.

Realtors' Comp Information

Usually, the best comparable sales data are in a Board of Realtors database (accessible by your agent) for the geographical area where you're looking. The database will list the sales price of houses that sold recently or are soon to close.

Comparable Sales Prices Available Online

Online services offer free, detailed—though not always up-to-date—comparable sales prices, based on information from county recorder's offices and property assessors, notably:

- Zillow, www.zillow.com, and
- Trulia, at www.trulia.com.

By entering your prospective new home's address on one of these websites, you can collect a fair amount of information, including an estimate of that house's value (which you should take with a huge grain of salt), each comparable house's address and location on an aerial photo, purchase price, year built, sales date, square footage, and numbers of bedrooms and bathrooms.

All of this information will help you decide which recently sold homes are truly comparable to the one in which you're interested, and how much a fair sales price would therefore be.

> ## CAUTION
>
> **Don't rely heavily on Zillow estimates.** Called "Zestimates," these home valuations can be fun to look at; but having been created without input from a live human, they're frequently off by a wide margin. In Berkeley, where Ira Serkes works, he's seen Zillow estimates differ from actual selling prices by as much as $400,000. How can a computer database know, for instance, from its limited data, whether the house is a dump or recently remodeled with state-of-the art everything? Do your own market research before coming to a conclusion about a home's value.

Is the Local Real Estate Market Hot or Cold?

To know whether your local real estate market is hot or cold, closely follow it for an extended period. (Even during the worst of the real estate slump, California has had some very hot local markets!)

This involves visiting lots of houses and reading MLS and comparative sales listings. If you don't have time for this, consult with one or more experienced local real estate people.

To do your own temperature research, keep in mind these rules:

- If 25% or more of the houses sell within a week or ten days of being listed, the market is hot.

- If more than 40% of the houses listed sold for more than the listing price, the market is sizzling.

- If more than half of the houses were on the market a month or more before selling, and most sold for less than their listing price, the market is cool.

- If the supply of houses on the market is steadily increasing, sales are slow, and prices of the houses you're looking at have decreased more than once, the market is cold.

Another driver of a market's temperature is the level of current mortgage interest rates. As rates jump substantially (usually one percentage point or more), most housing markets begin to cool—although at the beginning of the rise, people may rush to buy, hoping to lock in before rates climb even higher. Conversely, as rates drop, more people can afford houses, and the market perks up.

Chapter 17 includes several strategies for bidding on houses in a competitive market.

Is the House Itself Hot or Cold?

For many reasons, a particular house may be more or less attractive (hotter or colder) than those surrounding it. Here are some questions to ask:

- **How long has the house been on the market?** If it's more than 30 days, it's likely priced too high for the market, and you can probably buy it for less than the asking price.

- **Has the asking price dropped?** If it has been reduced once and it still hasn't sold (give it a month), the house is an icicle and may be ready for another reduction.

- **Does the house have serious structural problems requiring a hefty cash infusion?** If so, the house, even if otherwise attractive, may be hard to sell. If you have cash or can finance the purchase privately, the house may be yours. (See Chapter 3 for more on buying a house with structural problems.)

- **Has the seller, or perhaps the listing agent, tipped you off that a lower offer will be considered?** If you're told that the seller needs to sell quickly to close on a new house, perhaps because of a divorce or to move far away, you're almost surely being told to try a lower offer.

Or, if a real estate agent says the seller "hopes to receive" a certain amount, the agent is saying that the seller is being unrealistic and that a lower offer will probably (or eventually) be accepted.

- **Has the seller set a cut-off date by which all offers must be made?** This can be a good indication that the house is hot, and you may have to bid aggressively to get it. But be careful—the seller and his agent may attempt to create a bidding war, or at least the appearance of one. A seller may state that "five offers will be made" (or that "many people are considering bidding"), when only one or two are serious.

- **Is the house an ugly duckling?** In a hot market, interest in an unattractive house is likely to be lukewarm; in a cool market, icy. If you find a dowdy place you know how to turn into a swan, keep your passion to yourself and bid relatively low. (Again, see Chapter 3 for more on buying a homely house.)

- **How eager is the seller to sell?** It's to your advantage to figure out where the seller is coming from. For example, if you see a house where the price has been reduced substantially after only one month on the market, chances are the owner is anxious to sell and may be willing to reduce the price further.

- **Is the house very expensive?** The biggest fluctuations in price occur at the luxury end of the market. Houses that sell for $4 million at the very top of a market can often be purchased for 30% to 50% less during a recession. And, of course, the opposite is also true.

What Are the Seller's Needs?

The real estate business is structured to keep buyer and seller at arm's length. Unfortunately, this tradition can work to your disadvantage. You want to be able to size up the seller and structure your offer and your negotiating strategy accordingly, but obviously you can't if you never meet.

Your agent, however, may be able to glean useful information by talking to the seller's agent, such as how much room there is to negotiate on price or other items. Also, you may gain valuable insights by chatting with the neighbors while legitimately checking out the neighborhood.

If you have school-age children, talk to neighbors with kids about local schools. In casual conversation, they're likely to tell you why the seller is moving and lots of other useful information.

For example, sellers likely to want to close on the deal quickly, even if it means taking a lower price, include those who:

- have accepted a job in a different area
- have made an offer on another house contingent on selling the existing one
- are older people selling a long-time family home (sometimes with the help of a younger relative or friend)
- are families with small children, who are busy enough without the disruptions of the home-marketing process
- are divorcing or going through other major life changes, such as a loss of a job or retirement
- have inherited a house they don't plan to live in, or
- need a new home because of an expanded family.

We are not advocating taking advantage of a seller in distress. But, it's only common sense to find out if a seller needs to close quickly. If so, you may find a good house for a very reasonable price.

Is the House Uniquely Valuable to You?

A house's worth on the market isn't necessarily the same as its worth to you. A modest house listed at a price you can just handle, for example, may be worth it if you have three kids, the house is in a city that has excellent public schools, and the lot is large enough to add on a couple of rooms. The same house, however, may not be worth the price for a couple not planning to have children.

How Much Are You Willing to Pay?

Okay, now for the last and most important consideration. How much money do you really want to pay for the house? While tactical considerations (the temperature of the market, the seller's needs) are important, nothing should outweigh your own honest assessment of how much you are willing to fork over.

> ⓘ **CAUTION**
> **Find out whether the house will be hard to insure before you bid high—or bid at all.** Insuring a house with a history of problems, particularly from mold or water damage, has become surprisingly difficult. Ask about what claims the seller and previous owner have made, or, you can even request what's known as a "CLUE" report (Comprehensive Loss Underwriting Exchange) from the seller. These reports can also be obtained from www.propertyid.com (800-626-0106), but you'll need the seller's written permission first.

Making the Final Price Decision

The moment of truth has arrived: It's time to look at the many personal and market factors we discussed and come up with a dollar amount that you think is appropriate. There's nothing scientific or absolute about these factors.

Here's a method that clients of Ira Serkes find very helpful: Select a price that will put you at peace with the result. If your offer is accepted, you're happy. If it's not accepted, you will know that you offered the most you felt comfortable paying.

Other Ways to Make Your Offer Attractive

Though price is usually the most important part of your offer, the seller will be considering other aspects of the deal as well. Some sellers have even been known to choose a lower-priced offer because it met their other needs. Below are some strategies for making the nonmonetary terms of your offer as appealing as possible; you'll learn more about some of these offer terms in subsequent chapters, which describe the offer contract in detail.

Art: I Got a Bargain Without Being Too Greedy

I was on a tight budget when house hunting, and excited when a bargain surfaced. An acquaintance was moving out of the country and needed to sell his two-bedroom bungalow quickly. After visiting the house, and based on looking at dozens of houses in the area, I guessed that it was worth close to $425,000. The seller indicated he'd take about $385,000 for a quick sale.

Then I heard that another person was ready to make an offer. My spirits fell. I spoke to my dad, who had worked in real estate years before. His advice was not to be too greedy. "Bid a few thousand more than $385,000." I agonized about the exact amount and bid $392,000. I beat the other bidder by $4,000 and got a super house for the price.

To make your offer appealing:

- **Schedule a speedy closing.** If you've got all your financing lined up and are prepared to throw yourself into following up on other parts of the deal, such as inspections and appraisals, you may be able to offer a closing date that's a week or two earlier than the typical 30–45 days. That will be attractive to a seller who needs to get money out of the house quickly and move on. Realize, however, that getting final loan approval may require more time than you expect—talk to your mortgage broker before committing to an early date. Ira Serkes sold a home in Kensington to an all-cash buyer who was willing to close in less than two weeks. Ira explains, "The sellers actually countered the buyer back at a lower price, because they valued having the certainty of a quick close without an appraisal contingency!"

- **Give sellers ample time to move out.** Not all sellers want the deal to be tied up in a hurry. If, for example, your seller still needs to find a new home, you might offer a long closing period (60 days or more) or allow the seller to continue living in the home after the closing (for a low rent, or even free). If you offer a long closing period, however, make sure that your lender's commitment won't run out during this time. The lender may also limit the rent-back period, most likely to 30 days.

- **Show good financing prospects.** You'll need to start by being clear about what type of loan you'll apply for and what interest rate you plan to pay, so that the seller can ascertain whether this is realistic in the current market. In addition, a preapproval letter from a lender will help show the seller that your financing is likely to go through. And the higher your down payment, the more confidence the seller will have that your loan will go through. Offering a higher-than-normal earnest money deposit (discussed in Chapter 16) can also be used to show the sellers that you're serious about the deal and have the cash to follow through.

- **Offer to pay incidental expenses.** Every home sale requires someone to pay for various incidentals such as escrow fees, a title search, city transfer tax, and the like. These items can cost from a few hundred dollars to several thousand. By tradition, the seller usually picks up some of these costs, and the buyer picks up others (discussed in detail in Chapter 16). You could offer to pay for costs traditionally borne by the seller.

- **Write a letter to the seller.** It has become almost commonplace for prospective buyers, especially if competing against other bidders, to include a letter summarizing the main points of their offer and saying a bit about themselves—in particular, why they like the house and that they will take good care of it. You could also mention that you're ready to be flexible about the various terms of the offer. But don't put the seller in a position of having to discriminate in accepting or rejecting your offer, by including a photo or otherwise emphasizing your family composition (which might suggest gender, sexual orientation, or marital status), religion, or ethnicity.

- **Show that you'll be easy to work with.** Choose an agent with a good reputation, or the seller's agent may advise, "Let's avoid this offer, or we'll spend all our time in hardball negotiations." Beyond this, try not to be too demanding in the initial offer. If the seller sees that you're insisting that he or she pay all the transaction fees, purchase a home warranty, and leave the curtains and basketball hoop behind as well, you might be shooting yourself in the foot.

Some strategies are worth avoiding, however, as follows:

- **Don't unreasonably limit the time by which the seller must accept.** Some buyers (usually egged on by aggressive agents) add a clause to their offers insisting that the sellers accept (or reject) the offers "upon presentation" or within a few hours' time. Unfortunately, most sellers feel bullied. You can limit the time during which your offer remains open, but it's better to give the seller at least two or three days.

- **Don't waive the inspection contingencies.** Such a waiver would mean that you take the house without any inspections, or that, even if you conduct an inspection, you won't hold the seller responsible for any defects that are revealed. This is a risky proposition and most likely to be attractive to a seller who knows the home needs work. If you feel you must waive this contingency, ask to send in your own inspector *before* you make an offer.

- **Don't offer an open-ended amount.** Worried about being outbid, buyers have been known to resort to offers along the lines of, "We'll pay $5,000 more than your highest bidder." This is also known as a "relative bid" or "sharp" offer. In many areas, agents or sellers really dislike them, however, so be sure to ask your agent how the sellers' agent feels about them. If you are desperate enough to do this, at least get an attorney's help with drafting the contract, and put a cap on how high you'll go. Also add a provision giving you the right to review the other offer and preapproval letter to make sure it's legitimate. (However, viewing another buyer's offer materials raises confidentiality issues, and you may have to settle for seeing documents with portions blacked out.)

In Chapters 16 and 17 we delve further into the nitty-gritty of presenting your offer and dealing with counteroffers from the seller.

Putting Your Offer in Writing

What Makes an Offer Legally Valid 222

How California Offers and Counteroffers Are Made 223

What Your Purchase Agreement Should Cover...224

This chapter explains what should go into your written purchase offer. The next chapter discusses how to present it to the seller and suggests good negotiating techniques. Read both chapters carefully despite the fact that your real estate agent will likely prepare the paperwork for you. Many important decisions are being made here, and it's essential that you know how to protect your interests—before signing your offer form. If anything in the offer form isn't clear to you, ask your real estate agent or attorney to explain it.

We're going to assume that you'll use a standard form provided by your real estate agent and probably prepared by the California Association of Realtors. For that reason, this chapter will focus on all the topics that such a real estate offer form normally covers. (The actual clauses won't necessarily appear in the same order.)

What Makes an Offer Legally Valid

An offer to buy a house is legally useless unless it's in writing, has been delivered to the seller or the seller's agent, and contains specific financial and other terms so that if the seller says "yes," the deal can go through. The seller's acceptance, too, must be in writing.

Real estate offers almost always contain contingencies—events that must happen or else the deal won't become final. For example, your offer may be contingent on your qualifying for financing or the house's passing certain physical inspections.

Most offers give the seller a certain period of time within which to accept. During this time, you may revoke (take back) your offer in writing so long as the seller hasn't yet communicated an acceptance to you or your agent. (See Chapter 17, "Presenting Your Offer and Negotiating," for more on revoking.)

How California Offers and Counteroffers Are Made

Here are a few words on offer terminology and procedures in California. The exact same form may be called by different names, each with a different legal meaning, depending on when and by whom (buyer or seller) it's used.

Know this terminology:

- Making an *offer* is when you fill out a California purchase agreement form and give it to the seller.

- A *counteroffer* is made by a seller who is willing to accept some of your terms but only if you'll agree to modify others. The seller may respond, for example, with a higher price or a shorter time for you to arrange financing. A counteroffer is sometimes (but not always) made using exactly the same form as the buyer's purchase offer, with the title changed to reflect that it's a counteroffer. You're not in contract yet—in fact, the more legally accurate way to think about your position is that you've been rejected, but presented with a new offer.

- A *multiple counteroffer* is when the seller counters a number of offers simultaneously—though not always identically. The seller may submit a variety of counteroffers, including different prices, terms, or conditions, to different buyers. The seller will then ask for each buyer's "highest and best" offer in response. As if the seller wasn't already getting a good deal, the seller will draft the counteroffers so as not to become obligated to accept any of the buyers' return offers. As annoying as these multiple counteroffers can be, you can set yourself apart from the pack by swallowing your annoyance and countering with a slightly higher price. That gives the seller a solid incentive to single out your offer for acceptance. You're most likely to encounter this practice in Southern California.

- A *counter counteroffer* is when you state your willingness to accept some of the seller's counteroffer terms along with your wish to modify others. Again, you can do this using a redrafted version of the original offer form. (The back-and-forth dance can go on for a while with counter-counter counteroffers, and so forth.)

- The offer becomes a legally binding *contract* only when you and the seller agree on all the terms in the offer (or counteroffer, and so forth) and sign it. You can both sign the same offer form, or a separate written document stating that all terms of the offer (or counteroffer) are accepted. Not only must you both sign the agreement, you must both also initial every page.

EXAMPLE 1: Mitch gives Patricia a written offer to purchase her house for $450,000, which includes seven days to accept. Two days later, Patricia accepts in writing. A contract has been formed.

EXAMPLE 2: Now assume the same offer from Mitch, but before Patricia says "yes," Mitch finds a house he likes better. He immediately calls Patricia's agent and withdraws his offer. While this revokes his offer, he puts his revocation in writing and drops it off at Patricia's agent's office so there can be no misunderstanding. Mitch's offer has now been withdrawn; Patricia can't call Mitch up and say, "I accept," because no contract can be formed between them unless one or the other makes a second offer and the other accepts it in writing.

What Your Purchase Agreement Should Cover

Below is a review of the clauses traditionally found in a California purchase agreement.

Opening section. Your offer form will start with the obvious stuff: your name and the property's address. If you're married but buying a house using only your separate property (property acquired before marriage, by gift or inheritance during marriage, or after permanent separation), enter only your name. Normally, however, some community property (property acquired by either spouse during marriage, except gifts or inheritances) is used toward the down payment or monthly payments, so your spouse's name should also appear on the offer. (For more on this subject, see Chapter 20, Legal Ownership: How to Take Title.)

The street number, city, county, and state are sufficient for the address —a formal legal description isn't required. If the property has no street address, do your best to describe it ("the ten-acre Norris Ranch on County Road 305, two miles south of Andersonville").

You'll also be asked early on to state the purchase price you're offering, both written out (such as "four hundred seventeen thousand") and numerically ($417,000).

Financial terms. Time to talk money—not just what you're offering, but how you can get out of the deal if your intended financing doesn't come through. The agreement should cover:

- **Your deposit.** You'll normally accompany your offer with an "earnest money" deposit, the amount of which should be stated here. A seller who accepts your offer will hold the deposit (probably in an escrow account). The seller may be able to keep that money as damages if you back out of the deal for a reason not allowed by the contract. The deposit is usually about 1%–3% of the purchase price or sometimes a flat $1,000–$2,000 for lower-priced houses. The seller may counteroffer and ask for more. We advise limiting your initial deposit to 1%–3% of the purchase price. Also indicate the form of the deposit (personal check is most common).

- **Any increase to your deposit.** Buyers commonly increase the amount of the deposit after the offer is accepted, typically after 17 days or after removing the inspection contingencies (covered elsewhere in the agreement). For example, you might make an initial deposit of 1% of the purchase price and increase it to 3% upon removal of inspection contingencies.

- **Terms of the loans you'll be seeking.** If you already have your financing lined up, this will be easy. If a paragraph doesn't apply, enter N/A (for "not applicable") in the blank. If you're applying for a government loan, be ready to demonstrate to the seller that you're eligible.

- **Down payment.** Specify your proposed down payment balance— your total down payment less your deposit and deposit increase.

- **Total.** Your deposit, loans, and the down payment should total up to your offer price.

- **Financing time limits and contingencies.** For your and the seller's protection, you'll need to state the number of days within which you'll provide a copy of your loan preapproval letter (if you have to start from scratch, expect to spend several weeks getting this); provide verification that you can pay the down payment and closing costs; arrange your financing and remove the loan contingency; and get the property appraised and remove the appraisal contingency. Your strongest protection here (though one that few buyers use) is to state that you'll remove the loan contingency upon funding of the loan—most likely a day before closing. That guards against the possibility that last-minute demands from the lender will cause your financing to fall through. (Also, if you're able to pay all cash— which more people do than you might expect—you can waive the financing contingency, but might want to include an appraisal contingency regardless.)

Occupancy. You'll need to indicate whether you intend to occupy the property as your primary residence. The seller is interested in this because if you plan to rent out the property, you may have a harder time getting a loan. The agreement can also cover situations where tenants already live in the property, in which case you may agree to allow them to continue living there or propose a time by which they must move out.

Note that you buy subject to the tenants' rights and existing rental agreements. Many tenants will move on their own when they find out the house is being sold. In rent control areas, however, a long-term tenant with low rent may resist. After escrow closes, you may have to bring an eviction action on the grounds that you intend to occupy the house yourself.

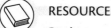

RESOURCE

Buying property subject to tenants' rights or rental property?
See *The California Landlord's Law Book: Rights & Responsibilities*, by David Brown, Janet Portman, and Ralph Warner (Nolo).

Although you'll probably want to take possession of the property on the day escrow closes, be prepared to give this up during your negotiations. Many sellers who are buying another house insist on not moving out until 60–90 days after escrow closes, normally in exchange for paying you rent. Some sellers who are renting new places won't want to move out until the first of the month when their lease begins—they, too, will pay you rent.

If you end up agreeing that the seller can stay on more than just a few days after closing, we suggest you and the seller sign a written rental agreement specifying a daily rent or security deposit, authorizing a final inspection, and indicating the rental term (length). (See Chapter 14 for resources on rental agreements.) Make sure your homeowners' insurance covers their stay; if not, you may need to buy short-term landlord's insurance and the seller may need to buy short-term tenant's insurance for personal possessions. The agreement should also state that you expect a per-day charge of your prorated monthly carrying costs.

Escrow. Escrow is a process in which a disinterested third party, usually a title or escrow company, transfers the funds and documents among the buyer, the seller, and their lenders, in accordance with instructions provided by the buyer and seller (or their agents). (Escrow is described more thoroughly in Chapter 18.)

The standard contract will give you a place to enter the name and address of the escrow holder you choose. It's wise to do some preliminary investigation beforehand, so that you'll have at least a tentative idea about which company you'll use. However, if the seller has already set up a "listing escrow" with a company (a preliminary step that some take to speed up the process by a week or so), the expectation is that you'll use that company. There's little reason to argue, unless you've heard something negative about the company the seller has chosen. But if you're buying and selling a house in the same area, you'll ideally want to use the same escrow holder for both properties, to coordinate the closings.

This section may also state the date upon which you intend escrow to close, usually within 30 to 90 days of the offer's acceptance. How much time you give yourself should depend both on your own needs and what you think will please the seller most, if you're competing against other offers. (The exact date may later need to be adjusted by a few days depending on how things go with removing contingencies and lining up your loan, but this isn't usually difficult to negotiate with the seller, who most likely wants the deal to go through as much as you do.)

Here are some money-saving tips for choosing the exact closing date:

- The later in the month your closing date, the less prorated interest you will owe in closing costs. If you close on the second of June, for example, you'll need to prepay interest from June 2 through the end of the month. If you close on June 28, you'll need to prepay interest for only a few days.

- Don't close escrow on a Monday (or a Tuesday following a three-day weekend). You may end up paying extra interest. Lenders must fund a loan, and start charging the buyer interest, the day before escrow closes. Closing on a Monday requires the lender to fund the loan on the previous Friday. This means you end up paying interest over the weekend, before you even own the property.

Who pays for what expenses. Your offer should indicate those items you agree to pay for, those you want the seller to pay for, and those you propose to split. Don't feel compelled to pay for every item—a lot depends on the particular house and market.

Use the chart below, "Who Pays for What," as a guide to how expenses are commonly divided. It's quite all right for you and the seller to agree to a different arrangement from that shown on the chart.

Property tax and insurance prorations; assessment bonds. This type of clause allocates payment of property taxes, insurance policies carried over from seller to buyer, rents, interests, and any homeowners' association (HOA) dues or regular assessments. Each owner pays only for the period of actual ownership during the year the house is sold.

This clause also provides that the buyer assumes certain bond liens to finance local improvements, such as curbs, gutters, or street lights. The seller may not even know whether the house has any such bond liens, but they'll show up on the title report.

Often bonds must be paid off when a house is sold, but sometimes they can't be. In that case, the buyer assumes responsibility to pay the lien, but the cost of doing so is credited by the seller to the buyer in escrow.

Who Pays for What		
Item	**Who usually pays**	**Comments**
Escrow fees	Buyer customarily pays in Northern California, seller in Southern California.	Not uncommon for fees to be divided
Title search	Buyer customarily pays in Northern California, seller in Southern California.	Buyer benefits—not unreasonable for buyer to pay.
Title insurance for buyer/owner	Buyer customarily pays in Northern California, seller in Southern California.	Buyer benefits—not unreasonable for buyer to pay.
Title insurance for lender	Buyer	Buyer benefits—buyer should pay.
Deed preparation fee	Buyer	Buyer benefits—buyer should pay.
Notary fee	Buyer usually pays for grant and trust deeds; seller usually pays for reconveyance deed on the property.	Grant and trust deeds help buyer purchase and finance property; seller receives reconveyance deed when paying off existing mortgage.
Recording fee	Buyer usually pays for grant and trust deeds; seller usually pays for reconveyance deed on the property.	Grant and trust deeds help buyer purchase and finance property; seller receives reconveyance deed when paying off existing mortgage.
Attorney's fee (if attorney hired to clarify title)	Whoever hired attorney	
Documentary transfer tax	Seller usually pays except in probate sales, where buyer is usually required to pay by the terms of the notice of sale.	
Transfer taxes	Buyer and seller usually split the cost of city transfer taxes, while the seller usually pays county transfer taxes.	These taxes can be surprisingly high—city transfer taxes, in particular, may run to 1.5% of the purchase price.

Who Pays for What (continued)		
Item	**Who usually pays**	**Comments**
Pest control inspection report	Buyer usually picks inspector and pays for inspection in Northern California; seller often has property inspected before listing it for sale in Southern California.	In Southern California, lenders usually won't process buyer's loan application without termite inspection because termites are a serious problem; if seller didn't do inspection, buyer should pay to ensure that report meets buyer's standard.
General contractor report	Buyer usually picks inspector and pays for inspection.	Buyer should pay to ensure that report meets buyer's standard.
Roof inspection report	Buyer usually picks inspector and pays.	Buyer should pay to ensure that report for inspection meets buyer's standard.
Other inspections	Buyer usually picks inspector and pays for inspection.	Buyer should pay to ensure that report meets buyer's standard.
One-year home warranty	Seller	Sometimes seller offers to purchase a policy when listing the property—if seller doesn't, buyer can purchase one if desired or negotiate this as part of the contract.
Real estate tax, fire insurance, bond liens (unless able to be paid off)	Buyer and seller usually prorate as of the date the deed is recorded (see these expenses listed in Clause 5).	Both parties benefit; costs should be prorated.

Fixtures included in the sale. Fixtures are items permanently attached to real property, like built-in appliances or bookshelves, chandeliers, and drapery rods (though usually not the drapes). If removing the item would cause damage, chances are it's a fixture. On the other hand, if the item is easily removed—like a refrigerator that can be unplugged and wheeled away—it's not a fixture, no matter how much it looks like a natural part of the house. Fixtures come with the house unless you and the seller agree that the seller can remove them. To avoid uncertainty, however, especially if there are fixtures that you'd be unhappy to see disappear, list the fixtures in the purchase contract. (The very process of negotiating over which items are fixtures can clear up misunderstandings.)

Buying a Potential Rental? Consider Impact of Rent Control

If you're buying a potential rental property in California, find out whether you'll be burdened with rent control. These laws affect your ability to raise the rent to market levels during a tenancy, terminate the leases of existing tenants, and even to simply refuse to renew their leases. Whether rent control will be a real consideration depends on the type of building you buy and where it's located.

California has no statewide rent control or eviction protection, but 19 cities have one form or another of rent control and/or eviction-protection ordinances (see the chart below). Eviction protection limits the bases upon which a landlord can terminate a lease to specified, "just-cause" reasons. Rent control limits how much a landlord can increase the rent on in-place tenants, and often includes just-cause protections as well.

But California law has, for many years, exempted single-family rentals (including most condos) from local rent control and eviction protection ordinances, as well as any property that obtained a certificate of occupancy after February 1, 1995. In addition, local ordinances usually exempt structures built after the effective date of the ordinance; many ordinances exempt owner-occupied buildings with four (or fewer) units; and a few cities exempt units that rent for more than a certain dollar amount.

If you're investing in a single-family home, chances are that any local rent control or eviction protection ordinance will not apply to you. But if you're purchasing another type of property, get a copy of the ordinance and become familiar with it. Be forewarned: These ordinances are convoluted and the subject of endless debate and litigation. Landlords chafe under the restrictions, and many have sold out in frustration. Bring the topic up with your real estate agent or attorney, who should be able to tell you whether you will be subject to any local controls. And if you decide to proceed, get in touch with a local landlords' association to learn how its members deal with common issues.

What Sellers Must Tell You About Registered Sex Offenders (Megan's Law)

Home sales contracts entered into after July 1, 1999 must include a notice, in eight-point type (at least), regarding the availability of a database maintained by law enforcement authorities on the location of registered sex offenders. (Civil Code § 2079.10a.)

The seller or broker is not required to provide additional information about the proximity of registered sex offenders. The law states, however, that it does not change the existing responsibilities of sellers and real estate brokers to make disclosures of "material facts" that would affect the "value and desirability" of a property. This arguably means that a seller or broker who knew for a fact that a registered sex offender lived nearby would be responsible for disclosing this "material" fact to the buyer. Since the law isn't clear, you should, if concerned, check the database yourself.

The California Department of Justice provides detailed information on Megan's Law and how to obtain information on sex offenders in your neighborhood (www.meganslaw.ca.gov).

Personal property included in the sale. Personal property doesn't come with the house unless the seller agrees in writing to include it. If the seller promises to include items such as rugs, beds, aboveground swimming pools, ladders, or appliances that aren't built in, list them in the agreement.

Contingencies. Contingencies are conditions that either the seller or buyer must meet (or the other party must waive) before the deal will close. Once both of you have agreed that the other party has met all contingencies (that is, you've "removed" the contingencies or, if you're no longer interested, "waived" them), you're legally bound to go forward with the purchase.

Sale contingent on selling your property. The sale of your current home is perhaps the most common noninspection contingency. It's also the most difficult contingency to get a seller to accept, particularly in a hot market. The rare seller who accepts this contingency will likely give you a short time period in which to sell your home, or ask you to prove that you have sufficient resources to go ahead with the purchase even without first selling your home.

Time Allowed for Removing Contingencies

Most offers call for the removal of all contingencies within 15–20 days after the seller's acceptance. You and the seller should decide depending on your time constraints and how long it will realistically take to remove each. If the house is in great physical shape, seven to ten days should be adequate to remove all contingencies relating to its physical condition. Just don't hamper your ability to thoroughly check out the house in your eagerness to keep negotiations with the seller going smoothly.

A contingency based on your selling an existing house or obtaining a loan you haven't yet applied for will normally need 30–90 days for removal. If any contingencies aren't met in the specified time, the deal is over unless you and the seller agree in writing to extend the contingency release time.

Chapter 18 gives more detail on how to remove contingencies.

Inspection contingencies and their removal. Your agreement will specify what inspections on the house you want and must approve before you complete the purchase (close escrow). You'll also note how soon after the acceptance of the offer the inspections must be done. Normally, seven to ten calendar days is reasonable. Most buyers request only a general contractor and a pest control report, unless the buyer or the general inspector suspects problems requiring an inspection by a specialist. As a very rough rule, you want to require more inspections when a house is older and expensive or vulnerable to special problems, such as being near an earthquake fault or a slide zone, or potentially containing toxic substances (lead, mold, or asbestos). With new houses, you should schedule inspections during key phases of construction, plus a final inspection. (See Chapter 7 regarding inspecting new houses.)

Other contingencies and their removal. The agreement will contain sections or allow space for you to specify other contingencies that must be met before you will close, and the dates by which you must agree to their removal:

- A title contingency is needed for all houses to make sure title is good, that is, no one has a lien on the house allowing them to foreclose, or claims an easement or other right that might impact your use or ownership of the property. (See Chapter 18, After the Contract Is Signed, for a discussion of these terms and preliminary title reports.) In most cases, the buyer orders the preliminary title report within three days of acceptance.

- The seller may buy you a home warranty, which will provide low-fee servicing, repair, or replacement of certain items in the house. If so, be sure to also check "Seller" under the list of costs associated with the sale.

- California home buyers may encounter difficulty purchasing hazard insurance with appropriate coverage (especially for earthquakes) at affordable rates. To protect yourself, you can make your purchase contingent upon your applying, and receiving a commitment in writing, for reasonably priced hazard insurance on the property as required by your lender. Ask for a week to remove this contingency.

- An appraisal contingency has become extremely important, to guard against the possibility that the lender-commissioned appraisal report comes in lower than the home's purchase price, in which case (depending on the amount of the loan), the lender may refuse to fund your mortgage. Even if you're paying all cash, however, you might want to insist on a home appraisal, to get an independent third party's confirmation that the house is worth what you're planning to pay for it. (That's assuming, naturally, that you choose an excellent appraiser, who's familiar with the area where you're buying.)

Condition of property. Your offer contract should require the seller to keep the property in its current condition until you take possession. You will also require the seller to clear out all personal belongings and debris.

Title. This standard clause assures you that title to (ownership of) the house will be "clear" when you take possession. Someone will need to order a preliminary title report, either you or the seller (depending on local custom). If any clouds on the title are revealed in the preliminary report, and the seller is unable to clear up these difficulties before the close of escrow or you can't obtain a title insurance policy, you have the right to get out of the contract. We discuss checking out the title in Chapter 18.

> ### How Clean Will It Be?
>
> Your contract will address the condition of the house and require the sellers to leave the premises vacant and undamaged, but not sparkling. Even if they have the house professionally cleaned before they leave (which some may do as a courtesy—feel free to ask), it may not look clean enough to you. After all, years of accumulated dirt and scuffs look invisible when they're in your own house but disgusting when created by someone else. As you plan your moving day, allow a day or two after the house is yours to tackle any cleaning tasks before your possessions arrive.

Final walk-through and possession. The agreement should let you have one last look at the property right before the close of escrow to make sure the seller (or tenant) didn't damage the place before moving out or leave an old stained sofa and other junk behind, and that all promised repairs have been done to your satisfaction. It will also explain the seller's obligation to give you the keys and other things needed for access at or after the close of escrow.

Agency disclosure and confirmation. Your offer contract must let you and the seller confirm your relationships with your agents. Long before you fill out this offer form, if you are working with an agent, you will have completed a Disclosure: Real Estate Agency Relationships form, which should have told you whether the agent is representing you, the seller, or both. In the agreement, you acknowledge that you've received that form, and confirm some of the information within.

Broker compensation. The contract may also clarify who pays which broker, and how much. Your options are outlined in Chapter 5.

Backup offer. If the seller has already accepted another offer and you'd like to make a backup offer, you will most likely need to prepare an addendum explaining this. For example, the San Francisco Association of Realtors provides a one-page form that simply references the would-be buyer's original offer and gives the seller a space to sign upon deciding to elevate the offer to primary position. If the seller does this, you'll normally be given a certain amount of time to approve the deal in writing. This lets you make more than one backup offer without being obligated to purchase more than one house if your offers are simultaneously accepted.

When offer expires. Your offer should give the seller a deadline to accept. If the seller doesn't accept by that time, your offer automatically expires unless you extend it in writing. (See Chapter 17 on how to extend an offer. Chapter 17 also covers revoking your offer before the seller accepts or the deadline expires.)

Liquidated damages. If you refuse to go through with the sale because a contingency can't be fulfilled, the seller must return your deposit. But if you back out simply because you change your mind, or you don't try in good faith to fulfill a contingency (for example, you don't even apply for a loan), it's considered a default. Assuming you both agreed to a liquidated damages provision, the seller need not return your deposit. Your deposit turns into "liquidated damages," which in legal terms means you and the seller have agreed in advance on the maximum amount of the damages if you default. By setting the maximum amount in the purchase contract, you and the seller can save both time and money by avoiding court or arbitration, and you are protected from the risk of a court or an arbitrator awarding the seller a larger amount.

California law generally prohibits sellers from keeping more than 3% of the agreed-upon sale price as liquidated damages. (Civil Code § 1675.) But the seller must prove that the damages somehow relate to that amount. In some situations, where the seller immediately gets another acceptable offer, the damage is zero—and the seller won't be entitled to anything.

If your contract includes a liquidated damages provision, it must be in at least ten-point boldface type and signed or initialed by you and the seller.

Mediation of disputes. This clause mandates that you first try to settle any disputes that arise under the contract by nonbinding mediation. Mediation is a process where you and the seller pick someone to help you reach a mutually agreeable decision. It is cheap, fast, and avoids the emotional drain and hostility of litigation.

Arbitration of disputes. You can choose to resolve your dispute by arbitration should your attempt to settle any dispute informally or by mediation not succeed. You give up your right to a court trial, but like mediation, it's cheaper, faster, and less hostile than litigation.

In arbitration, you submit your dispute to one or more arbitrators for a decision. In the standard provision, most agreements are governed by either the American Arbitration Association (AAA) or the Judicial Arbitration and Mediation Services, Inc. (JAMS), both of which provide that the parties may get lawyers to represent them (but don't have to) and that the decision is final—neither party can appeal it to a court.

Attorneys' fees. In any standard real estate purchase contract, the losing party in arbitration or litigation (you could wind up in litigation if you choose arbitration and the seller doesn't agree, or vice versa) is responsible for his or her own—and the other side's—attorneys' fees and court costs.

Entire agreement. A standard contract will state that it is the entire and final agreement between you and the seller, and that all modifications to the contract must be in writing—in other words, that any other written or oral agreements floating around in the world don't count.

Time is of the essence. The statement that time is of the essence is standard contract language emphasizing the importance of the dates to which you and the seller agree. It means that a missed deadline by either party is considered a substantial breach of the contract, which can result in the other party being given money damages or being allowed to cancel the contract.

TIP

Put away your stopwatch. Despite this provision, many courts reject cries of "he breached the 'time is of the essence' clause" for a delay of a few hours or days, unless you can show that you have suffered, or will suffer, damages as a result.

Disclosures. Some parts of the standard offer form don't need to be filled out—for example, clauses intended to alert you to the seller's obligation to give you various disclosure statements within a certain time. Some of these seller disclosure statements are generic (like a pamphlet on lead paint hazards), while others are specific to the property (see the "Real Estate Transfer Disclosure Statement," in Chapter 19).

If you're buying a condo or a house in a planned development, the seller should provide you with all the rules and regulations, financial documents, and other pertinent paperwork. Study them carefully—you'll have an opportunity to cancel the agreement if you're not happy with them.

Buyer's signature. By signing and dating the purchase agreement form, you agree to make your offer a binding contract if it's accepted by the seller. All buyers must sign, including your spouse if you're using community property to make the purchase. If you have a broker, the broker (or agent) must sign too (sometimes your broker will be referred to as "Selling Firm").

Seller's acceptance of offer. If the seller signs, it means your offer has been accepted, and the seller promises that he or she owns the property and has the right to sell it to you. If the sellers are a married couple, they both must sign, even if one spouse claims the house is separate property. A title company won't want to get involved in the complexities of California community property law and will want to see both signatures.

Seller's rejection of offer. Your offer form may provide a place for the seller to formally reject your offer. It will definitely make your life easier to know whether and when your offer is no longer being considered by the seller. However, not all sellers will take the time to fill this in and return it to you.

Other advisories. Your offer form may also contain various clauses whose primary purpose is to advise you and the seller of your rights and responsibilities. Most of these are warnings that you, as the buyer, can't rely on every word that the seller or any broker says and should be a cautious consumer and investigate matters on your own.

Addenda containing other terms and conditions. Standard contracts don't necessarily contain space for every term that you might want to include in your agreement. You can create supplementary documents that are part of the agreement, for example to cover such issues as:

- your acknowledgment that the property contains unpermitted units
- details outlining a probate or foreclosure sale (get help from a real estate agent or attorney experienced in these matters), or
- specification of who will pay to pump and certify a septic system or connect a sewer.

Presenting Your Offer and Negotiating

Notify the Seller of Your Offer..240

Strategies in a Cold Market 241

Strategies in a Competitive Market 241

Present Your Offer..243

The Seller's Response to Your Offer 244

The Seller Accepts on the Spot 245

The Seller Rejects on the Spot 245

The Seller Asks for More Time 246

The Seller Is Waiting for Other Bids..247

The Seller Has Received a Higher Bid 248

The Seller Responds With a Counteroffer 248

Negotiate by Counteroffers..250

An Offer Is Accepted—A Contract Is Formed..252

Revoking an Offer or Counteroffer..252

Making a Backup Offer 252

This chapter discusses presenting your offer to the seller and, if necessary, negotiating the price and other terms. If you haven't done so already, read Chapter 16, Putting Your Offer in Writing.

GO BACK
If you're looking to buy a new house. This chapter focuses on negotiating to purchase an existing house. We discuss negotiating with the developer to purchase a new house in Chapter 7.

Of course, you personally will probably not be handling the drafting or presentation of the actual offer, nor conducting the face-to-face (or phone-to-phone) negotiations. These are all tasks your agent will be responsible for, with you in the background. By tradition and basic principles of agency relationships, once home buyers and sellers are represented by agents, they do not communicate with one another directly.

Nevertheless, your agent will (and should) be regularly consulting with you about key terms of your offer, reporting to you on the latest counteroffers or requests by the seller, and asking for your decisions on all key terms and strategies. Reading this chapter will help you prepare for your role—as well as for the possibility that you chose not to be represented by a real estate agent.

Notify the Seller of Your Offer

Once you notify your agent that you are ready to make an offer and draw it up, your agent will contact the seller's agent (or the seller directly, if the house is for sale by owner). A good agent will not reveal any of the terms of that offer in advance, but will simply request an appointment at which to formally present it. (Any information the seller's agent or the seller receives in advance of a written offer could be used to dismiss your proposal out of hand or to begin oral dickering without the safeguards provided by written offers and counteroffers.) The seller or agent may respond by either:

- setting up an appointment at which your agent can present your offer (common in cold markets)
- telling you a date and time when offers will be accepted (common in hot markets, when sellers expect multiple offers), or
- stringing you along or coming up with a delaying strategy, if the seller thinks he or she may get a better deal by waiting.

No matter which strategy the seller employs, unless your offer is rejected outright, you should eventually be able to coordinate a meeting so your offer can be presented.

Strategies in a Cold Market

When prices are dropping, you can bid less than the sellers' asking price. Assuming the sellers are anxious to close the deal, they will probably counter with a price somewhere between their most recent offering price and the amount you proposed. For example, let's say you bid $550,000 on a house offered at $625,000. The sellers counter by lowering their price to $595,000.

Your next step is to decide whether you want to raise your offer. Hide your eagerness to buy the house. Here are some ways to do this:

- Don't respond immediately. Instead, either wait until the sellers' deadline for a response or ask for a little more time.
- Make it clear, either directly or through your agent, that you are still looking at other properties.
- If you are willing to risk losing the property, consider breaking off negotiations for a week or two.

When you make a counteroffer, make it on the low side to get the best deal you can. You can raise your offer later if the seller says no.

Strategies in a Competitive Market

In real estate markets where demand is high, homes sell quickly—often 15% to 40% above the asking price—as bidding wars erupt. If you're buying in a competitive market, it's crucial to develop a bidding strategy.

For situations where your Realtor is preparing to present your offer without having received clear information on how many other offers will be on the table, you might prepare several bids at different prices. Present the lowest bid if you're the only one making an offer, the next highest if there are only one or two other people making offers, and your highest price if there are three or more bidders. (In most multiple-offer situations, however, your agent will simply keep in close touch with the seller's agent to find out how many people have made appointments to present offers, and you can plan accordingly.)

> **CAUTION**
>
> **Don't lose your head in a bidding war.** When a number of people bid on a house, competitive juices begin to flow, and a kind of "auction mentality" prevails. Be careful not to exceed your budget.

Remember, price is not the only consideration for sellers. Your ability to close the deal quickly and smoothly—for example, by getting loan approval—is crucial in hot markets. Finally, your flexibility and sensitivity to the seller's needs—whether it's extending the closing date for a seller who can't move for a few months or paying for repairs—may make or break your offer.

What to Bring to the Offer Conference

Your agent will, with your help, prepare the following materials for the offer conference:

- a completed offer
- proof that you can afford the purchase, such as, in order of effectiveness:
  - a preapproval letter
  - a credit report, or
  - a family financial statement (see Chapter 2), and
- a brief letter about you and why you love the house and will take great care of it yourself.

Present Your Offer

Buyers don't usually accompany the agent to the offer presentation or subsequent negotiations. Most real estate people believe it's unwise for buyers to be there, fearing that you'll muck up the process or say something that the seller or agent (who will likely both be there) could use against you. But it's your purchase; talk to the agent if you really want to be there.

If you are attending the conference, or representing yourself, you have two goals, in addition to presenting your offer:

- to fully understand the seller's needs so you can adjust your offer to meet them, without compromising your own objectives, and
- to convince the seller that you can afford to buy the house and are a reasonable person to work with.

Starting Off on the Right Foot

Don't overlook the basics when meeting with a seller to negotiate:
- Show up on time.
- Dress reasonably, but conservatively.
- Turn off all phones and devices.
- If you don't own a decent car, borrow one (or ride with your agent).
- Leave your kids at home.

You want to convey to the seller that you are reasonably knowledgeable about the real estate market—though you don't want to come off like a know-it-all.

Approach the seller in a straightforward, friendly manner. As an opener, say something nice about an aspect of the house that reflects the owner's personal taste, such as the garden or artwork. But don't gush—you'll only drive up the price. On the other hand, don't criticize anything that reflects the seller's taste.

Bring a preapproval letter for an amount that shows you can afford the home. Another way to establish your economic bona fides is to casually mention your job, or jobs, such as, "One reason we like this house is that it's a convenient commute to both of our jobs—Sidney is a law librarian at the county courthouse, and I'm a nurse at the hospital, which is only about 20 minutes away."

Even though you have decided on the terms you need, it's not too late to glean useful information from the seller. Encourage the seller to talk. If the seller needs to move quickly to close on another house, relocate before school starts, or cope with a divorce, you may be able to get a better price if you can close quickly.

> **TIP**
>
> **Need to regroup?** If you get information from the seller that surprises you and you want to modify your offer, ask to speak privately with your agent. This may mean no more than walking around the block or it could mean recessing for hours or even days to get legal, tax, or other specialized advice.

The Seller's Response to Your Offer

The seller and his or her agent will read your offer and any others that are submitted. Sellers normally focus on price, financing, and contingencies:

- **Price.** If it's in the ballpark of what the seller expected, the negotiation process will likely begin. If your bid is way out of line, the seller may reject it or not bother to respond at all. If there are several bidders, the seller will normally take some time to look at which is highest and then focus on the quality of the offers—seeking, for example, a buyer who is preapproved by a mortgage lender, will make a substantial down payment, has few contingencies in the offer, and can close within a short period of time.

- **Financing.** The seller will look at your financing information and is likely to reject your offer on the spot if it seems unrealistic. If multiple offers come in at similar prices, a seller will probably prefer the buyer with the strongest financial profile.

- **Contingencies.** A seller who wants to sell fast will be particularly concerned with any difficult or time-consuming contingency, such as your need to sell an existing house.

The Seller Accepts on the Spot

If the seller says "yes" to your entire offer, make sure he or she immediately follows up by putting it in writing. An oral acceptance is not legally enforceable.

Your first reaction at this point may be that you paid too high a price. "That's normal," says Ira Serkes. "Focus on the fact that you offered the amount you felt comfortable with at the time."

The seller will ordinarily accept by completing the acceptance blank at the bottom of your Contract to Purchase Real Property form. If the seller accepts all but even one term, it technically isn't an acceptance, but a counteroffer, which you, in turn, can accept or reject. In fact, it is rare for a seller to say yes to all of the terms of an offer on the spot.

The Seller Rejects on the Spot

If the seller chooses not to accept your offer, you should get notification in writing. An oral rejection can cause problems if your original offer gives the seller additional time to accept. In theory, the seller could change his or her mind and accept your offer in writing two days later, when you may no longer want the house.

If the seller refuses to go to the trouble of putting a rejection in writing (which is very little trouble at all, since there's a section in the standard offer form for it), simply withdraw your offer using a written Revocation of Offer to Purchase Real Property form. (See "Revoking an Offer or Counteroffer," below.)

Normally, if the seller thinks a deal can be made, the seller will counter your offer, not reject it outright. Most outright rejections happen when the seller already has a better offer or thinks the buyer's offer is ridiculously low or otherwise weak. If you think you can make your offer more attractive—for example, by upping the price or getting rid of a contingency that you sell your current home—and you're willing to follow through, you can write another offer.

The Seller Asks for More Time

It's reasonable (although not required) to give the seller one to three days to decide whether to accept, reject, or counter your offer. If the seller wants more time than you have specified in your offer, and you are so anxious to get the house you decide to oblige, prepare an Extension of Offer to Purchase Real Property form. A sample is shown below.

If you make a take-it-or-leave-it offer to force a quick decision, you won't want to give the seller extra time. This preemptive bid strategy is a good one in a hot market, if you bid aggressively on a new listing (maybe even overbid the asking price) in an effort to grab the house fast. In addition, the strategy may be necessary if you're interested in more than one house and want to force a quick decision on one so you can bid on another if the first seller says no.

Extension of Offer to Purchase Real Property

(Buyer) _____

extends the offer made to purchase the real property at (address) _____

_____

_____

made on (date) _____ , until (time) ____ ☐ a.m. ☐ p.m.

on (date) _____ .

_____   _____

Offerer/Buyer   Date

_____   _____

Offerer/Buyer   Date

True
Story

Chuck and Ming: Buying a Good House in a Bad Way

Chuck and Ming spot a house they like. Frederick, their agent, arranges with the sellers' agent, Shirley, to present the offer to the sellers, Mike and Gail, at 11:00 a.m. the next day. Chuck and Ming will meet him there. But Frederick arrives 20 minutes late.

He bursts in and slaps the offer on the table, barely saying hello. The offer is $15,000 less than the list price, but Chuck and Ming love the house and will meet the asking price, if necessary.

Shirley asks Chuck how they like the house. Ming interrupts, saying they really love it and adds that they're exhausted from looking at dozens of others.

Shirley, Mike, and Gail excuse themselves. They're hardly out of the room when Chuck and Ming criticize Frederick for being late; he, in turn, expresses anger at Ming for not letting a more knowledgeable person do the negotiating.

In the meantime, Shirley, Mike, and Gail are pleased; Ming and Chuck have offered a good price, they can obviously afford the purchase, and the only contingency is a routine inspection. The offer is so solid, Mike and Gail probably would have accepted it as is, but based on Ming's revelations about how they love the house, they counteroffer $13,000 higher than Chuck and Ming's offer. After some negotiating a deal is finally struck for $9,000 above the first offer. Ming and Chuck overpaid because they weren't prepared to negotiate properly.

The Seller Is Waiting for Other Bids

If a seller is expecting other offers, he or she is unlikely to make a decision until all offers are in (unless the seller receives one too good to resist). If you want the house, there's nothing you can do but wait, unless you want to force the matter by making an attractive offer that requires an immediate decision.

The Seller Has Received a Higher Bid

A seller may say that he or she has already received a higher offer and that you'll need to raise yours to be seriously considered. Ask to see the higher written offer, so you know what you're bidding against, and then ask the seller to give you a written counteroffer. The seller is unlikely to show you the competing offer; but it doesn't hurt to ask.

If you're shown another offer contract, don't stop reading when you find out the amount offered. Check whether the financing is solid and whether there are any contingencies that make the offer chancy. If the offer has problems, the seller may accept your more solid, lower offer, or you may get another chance if the first deal falls through.

If the higher offer has real potential, and the seller counters your offer at, or above, the amount of the other offer, consider how much you can afford, how much you believe the house is worth, and your overall house purchase strategy.

Don't get so caught up in negotiating that you make a decision you'll regret later. If you do bid higher, take time away from the negotiating table to carefully consider each increase. A house you concluded was worth $600,000 on Sunday is unlikely to be worth $700,000 on Tuesday just because another buyer wants it.

Your other option if you appear to be second in line is to accept a backup offer position, as discussed later in this chapter.

The Seller Responds With a Counteroffer

Typically, the seller responds with a written counteroffer accepting most of the offer terms but proposing certain changes. If the seller orally states a counteroffer, insist that it be put in writing before you consider or discuss it.

Major Provisions of a Typical Counteroffer

Most counteroffers correspond to these provisions of an offer:

- **Price.** Unless your offer meets or exceeds the asking price, the seller may ask for more money. If you decide to increase your initial bid (in a counter counteroffer or by accepting the counteroffer):

- Make the increases small.
- Try to get something in return for each increase. For example, ask the seller to pay for certain repairs.
- Walk away if the price and the terms aren't right and you can't reasonably expect to come to agreement—for instance, the seller flatly refuses to pay for expensive mold remediation.

- **Financing.** If the seller believes your financing is impractical, he or she will likely propose a change. Similarly, if you offer to put 10% down with the seller taking back a second mortgage, and the seller wants all of his or her equity in cash, he or she will counteroffer.

- **Occupancy.** The seller may want additional time to move out. Or, if there's any hint that the deal might fall apart due to financing troubles, the seller may want to simply put off moving day until after you've successfully closed.

- **Your selling a current house.** If your offer is contingent on selling a current home, the seller may reject this in a counteroffer if the market is hot and the seller believes it will be easy to find another buyer. Or the seller may counteroffer with a wipe-out clause (see Chapter 18).

- **Inspections.** A seller's counteroffer for dealing with inspections may suggest a shorter period of time, eliminate one or more of your proposed inspections, or offer the house for sale "as is," meaning the seller won't pay for any defects the inspections turn up. Another possible scenario is for the seller to propose that the buyer be responsible for the first "X" dollars of any needed repairs. While it's reasonable for you to complete inspections in a timely manner, it's completely unreasonable (and a possible red flag indicating physical problems) for the seller to limit the type of inspections you can conduct or insist that you purchase "as is."

Counteroffer Form

When only limited changes are proposed in the counteroffer (or counter counteroffer), an abbreviated form may be used. (The California Association of Realtors offers a one-page counteroffer.) A seller can also counteroffer using a detailed offer form.

> ## Concerned About Discrimination?
>
> What are your rights if the seller refuses your offer and then promptly sells to another buyer at the same or a lower price, or on less favorable terms? If you think the seller's decision not to sell to you was based on your race, ethnic background, religion, sex, sexual orientation, marital status, age, family status, or disability, the seller may be violating laws prohibiting discrimination. Contact the California Department of Fair Employment and Housing (www.dfeh.ca.gov).

Study any new form carefully—no two are exactly the same. An experienced broker or real estate lawyer should review the paperwork. If one provision of the counteroffer is unacceptable and you no longer want the house, do nothing. A counteroffer not accepted by the deadline simply expires.

> EXAMPLE: Leili offers to buy Jorge and Jackie's house for $680,000, leaving the offer open for 48 hours. They counteroffer for $710,000 and permission to remove some built-in bookshelves. In addition, they require Leili to drop her contingency to sell her existing house first. Jorge and Jackie give Leili 12 hours to accept the counteroffer. Leili, who has found a house she likes better, does nothing, and the counteroffer simply expires.

Negotiate by Counteroffers

For many sales, the written offer acceptance process is completed relatively quickly: The buyer makes an offer, the seller suggests a few changes, the buyer agrees. Sometimes, however, the process drags on, with counteroffers, counter counteroffers, and counter counter counteroffers flying back and forth for days, or even weeks. This can work well, if you and the seller narrow your differences with each counteroffer. But don't get so caught up in negotiating that you pay more than the house is worth, make a bad deal, or leave the door open for another buyer who offers more.

If you participate in a counteroffer dance, make sure:

- All counteroffers are in writing.
- You and the seller meet all deadlines.
- All counteroffers contain a time limit by which responses must be accepted.
- You and the seller keep clear on what's being offered and what's being accepted. At some point, using short counteroffer forms that don't restate the entire offer will become confusing. Before that happens, use a new purchase agreement form. Retitle it "Counteroffer" (or "Counter Counteroffer" or whatever), state the terms you and the seller have agreed on, and make appropriate changes.

True Story

Christina: I'm Glad Our First Few Offers Fell Through

After eight years of renting a small apartment my husband and I decided we wanted a larger place with more grass and trees—someplace good to raise the kids we planned to have in a few years.

Our first weekend house hunting, we fell in love with a beautiful house in a nearby suburb, but it was $30,000 above our maximum price and needed some major structural work. The sellers were anxious to sell quickly for full price and "as is," because they had already bought a second house.

We made the classic mistake of thinking this house was the only one in the world; we counteroffered for days. Our real estate agent, who was anxious for a quick sale, fanned the flames. When this deal fell through, we repeated the same mistake with the next house.

A few weeks later, we finally came to our senses and realized there were lots of houses out there. We got a new agent and became more realistic—after, all, we were in no real hurry to move. Once we relaxed, we found a lovely place—much nicer than the first one—for $15,000 less than we expected to pay.

An Offer Is Accepted—A Contract Is Formed

A contract is formed when either the buyer or the seller accepts all of the terms of the other's offer or counteroffer in writing within the time allowed. After this happens:

1. Make copies of the contract; keep one and make sure the seller has or gets one. If short-form counteroffers were used to change a long offer, all contract terms won't be stated in one document. It's best to enter all the accepted terms onto one form.

2. Give the seller's agent a deposit check made out to an escrow or title company in the amount called for in the contract.

3. Give copies of documents to any real estate agent, attorney, or tax adviser who's assisting you.

4. Take steps to begin removing the contingencies—you usually have only a few days to act. At the least, you'll need to arrange inspections and apply for financing if you haven't already done so.

Revoking an Offer or Counteroffer

You may revoke (take back) your offer in writing any time before the seller accepts in writing. You needn't state a reason. If you want to revoke an offer (or counter counteroffer), do so immediately. Your agent or you should call the seller or her agent and say that you're revoking your offer; immediately follow up in writing. The best ways to do this are by email or fax (follow up by sending a signed original to the seller or agent), hand delivery, or overnight mail.

A sample Revocation of Offer to Purchase Real Property form is shown below.

Making a Backup Offer

If you locate a house you love, but end up losing out to another bidder, consider making a backup offer.

Revocation of Offer to Purchase Real Property

(Buyer) _____

hereby revokes the offer made to purchase the real property at (address)

_____ ,

made on (date) _____ .

_____   _____
Offerer/Buyer   Date

_____   _____
Offerer/Buyer   Date

One way to do this is by submitting a short addendum to your original purchase offer. Your addenda should give you the right to say yes or no in writing within a certain number of hours should the seller inform you in writing that the primary offer has fallen through and the seller now wants to accept yours. Be sure that your inspection, loan, insurance, and appraisal contingency time periods do not kick in until you move into primary-offer position.

Many cautious sellers are delighted to receive backup offers and accept desirable ones. If a seller accepts more than one, priority is set by the date and time of acceptance.

CAUTION

It's tough being the primary offer when there's a backup. The seller in such a situation tends to become less likely to negotiate over price or credits. If you act hastily, you may lose out. Ira Serkes remembers a situation where, "Our buyers asked the seller to reduce the price, but the seller had a backup offer, so said no. Our buyers said, 'We're canceling the agreement, then.' About 30 minutes after we submitted the cancellation for them, our clients called to say they'd changed their minds. Too late—the home was already sold to the backup buyer."

18

After the Contract Is Signed: Escrow, Contingencies, and Insurance

Open Escrow 256

How to Open Escrow 257

How to Find an Escrow Holder 260

How to Work With the Escrow Holder...260

Ordering Title Insurance..261

The Cost of Escrow 261

Complying With IRS Foreign Investor Rules...262

Remove Contingencies..262

Inspection Contingencies..262

Financing Contingencies...265

Extending Time to Meet a Contingency..265

Releasing Contingencies...267

Release Clauses (Wipe-Outs)..268

When You Can't Fulfill a Contingency..268

Obtain Homeowners' Insurance 271

Typical Coverage 271

Earthquakes and Floods..273

Condominiums..274

Shop Around for Insurance...276

How Insurance Relates to the Closing..279

Obtain Title Report and Title Insurance..279

Conduct Final Physical Inspection of Property 282

Closing Escrow...286

ongratulations! Your offer to purchase a house has been accepted. But it's not yet time to buy a new doormat. Many tasks remain before the house is yours—opening an escrow account, removing contingencies, obtaining title insurance, and closing escrow—and all are discussed in this chapter.

The time it takes between the contract signing and the close of escrow (when you become the owner) depends on what deadline you and the seller agreed to, probably based on what remains to be done following the signing. If you have your financing lined up in advance and the house is in excellent condition, you shouldn't have any trouble meeting the standard 30- to 60-day closing date.

If, however, your offer is contingent upon your selling an existing house, the inspections turn up lots of physical problems, the appraisal comes in low, or you need to arrange a complicated financing package, it could take several months or more. If your deadline turns out to be too soon, you and the seller can agree to extend it.

> **CAUTION**
>
> **Make an escrow to-do list.** Opening and successfully closing escrow involves detailed, picky, and often overlapping steps. Read through your purchase contract and draw up a list, calendar, or flowchart that shows you who needs to perform what tasks, and when. Your agent or escrow officer should help you keep track, too.

Open Escrow

In finalizing the purchase of your house, you and the seller need a neutral third party to hold onto, and then exchange, deeds and money, pay off existing loans, record deeds, prorate the property tax payments, and help with other transfer details.

To begin this process, you and the seller "open an escrow account" with a person or an organization legally empowered to act as an escrow agent. Lawyers need not be involved with escrow in California, and usually aren't, unless an unusual problem arises (for example, the seller's title isn't clear)—in which case, either buyer or seller may wish to consult an attorney.

By custom, escrow is done differently in Northern and Southern California. The common "dividing line" is somewhere near the Tehachapi Mountains. Nevertheless, both escrow styles routinely appear in the middle of the state, and some Northern California escrow agents are beginning to adopt Southern California practices.

Northern California. An escrow account is normally opened with a title insurance company (often just called a title company) immediately after the purchase contract is signed. Title companies not only provide the necessary title insurance, but also handle financing arrangements, such as collecting your down payment and funds for your lender, paying off the seller's lender, and preparing and recording a deed from the seller to you and a deed of trust for your lender.

Southern California. An escrow account is usually opened by the buyer and seller with an escrow company, which prepares the necessary papers and exchanges the seller's ownership interest for your money after deducting the amount needed to pay off the seller's existing mortgage, past taxes, and other liens. Title insurance is obtained from a title insurance company, which isn't usually otherwise involved in the escrow process.

Other escrow holders. Although it's unusual, escrow can be legally handled by someone other than a title or an escrow company. The buyer or seller's attorney, a real estate broker who has a trust account for supervising escrows, or the escrow department of a bank are all legally empowered to do the job.

How to Open Escrow

When the seller accepts your offer, you'll normally give your agent a deposit check made out to the escrow holder. The deposit is taken to the title or escrow company, and an escrow account is opened. The deposit will be applied to the purchase price, or it will be returned to you if you back out of the deal for a valid reason allowed by the contract—for example, a contingency can't be met.

Escrow Terminology

Here are common real estate terms used during escrow.

Close of escrow or closing. The final transfer of ownership of the house to the buyer. It occurs after both the buyer and seller have met all terms of the contract and the deed is recorded. "Closing" also refers to the time when the transfer will occur, such as, "The closing on my house will happen on January 27 at 10:00 a.m."

Closing costs. Expenses involved in the closing process, such as commissions, title insurance, loan, appraisal and inspection fees, private mortgage insurance, deed recording, and incidental fees charged by the escrow agent and lender.

Closing statement. A document prepared by the escrow holder containing a complete accounting of all funds, credits, and debts involved in the escrow process. Basically this amounts to a statement of the amount of cash the buyer and the buyer's lender have put into escrow, how much the seller has received, and how much money was used for other expenses.

Demand or request for beneficiary statement. A letter from the seller's lender stating how much it will cost to pay the seller's existing mortgage in full. The lender sends it after being notified by the escrow holder that the seller is selling the house and expects to close by a certain date. If the time between opening and closing escrow is reasonably short, the seller wants to receive the demand fast, in order to include the calculations in the closing. If the time between opening and closing will take some time, however, the seller won't rush the demand. A demand is typically good for only 30 days; if it comes too soon, it will expire before escrow closes and the seller will have to request a second one.

Final title report or final. Just before the close of escrow, the title company rechecks the condition of the title established in the preliminary title report. If it's the same (it usually is), the preliminary title report becomes the final report, and title insurance policies are issued.

Funding the loan. California law requires that checks and drafts be collected prior to disbursement. This means that to close escrow, funds must be deposited with the escrow holder one or more days prior to the close of escrow, except for cash and funds deposited by electronic transfer.

Escrow Terminology (continued)

Legal description or legal. The description of the parcel of land being sold that appears on the deed to the property. It has nothing to do with the buildings, but rather the land itself. The legal may specify lot and block numbers or metes and bounds (a complicated exercise in map reading), none of which should concern you.

Loan commitment. A written statement from a lender promising to lend you a certain sum of money on certain terms.

Opening escrow. Escrow is opened when you and the seller select an escrow agent to hold onto and transfer documents and money during the house purchase process.

Preliminary, prelim, or pre. The preliminary title report issued by a title company soon after escrow opens. It shows current ownership information on the property (including any liens or encumbrances). If any problems are found, the seller can take steps to resolve them before escrow closes. The title insurance policy issued at the close of escrow is usually based on this report.

Taking title. Describes the transfer of ownership from seller to buyer. For example, "The buyer takes title [gets his or her name on the deed] next Tuesday."

TIP

Will you be away for the closing? Your absence, for example if you live far away or will be traveling on the closing date, isn't necessarily a barrier to completing the purchase. But you will need Internet access. First, you might want to set up a free Skype account so as to hold video conference calls with your agent. You will then use a program such as DocuSign to digitally ratify the contract. If you're overseas, however, you may need to go to a U.S. embassy to have documents notarized, which can be difficult or time-consuming to arrange. Another option is to give someone local a "power of attorney" with which to sign the papers. Ask your escrow company to draft the power of attorney.

How to Find an Escrow Holder

In your offer contract, you'll enter the name and address of the escrow holder you choose. In some situations, the seller may disagree and list his or her choice in the counteroffer. As the basic task to be accomplished and prices charged are similar, this should not be an issue to hold up the acceptance of an offer. Unless you feel very strongly about using "your" escrow agent or not using the seller's, give in.

How do you know which title company or escrow company to enter on the offer form? As with finding any service provider, it's best to get a recommendation from someone you trust, most likely your agent. But be sure to confirm that your escrow officer won't be taking any long leaves or vacations during your escrow period.

If you are considering several recommended firms, you may be inclined to call around and compare prices. You may save a few dollars, but prices tend to be pretty similar. Concentrate on finding a company that offers superior service.

How to Work With the Escrow Holder

What happens after escrow opens depends on your escrow agent, whether you're in Northern or Southern California, and your contract with the seller.

If the contract contains contingencies, the escrow holder may do very little until you and the seller remove them, although many escrow holders in Southern California routinely confer with agents, or with sellers and buyers without agents, to make sure steps are being taken to remove contingencies. Southern California escrow holders also frequently try to help resolve any title disputes.

Even if your escrow holder is less involved, be sure the escrow holder gives you a list of what you need to provide and the dates when you need to provide each item.

Your agent should help the escrow process go smoothly. If neither you nor the seller is working with an agent, however, you'll need to handle the details yourselves. Fortunately, it's not difficult. Make an initial appointment with the escrow agent. Bring the timeline from Chapter 13, "Obtaining a Mortgage," and use it as your guide to ask questions. Check in regularly—about once a week—to be sure you're doing what's expected and that everything is on track.

If a dispute arises between you and the seller during escrow, don't look to the escrow holder to resolve it—or to transfer the money and deed. The escrow holder is a neutral party. You'll have to solve the problem (see Chapter 21, "If Something Goes Wrong During Escrow"); until you do, the escrow holder sits still. If the dispute drags on long enough, the escrow holder may get tired of being stuck in the middle and may initiate a lawsuit (called an "interpleader") to have the court resolve the dispute and direct the distribution of the deposited money.

Ordering Title Insurance

Ordering title insurance from a title insurance company (usually the same company handling the escrow in Northern California) is the buyer's responsibility. The title company issues a preliminary title report and then, just before closing, a final title report and two title insurance policies. If you're represented by a real estate professional, he or she will be able to help you with this.

The Cost of Escrow

Closing costs are typically about 2%–5% of the purchase price, with the lion's share made up of loan points and fees. Escrow costs—that is, the costs directly attributable to the escrow company—are considered part of closing costs, and tend to be under 1% of the purchase price. (In Southern California, the costs are divided between the escrow company and a title insurance company.)

Included in the escrow costs are fees for the preliminary and final title reports, recording of the deed, notarization, the title company, the escrow company (if necessary), and two title insurance policies. One policy is for the buyer (CLTA policy), and one is for the lender (ALTA policy). (See "Obtain Title Report and Title Insurance," below, for more.)

No law specifies who pays escrow costs; you and the seller negotiate this as part of the forming of the contract. For our discussion on who *customarily* pays which fee, see Chapter 16.

Complying With IRS Foreign Investor Rules

The seller must complete a form, available from the escrow or title company or the IRS, stating whether he or she is a foreign investor as defined by law. (This is required by a federal law called FIRPTA, the Foreign Investment in Real Property Tax Act, Internal Revenue Code § 1445.) If the seller is a foreign investor, you must withhold in escrow 10% of the sale price of the house and fill out and file some papers with the IRS. The escrow agent can help you.

If the seller is located outside of California or the proceeds of the sale will be paid to an intermediary of the seller, you must withhold and send some money to the Franchise Tax Board (California's taxing authority). Again, the escrow agent can help you.

Remove Contingencies

If your contract contains contingencies, you must remove them in writing and let the escrow holder know they've been removed before the purchase becomes final. Removing the most common contingencies, and extending the time for doing so, is discussed below. (The seller may need to work on removing some contingencies, as well.)

Inspection Contingencies

Most house purchase contracts give the buyer the right to have the house inspected by specified inspectors, and approve the findings within their reports, before going through with the sale. This is an important part of the process, in which you'll learn a lot about your new house's foundation, structure, internal systems such as heating and electrical, and pest activity. You will normally hire one or more professional inspectors, including at a minimum a general contractor and a pest inspector.

Give each inspector a copy of the seller's Real Estate Transfer Disclosure Statement, Natural Hazard Disclosure Statement, and any other inspection reports and disclosures the seller provides you. The seller must let the inspectors have access to the house, although you may need authorization from a homeowners' association for the contractor to inspect common areas of a condominium or another property within a common interest development.

We suggest that you accompany the inspectors on their rounds. Chapter 19 discusses the seller's legally required disclosures and the house inspection system in detail.

Inspections often find problems. For example, the house may have termite damage, need new wiring, or require roof repairs. You have various options to deal with such problems:

- **Ignore them.** The inspector wouldn't be doing his or her job without alerting you to home defects of every scale, down to missing switchplates and cracked tiles. Many of these are natural results of an aging house, and not worth making a big deal over in negotiations.

- **Back out.** If your offer is contingent upon your approving inspection reports, and a report indicates serious problems, you can back out of the deal.

- **Negotiate over repairs.** This is the most common approach, assuming you still want the house. (If the problem was disclosed before you made your offer, however, and you nevertheless offered to purchase the house "as is," you can't legally claim that it must be repaired at the seller's expense before you'll buy.) If the problem is extremely serious, you may say, "No." But if you still want the house, you and the seller must negotiate over who pays for what.

Negotiating the Cost of Repairs

By the time an offer has been accepted and inspections have been done, neither you nor the seller wants to spend more money. At the same time, both of you have already invested considerable time and energy in the transaction and don't want to walk away and start over. If either of you needs the sale to go through to meet other commitments, time pressure (and, often, the other's leverage) can cause great stress and short tempers.

Who pays what usually comes down to who is perceived to have more negotiating clout. A seller who thinks he or she has agreed to sell at too low a price or can easily find another buyer will probably refuse to pay for all or most repairs. If you think the seller is right, you'd be smart to share modest repair costs. If, however, you believe you've offered top dollar for the house and don't think it's worth a penny more, you'll want to insist that the seller pay for most or all of the repairs and refuse to finalize the deal otherwise.

Paying for Repairs

A seller willing to allow for the cost of repairs normally does so through either lowering the purchase price (which the agents might not like because it lowers their commissions—it's most commonly done if the buyer is making a large down payment or paying all cash) or by an "escrow credit." This means the seller agrees to leave money in escrow from the sale proceeds to cover the amount of the repairs. The exact amount the repairs will cost is normally agreed to by all parties based on contractors' bids. You want to be sure that the cost reflects all needed work using quality labor and materials.

If extensive repairs are needed to make the place habitable, the lender may require that work be done before escrow closes. Assuming the seller has agreed to cover the cost, a portion of the money placed in escrow can be paid to a contractor before the close of escrow, or held by the escrow holder after the sale closes, pending the contractor's completing the work.

Where repairs aren't major, a lender will let escrow close without requiring the repairs to be made first. If the seller has agreed to pay a credit into escrow for the work, the buyer is free to use this money for other purposes, such as contributing to the down payment.

> **EXAMPLE:** Mary agrees to sell her house to Alvin for $581,000. Alvin's offer is contingent upon his approval of a pest control and general contractor's inspection. The inspections turn up $30,000 worth of beetle damage and drainage problems. Alvin refuses to go through with the sale unless Mary credits him $30,000 in escrow for the repairs. They negotiate and agree to share the costs, with Mary paying $24,000 and Alvin $6,000. The compromise reflects the fact that Alvin was ready to walk away from

the deal if Mary didn't pay most of the cost. Mary, on the other hand, needed to move and didn't have time to find another buyer.

If the lender doesn't require that work be done, and you have enough cash to pay for the repairs yourself, consider asking the seller to reduce the asking price instead of giving you a credit in escrow. This saves you money because escrow and title fees, as well as annual property taxes, are based on the purchase price. The seller is often pleased, because the commission the sellers pay is based on the sale price. However, since the real estate commissions are reduced, the agents might not be excited about this arrangement.

Removing Inspection Contingencies

As you satisfy or waive an inspection contingency, you must remove it in writing. See "Releasing Contingencies," below, to learn how and see a sample form.

Financing Contingencies

In any standard purchase contract, the buyer makes the offer to buy contingent on arranging satisfactory financing. To remove (release) this contingency you should provide the seller written evidence that you have obtained financing sufficient to purchase the house, along with a contingency release form.

Evidence of financing is usually a loan commitment letter from a lender or a bank confirmation if you arrange private financing. If you're assuming the seller's mortgage, order the assumption documents from the lender to start the process of taking over the loan.

Extending Time to Meet a Contingency

Buyers frequently find they need extra time to satisfy a contract contingency. Without the extra time, the contract ends (the deal falls through) unless you and the seller agree to extend it. A seller who wants out won't extend the time. More commonly, however, the seller wants the deal to go through but needs reassurance that you're still serious about buying the house. The seller may demand that you increase your deposit in exchange. The amounts vary, but 1% is reasonable.

Any agreement to extend the time to meet a contingency (or to change any other term of the contract) must be in writing and signed. A sample is below.

> **EXAMPLE:** Julie agrees to buy Shawn's house for $600,000, contingent upon securing an adjustable rate mortgage at 4% or lower for 80% of the purchase price and selling her own house within 90 days. Julie arranges the financing easily but has trouble selling her house. She offers Shawn $3,000 cash to extend her time to purchase (to let her sell her existing house) for another 60 days. Shawn agrees.

Extending Time to Meet Contingencies

The material set out below is hereby made a part of the contract dated _____ between (Buyer) _____ and (Seller) _____ to purchase real property located at _____

_____

_____

The final date for Buyer's removal of all contingencies set out in Clause _____ of the contract, is hereby extended until (month, day, year) _____ at _____ (time) _____ ☐ a.m. ☐ p.m.

_____   _____
Signature of Buyer   Date

_____   _____
Signature of Buyer   Date

_____   _____
Signature of Seller   Date

_____   _____
Signature of Seller   Date

Releasing Contingencies

As you satisfy or abandon (waive) a contingency, you must remove (or release) it in writing. Don't wait until all contingencies are met to do this. Remove each one as it is satisfied or abandoned.

You remove a contingency by executing a contingency release form such as the one below. Give the original to the seller and keep a copy for yourself.

Contingency Release

(Buyer) _____

of the property at (address), _____ hereby removes the

following contingency(ies) from the purchase contract dated _____ ;

_____

_____

If this release is based on accepting any inspection report, a copy of the report, signed by Buyer, is attached, and Buyer releases Seller from liability for any physical defects disclosed by the attached report.

_____   _____
Signature of Buyer   Date

_____   _____
Signature of Buyer   Date

_____   _____
Signature of Seller   Date

_____   _____
Signature of Seller   Date

If the seller has agreed to credit you for the cost of any repairs, add the following to the release, after the final word "report":

"providing that by ____ __.m. on _____ ,
Seller agrees in writing to extend to Buyer an escrow credit in the amount of
$_____

against the purchase price to cover the cost of needed repair and
rehabilitation work to be paid by Buyer."

Release Clauses (Wipe-Outs)

Some contracts let the seller demand in writing that you remove all contingencies within a certain time (usually between 24 and 72 hours). This is sometimes called a "notice to perform" or a "72-hour release clause," and we call it a "Seller's Demand for Removal of Contingencies" in the sample below.

If you can't, the seller can give you written notice ending your contract (wiping it out) and then perhaps go ahead with a backup offer. The seller can do this to you only if a wipe-out clause was included in the original contract. Wipe-out clauses are most common when an offer is contingent upon your selling an existing house or arranging financing that the seller believes may not come through.

When You Can't Fulfill a Contingency

If, after trying in good faith, you or the seller can't meet a contingency, the deal is over. The most likely reasons your sales might fall through are:

- An inspection turns up expensive physical problems and you decide you no longer want the house, or you and the seller can't agree who will pay.
- You're unable to sell your existing house within the time provided.
- You can't secure adequate financing within the time provided.
- The appraisal comes in low, and either the seller won't lower the price or your lender won't make the full loan.

You and the seller should sign a release canceling the contract and authorizing the return of your deposit. The seller has no right to keep your deposit if the deal falls through for failure to meet a contingency spelled out in the contract. If the seller refuses, or you refuse, to sign the release within 30 days following a written demand, the person who refuses to sign may be liable to the other for attorneys' fees and damages of three times the amount deposited in escrow, no more than $1,000 and no less than $100. (Civil Code § 1057.3.)

Seller's Demand for Removal of Contingencies

Under the terms of the contract dated _____ , between (Buyer) _____ and (Seller) _____ for the purchase of the real property at (address) _____ , _____ , Seller hereby demands that Buyer remove the following contingency specified in Clause _____ of the contract:

_____

_____

_____

within ☐ ninety-six (96) hours from receipt of this demand if personally delivered.

     ☐ five (5) days from mailing this demand if mailed by certified mail.

If Buyer does not remove this contingency within the time specified, the contract shall become void. Seller shall promptly return Buyer's deposit upon Buyer's execution of a release, releasing Buyer and Seller from all obligations under the contract.

Signature of Seller _____ Date _____

Signature of Seller _____ Date _____

Personally delivered on: _____

Mailed by certified mail on: _____

Release of Real Estate Purchase Contract

(Buyer) _____

and (Seller) _____

hereby mutually release each other from any and all claims with respect to

the real estate purchase contract dated _____

for the property located at: _____

_____ .

It is the intent of this release to declare all rights and obligations arising
out of the real estate purchase contract null and void.

☐ Buyer has received his/her deposit.

☐ Seller has directed the escrow holder to return Buyer's deposit.

_____   _____
Signature of Buyer   Date

_____   _____
Signature of Buyer   Date

_____   _____
Signature of Seller   Date

_____   _____
Signature of Seller   Date

If an inspection turns up negligible problems and you refuse to go
ahead with the purchase (or you refuse to proceed for another non-
legitimate reason), the seller can keep your deposit. A seller rarely
keeps an entire deposit, however, because the seller will have trouble
completing a subsequent sale until the escrow with you terminates;
and termination of escrow normally can't happen until your deposit is
released. Also, state law generally limits the amount sellers can keep if
you default. (See Chapter 16 for our discussion of liquidated damages.)

> ⚠ **CAUTION**
>
> **If you've removed all your contingencies and then decide not to go through with the sale, your deposit could be at risk.** This is true even if the reasons were beyond your control—for example, your financing fell through after you released the contingency. Consult a real estate attorney—but don't panic yet. Even if a buyer withdraws for a nonlegitimate reason, it's common for the buyer and seller to compromise, with the seller keeping part of the deposit and some of it being returned to the buyer.

A sample release form is shown above.

Obtain Homeowners' Insurance

Before finalizing your loan, your lender will require that you purchase hazard coverage to pay the lender in the event your house is damaged or destroyed by fire, smoke, wind, hail, riot, vandalism, or another similar act. Don't balk at the insurance. You're going to want what's required, and probably more.

In fact, even if you're paying all cash and therefore have no lender leaning on you to buy insurance, you should buy insurance.

Don't wait until right before escrow closes to start shopping for insurance—it can be hard to find a good policy at a reasonable price, due to various losses and clampdowns in the insurance industry.

Typical Coverage

Virtually all homeowners buy comprehensive homeowners' insurance, not just the minimum required by the lender. In addition to covering your house, homeowners' insurance protects other structures on the property (such as a pool or an in-law unit) and your personal property, usually for 50% of the coverage limit on your house, unless you pay extra.

A few valuable items, such as art, computer equipment, and antiques, are covered to a specific (low) amount; if you own more, you'll have to itemize them and pay extra. But this may not be the time to skimp—if everything you own is destroyed, say in a fire, being able to rebuild the bare house will be small comfort.

A comprehensive policy will also cover you for some types of personal liability—if the letter carrier trips over your kid's skateboard or a neighbor gets bitten by your dog, your policy will pay for medical expenses and other losses. In addition, if you injure someone off your property, you will likely be covered if the injury doesn't involve a motor vehicle or your business.

Special Insurance Concerns for Home-Based Businesses

Many homeowners earn extra cash by starting a home business, anything from a therapist's practice to renting out rooms occasionally through a service like Airbnb. If you run a home-based business, don't rely on the standard homeowners' policy to cover business-related losses.

If you'll have business-related visitors, consider buying liability coverage in case they're injured. You may also need a landlord or rental dwelling policy if you'll be renting the place out for days, weeks, or months at a time.

And whether or not your home is not your business's central location, inventory or equipment that you keep at home, particularly if it's worth more than $5,000, will not be covered by the standard homeowners' policy. Ask your insurance broker for more information about getting a business owner's policy.

CAUTION

Beware of dogs raising your premiums. Most insurance companies are attaching canine exclusions for dog breeds that are particularly large or have bad reputations, or for individual dogs with a history of violent behavior. While the various insurance companies are not consistent about which pooches they prohibit, owning an "ineligible" breed could impair your chances of purchasing a policy or result in your paying a surcharge.

How much insurance do you need? You should cover the full replacement value of your real property (not including the land) and your personal property. (At least 40%, and often more, of the value is the land itself, which will likely still be there even if your house is destroyed.) The coverage most people select is "extended replacement cost." This pays for replacement of your house up to a certain percentage (often 125%) of what the policy states is the coverage limit. Such coverage helps protect you if your house costs more to actually rebuild than the amount you insured it for.

For added protection, you can also buy what's called an "inflation guard." This automatically amends your policy to raise its face value by a fixed percentage every year. You choose the percentage when you buy the inflation guard.

It's rare for insurance companies to write policies for "100% guaranteed replacement." This is because such a policy replaces your house at full value even if construction and labor costs have skyrocketed past the house's insured value as stated in the policy.

Earthquakes and Floods

Two of the greatest risks facing California homeowners are not even covered in the standard homeowners' insurance policy: earthquakes and floods.

Because of the huge losses earthquakes have caused Californians in the past, the state of California now mandates that your insurance company offer you state-sponsored earthquake insurance, both when you first buy the policy and at every alternate renewal. The offered policy must cover loss or damage to the dwelling and its contents and living expenses for the occupants if the house is temporarily uninhabitable. (Insurance Code §§ 10081, 10089.) You actually have to sign something to decline this coverage.

Unfortunately, the state-sponsored coverage is not highly regarded, so you're better off looking for a private earthquake insurer. Whether you can find private coverage at a price you can afford will depend on where you live and when the last earthquake occurred (immediately after an earthquake, insurance companies stop selling earthquake coverage for a while).

Buying earthquake coverage typically costs several hundred dollars per year. Houses near active faults or made of brick may be more expensive to insure. The problem with earthquake insurance is the high deductible— typically 10% to 15% of the policy amount. That means if you have a $200,000 policy, you won't get any benefits unless the damage is more than $20,000 (with a 10% deductible) or $30,000 (with a 15% deductible).

Another endorsement to consider, if you're one of the thousands of California residents buying a home in a flood zone, is flood coverage. Unfortunately, the extra coverage can be expensive and contain high deductibles. However, lenders require flood insurance for property in designated flood hazard areas. This is an irritant to property owners who live in designated flood areas but who haven't seen a real flood in years. If you're buying a house in such an area, you may be able to avoid buying flood insurance by having your property surveyed to show that it lies above the flood plain. (And, though it's many years away, once your house is paid off, the lender will have no say in whether you buy flood insurance!)

Then again, no matter what the lender says, you may want to buy flood insurance if your own research shows a chance of flooding in your area—take a lesson from Hurricane Katrina, where many homeowners found themselves out of luck because their lenders hadn't mandated flood insurance, and they had relied on that in not purchasing insurance. Floods can happen for a myriad of reasons, from snow melt to being near a creek that's been disturbed due to a new housing development.

See Chapter 19 for a discussion of seller disclosures regarding flood, fire, and seismic hazards. Also, see Appendix A for information on the areas of California susceptible to earthquakes, fires, and floods.

Condominiums

If you are buying a condominium, a town house, or some other planned unit development property, consult the CC&Rs to determine what type of insurance protection you should or must buy. Often the home-owners' association buys a master insurance policy for all the buildings and the common areas. That leaves you responsible for buying coverage (including earthquake insurance) for the contents of your unit (interior

How to Make Sure Your Policy Gets Renewed

After making the important decision of which home insurance policy to buy, it's worth taking steps to hang onto it for more than a year. Try to:

- **Pay your premiums when they are due.** Don't allow your insurance policy to lapse or be cancelled due to late payments. Once you've had a policy cancelled for any reason, finding a replacement policy will be an uphill battle.
- **Think twice about turning in claims.** Unless your house has gone through major damage, any money that you realize by filing a claim may be wiped out by a resulting increase in your premium, or the cancellation of your insurance when it's time for renewal. With this in mind, ask your agent to increase your policy deductible—up to $2,500 to $5,000 is a safe amount, if your lender will allow it—and take advantage of the premium credit that will result. (Why have a low deductible if you won't be filing claims for these relatively low amounts, anyway?) Then save up money for home maintenance and fix those minor problems yourself, without even contacting your insurance company.
- **Cooperate with your insurance company.** If your insurance underwriter asks numerous questions during the application process, or sends you a questionnaire about you and your home at renewal time, call your agent. Find out what's going on and get back to the underwriter as soon as you can. Don't give the company an excuse to cancel your policy based on noncooperation.
- **Keep up with basic home maintenance.** Don't ignore little problems that could turn into big ones, such as leaking roofs and plumbing problems. If you aren't attuned to home repair issues, bring in a professional to assess your home's condition.
- **If you need additional help, get in touch with an experienced insurance broker.**

By the way, if you've got a decent insurance policy, hang onto it. Jumping from one insurance company to another in an effort to save a few dollars is not worth your time. Just when you get another policy, your new company is likely to institute a rate increase to catch up with the competition.

walls, plumbing, cabinetry, appliances, and personal property) and personal liability (that is, claims made against you). But check carefully to see where the HOA insurance ends and yours should begin.

If you have any thoughts of replacing or improving the features of your unit, you should also invest in what's called "alterations and additions" coverage. For example, if you were to replace the unit's existing cheap painted cabinetry with polished teak, and your unit burned, the association's homeowners' insurance would cover only the value of the cheap cabinets.

> ⚠ **CAUTION**
>
> **Be ready for CC&Rs that make you responsible for holes in the homeowners' association's insurance coverage.** For example, if the clubhouse burns down and the association insurance won't cover the entire loss, a typical set of CC&Rs would allow the association to collect the shortfall from the unit owners. Insurance for this type of unhappy event, called "loss assessment" coverage, can be very cheaply included in your policy.

Shop Around for Insurance

Homeowners' insurance rates can vary greatly from company to company, so try to compare rates of several companies. Another way to save money is to opt for a larger-than-usual deductible. By increasing your deductible to $1,000 or more, you may save 10% or more on your premiums.

Also, ask your insurance agent what discounts are available for new or remodeled houses, houses with a security system or within a gated community, or near a fire hydrant. Some companies also offer discounts if you buy more than one policy from them, for example, an auto as well as a business and home policy. Nonsmokers may also receive a discount. And, if you're a retiree age 55 or over, you may qualify for a discount of 10% or more at some companies.

Price isn't the only factor to consider. Some insurance companies are better than others at processing claims fairly and quickly. If you live near an area where there was a severe fire, earthquake, or flood, ask community organizations which insurers were most responsive to consumers.

And then there's the matter of convincing the insurance company that you qualify at all. Having taken some economic hits over the years, the California insurance industry has gotten skittish about doing the very thing it's supposed to do: sell insurance. You may be refused affordable coverage, or any coverage, based on your home's location and history of mold, water damage, or other claims, your credit score, or your history of filing other homeowners' insurance claims.

Your Home's Location

The insurance industry is not allowed to use outright discrimination (known as redlining) when deciding which localities it will offer policies within. However, insurance underwriters come close to the wire, by following their home offices' guidelines stating that no insurance can be offered in certain "capacity exposure areas."

When you apply for homeowners' insurance, the first thing the underwriter will do is to "map" the property. If you reside in a brush area, for example, the underwriter may turn down your application for insurance. If you promise to clear the brush away from your home, you may get a second chance, but woe unto you (and your coverage) if you fail to clear the brush or you allow it to grow back.

Soil instability in the area where your new home is located could also make the home difficult to insure. This seems especially odd given that most homeowner's policies do not even pay claims for earth movement, earthquakes, or soil slippage. However, some underwriters fear that our courts will be overly generous to a homeowner whose house has just been shaken into the mud, and they refuse to issue insurance policies in unstable soil areas.

Your Credit Score

Most insurance companies and their underwriters now order a copy of your credit report before they decide whether to sell you coverage. (That's why they'll ask you for your Social Security number.) Their theory is that if you have bad credit, you might turn in maintenance claims to the insurance company instead of taking care of the property yourself. They call this the "moral hazard."

Past Claims for Water Damage and Mold

The prospect of mushrooming mold claims has made the insurance industry nervous—especially given the lack of medical information about which molds are dangerously toxic. If you have ever submitted a claim for water damage (in a past home), or if the home you are buying has had any history of water damage, you may have difficulty in getting the underwriters to insure your property. Or, if they do agree to insure you, the policy may contain a mold exclusion or a low amount of coverage for any future mold claims, plus a large deductible for claims based on mold or water damage.

Other Past Claims

You might have thought that the purpose of insurance was to collect on it when you need to—but think again. To keep their risks low, insurance companies try to insure those homeowners least likely to actually use the insurance! Your history of filing claims on the home you are leaving, as well as the seller's history of filing claims on the home you are buying, will all be taken into account. Yes, you heard right: Even claims on your former home and claims that someone else made will be counted against you in the underwriting process. (Of course, if you are purchasing a brand new home or one in which you are the first owner, you'll have only your own past claims to contend with.)

Do You Need Life Insurance?

Some insurance companies will try to sell you life insurance or credit insurance so your heirs can pay off the mortgage if you die. Unless your survivors could not afford the monthly payments without you, don't bother. Even then, look for a policy that lets your survivors use the money as they wish, not just to pay off the mortgage. For this purpose, a term policy covering the period for which survivors (often small children) are vulnerable to losing the house if you die is far cheaper than a whole life policy, and just as good.

How Insurance Relates to the Closing

Once you arrange your insurance, have your insurance agent deliver your policy to the escrow holder before closing. Your lender will not approve your loan until your insurance takes effect. Many lenders will want you to prepay the first year of insurance by the closing; ask if you can pay semiannually, quarterly, or monthly, if your budget is tight.

RESOURCE

Insurance information. For general information on homeowners' insurance, including premium comparisons among some of the state's larger companies, or to file a complaint about an insurance company, contact the Department of Insurance Consumer Hotline at 800-927-4357; www.insurance. ca.gov. Also, www.uphelp.org has useful information on homeowners' insurance. Check the websites of individual companies, such as State Farm or Allstate, as well.

CAUTION

Even after you find earthquake insurance, your mortgage lender may claim first dibs on the proceeds. Some mortgage agreements (deeds of trust) require that the lender be the primary payee of any earthquake insurance proceeds. The lender then collects amounts owing on the mortgage and dictates how whatever is left will be used for repairs. Worse yet, a California court has upheld this practice. (*Martin v. World Savings*, 92 Cal.App.4th 803 (2001).) Read your loan paperwork carefully.

Obtain Title Report and Title Insurance

Title insurance protects both you and your lender against unknown clouds on the legal title to the property. It insures against the possibility of undisclosed legal challenges or liens against the property, such as an unrecorded deed, a forged deed, or an unrecorded easement—the right of someone else to use your property for a specific purpose (for example, the right the previous owner granted your neighbor to share your extra-wide driveway).

If you think you might sell the house within the next two years, ask your title insurer about a "binder" policy that will give you a refund when you resell.

What Are Liens?

A lien is a claim for money, with property as security (collateral) for payment. Other common liens are for unpaid taxes and debts owed to contractors who worked on the property but were never paid (called mechanic's liens).

Financial institutions require title insurance whenever they finance a house sale. As soon as you and the seller sign the house purchase contract, you should order a preliminary title report (also called a prelim or pre) on the property. Your offer should make your approval of a preliminary title report a contingency. (In Northern California, the escrow holder—a title insurance company—will often order the policy itself.) This report is a statement summarizing the current condition of the title to the property, including liens; encumbrances; covenants, conditions, and restrictions (CC&Rs); and easements. You want the prelim early in escrow so that you, the seller, and the lender have time to address any problems that turn up.

The most common problems require the seller to pay off liens (perhaps for past-due child support or property taxes) from the sale proceeds. These problems threaten your deal only if the seller disputes the lien and refuses to instruct the escrow holder to pay the lienholder.

Other likely problems include a newly discovered easement, lawsuits disputing the boundary line or filed against the seller, an unknown heir (if the previous owner recently died), or an unexpected owner (such as a previous spouse). If any of these situations come up, the seller will likely need the help of a lawyer.

If problems arise with the title that the seller cannot quickly resolve, you can either refuse to go through with the sale, give the seller an extension of time (if you think the extra time will help), or buy the house with less-than-perfect title. Deciding to do this is beyond the scope of this book; consult an experienced real estate lawyer.

If you pay all cash or borrow from your Uncle Stanley, or if the seller takes back a second, you (or you and Uncle Stanley or you and the seller) must decide whether to buy title insurance. We recommend it, even if you search the title yourself at the county recorder's office and believe title is clear. In the future, you don't want any unpleasant surprises.

Financial institutions require a California Land Title Association (CLTA) policy and an American Land Title Association (ALTA) policy. The CLTA policy covers items in the public record, such as mortgage liens, trust deed liens, or judgment liens. The ALTA policy is more extensive, insuring against claims found both in the public record and by physically inspecting the house, such as unrecorded easements, boundary disputes, and physical encroachments.

The policies also differ regarding how much they cover and whom they benefit. The CLTA policy insures to the amount of the purchase price and benefits you. The ALTA policy insures to the amount of the loan and benefits the lender. If you'll occupy the house, the CLTA policy you receive will include the same extended coverage the lender gets on the ALTA policy. If you won't be occupying the house, you can pay a little more for the extended coverage.

RESOURCE

CLTA and ALTA policies. For more information check the CLTA website at www.clta.org or the ALTA website at www.alta.org.

Before closing, the title insurance company will check the public records for any changes since the prelim was issued. If all is the same (as is the usual case), the prelim becomes the final title report. If there are any changes, they'll be reported in a supplemental title report. You and your lender must decide whether to close or to call the deal off.

Conduct Final Physical Inspection of Property

A few days before escrow closes, reinspect the property to make sure everything is in order. Your contract should give you the right to this "walk-through." You'll want to make sure:

- No damage has occurred to the house since you agreed to buy it.

- The fixtures and personal property the seller agreed to sell you are still in the house.

- Smoke detectors (preferably photoelectric and with ten-year batteries) are installed in all sleeping rooms as required by state law. (Health and Safety Code §§ 13113.7 and 13113.8.)

- Carbon monoxide detectors are installed outside of each sleeping area, in compliance with state law. (Cal. Health & Safety Code § 17926(a).) These may be combined smoke detector/carbon monoxide detectors.

- The water heater has been braced, anchored, or strapped to resist falling or displacement during an earthquake. (Health and Safety Code § 19211.)

- All agreed-upon work has been done to your satisfaction (this is especially important with new houses).

- The house is empty—that is, the seller (or tenant) has moved (unless your agreement lets him or her stay longer) and hasn't left piles of unwanted possessions behind.

If you discover a problem during this final inspection, you can:

- Insist that the closing be delayed until the seller fixes the problem.

- Insist that the seller credit you in escrow with a sum of money sufficient for you to remedy the problem—this means you pay that much less for the house.

- Conclude that the problem isn't significant and close anyway.

If you're at a real deadlock, consider mediation, as many standard real estate contracts require.

If you're buying a new house, be sure to reread Chapter 7 on dealing with final inspections, construction delays, and other problems.

County Property Taxes and Exemptions

When real estate is sold in California, the county assesses the value of the property and imposes property taxes accordingly. This will be done shortly after you close on the sale.

Take a careful look at the assessment statement. If you will live in the house, most counties allow you a yearly homeowner's property tax exemption of up to $7,000 on the assessed value of the property. If you move in after March 1, you are entitled to 80% of the full amount for the first year. If the assessment statement does not include the exemption, call your county tax assessor's office and find out how to file for it.

When a house sells for more than the previous assessed value, the county will issue a supplemental tax bill that accounts for the difference in price. The county issues this bill during the first year after you buy your home. If, for example, the house was previously assessed at $180,000, and you paid $640,000, you'll receive a supplementary tax bill representing the $460,000 difference. The bill will be prorated according to how many months into the tax year you bought the house. Tax years run from July 1st to June 30th of the following year. So if you purchase your home on September 30, 2017, your tax bill will cover only the period from October 1, 2017 through June 30, 2018.

TIP

Ask the sellers to accompany you during the final inspection or to give you a post-inspection "tour." Every house has its quirks and mysteries —how to light the old gas oven, the identity of garden plants, and more. If negotiations have remained friendly, going through the house with the sellers can yield a wealth of information. Prepare questions in advance. If you're happy with how the house has been maintained, ask for the names of the sellers' gardener, painter, and other servicepeople.

Closing Costs and Loan Fees

Closing costs and loan fees usually add up to 2%–5% of your purchase price —and California is known for having some of the highest closing costs in the country. Some fees are paid when you take out the loan, or at the same time you arrange inspection reports, but most are paid the day you close escrow. Not all lenders and escrow holders require all the fees (some are waived as part of special offers). When escrow closes, you'll receive a statement with an itemized list of the closing costs.

Here are typical closing costs and loan fees.

Appraisal fees. Charged by an appraiser hired by the lender to be sure the property is worth what you've agreed to pay. Fees usually run between $300 and $600 for a regular-sized single-family home, and somewhat more for a very large or multiple-unit building. (See Chapter 13 for more on appraisals.)

Lender fee. Loan application fees (typically $650 to $1,300) cover the lender's cost of processing your loan.

Assumption fee. Typically 1% of the loan balance to assume the seller's existing loan.

Attorneys' fees. If problems develop, such as the need to evaluate or clear title, you may need to hire an attorney, at around $250 per hour.

Credit report. Should cost around $20 to check your credit. While standard credit checks cost less, for home loans, a lender checks information from three credit reporting agencies, as well as the county records for judgment and tax liens.

Escrow company fees. An escrow or title insurance company will charge a fee, based on the purchase price. Typical fees start at around $350 and go up from there.

Loan fees. This includes points (one point is 1% of the loan principal) and an additional fee, usually between $100 and $450.

Physical inspection reports. May add several hundred dollars or more, depending on how many are requested. If you pay these at the time of the inspections directly to the inspectors, you can save a few dollars. Escrow companies will charge $25–$50 if they pay off your inspectors in escrow.

Closing Costs and Loan Fees (continued)

Prepaid homeowners' insurance. Amount as required by lenders, typically one year; depends on the house's value, level of coverage, and location.

Prepaid interest on the loan. You'll be asked to pay per diem interest in advance, from the date your loan is funded to the end of that month. The maximum you'll be charged is 30 days of interest.

Prepaid property taxes. Depends on tax assessment; covers the time period between closing and your first monthly mortgage payment. Some lenders have you prepay one or two months' in addition.

Private mortgage insurance. As discussed in Chapter 4, if you make a down payment of less than 20%, most lenders will require private mortgage insurance, or PMI. You will probably need to pay a few months' worth of PMI premiums at the close of escrow. It's usually calculated at 0.52% of the loan amount, divided by 12. On a $600,000 loan, that's $260 per month.

Recording and filing fees. The escrow holder will charge about $100 for drawing up, reviewing, and recording the deed of trust and other legal documents. The total escrow and title fees can amount to 0.5% of the loan.

Survey fee. May be needed to show plot measurements if house has easements; will run about $300.

Tax service fee. Issued to notify the lender if you default on your property taxes; usually costs about $75.

Title search and title insurance. Only in Northern California does the buyer pay the title costs. Most lenders require title insurance for the face amount of their mortgage or for the value of their loan. Title insurance is a one-time premium that averages about $2,500.

Transfer tax. Tax assessed by the county when the property changes hands. Usually split with seller, in which case it costs about $1.10 per $1,000. Many cities also charge transfer tax; it varies city to city, but can be as much as 1.5% of the purchase price.

Closing Escrow

Until all contingencies in your offer are removed, no firm closing date can be set. Thus, during the early and middle stages of an escrow, the closing date is projected, not firm.

The paperwork necessary for closing escrow should be completed a minimum of four working days before the expected closing date. This allows for delays in the transmittal of the loan documents between the lender(s) and the escrow holder. The buyers and sellers in California usually sign closing documents at different times, making separate visits to the escrow holder's office.

For safety's sake, it's also best to arrange to have any down payment money and other cash that will be part of your purchase arrive at the escrow office a day or two before the closing. Especially if you will use a nonlocal check, ask the escrow holder how many days in advance of closing your check must be submitted. Using a cashier's check is usually cheaper than arranging for a wire transfer from your bank to the escrow holder's bank.

Once the escrow officer has the necessary documents from both seller and you, along with your down payment and the loan proceeds, the officer will prepare a new deed, naming you as the owner. The escrow officer will send the new deed to the county recorder's office, which will record the deed the next day. The seller will receive his or her check late in the day that escrow closes. Others may also be paid out of the sale proceeds, for example, the seller's lender and any lienholders. (These procedures are very different from those in many other states, where the buyer, seller, and agents sit around the closing table, swap deeds and cashier's checks, and complete the sale the same day.)

The forms you'll be required to sign may include:

- final escrow instructions. In Northern California, the escrow holder prepares two slightly different sets of instructions—one for the seller and one for the buyer—so read them carefully to be sure that you and the seller are in agreement; in Southern California, the buyer and seller sign identical escrow instructions.
- copy of the preliminary title report
- deed of trust (and other forms) from the lender

- copies of structural pest control and other inspection reports
- FIRPTA (Foreign Investment in Real Property Tax Act) statement
- fund disbursement (or loan assumption) documents provided by the lender
- any rental agreement between you and the seller if the seller will live in the house for a while after the close
- settlement statement listing all costs, prepared by the escrow holder
- statements authorizing an impound account
- a perjury statement where you attest to the truth of the information you provided, and
- statement showing your homeowners' insurance coverage.

If rehabilitation work must be done to repair damage or substandard conditions discovered in an inspection report, money may be held by the escrow holder after the sale closes to pay the contractor.

Chapter 21 covers what happens if there are delays or problems during escrow.

RESOURCE

Where to complain about an escrow or title insurance company.
If you have any problem with your escrow company, contact the Department of Business Oversight at www.dbo.ca.gov (click "Consumers" then "Submit a Complaint"); this state agency regulates independent escrow companies. The Department of Insurance oversees title insurance companies; go to www.insurance.ca.gov.

Check Out a House's Condition

Evolution of California's Disclosure Requirements................................290

Real Estate Transfer Disclosure Statement..291

    Examining the Seller's Disclosure Statement 298

    When to Go Beyond the Real Estate Transfer Disclosure Statement........300

    Handling Problems With the Transfer Disclosure Statement...................301

    Water Heater Bracing...302

Natural Hazard Disclosure Statement..303

Earthquake and Seismic Disclosures 306

    Residential Earthquake Hazards Report 307

Environmental Hazards...307

Lead..308

Disclosure of Deaths...308

Disclosure of Military Ordnance..309

Local Disclosures..309

Inspecting the Property Yourself...310

Arranging Professional Inspections 311

    Structural Pest Control Inspection 313

    General Inspection...313

    How to Find a Good Inspector..314

    Inspections and Reports 315

    Specialized Inspections Common in California.................................316

    Which Inspections Do You Really Need? 319

    Who Pays for Inspections? 321

Are the Repairs Really Needed? 321

Who Pays for Defects?...322

Ask for a Home Warranty 322

B efore you finalize your house purchase, check out its condition. If the house is in good shape, you can proceed knowing that you're getting what you paid for. But the few hundred dollars you spend on professional inspections may save you thousands later. If inspections discover problems, you can negotiate with the seller to pay for repairs, or back out of the deal, assuming your contract is written to allow that.

> (!) CAUTION
>
> **Don't rely solely on inspection reports from the seller.** Sellers often commission a full set of inspections and provide buyers with a comprehensive "Disclosure Package," all of which can be around 100 to 200 pages long. Read these carefully, but don't rely on them solely. The seller's report may be from the most optimistic inspector they could find. Even if the inspector spots a problem, his or her analysis of what's needed to correct it may tend toward the low-cost solutions. What's more, the California Bureau of Real Estate reports that it is "not uncommon" for sellers who don't like the results of one report to commission a second one, and then present the more favorable-looking one to buyers.

Evolution of California's Disclosure Requirements

Until the mid-1980s, California houses, like houses in most states, were sold with a caveat emptor (buyer beware) approach. As long as the seller didn't fraudulently conceal defects, the buyer was responsible for discovering the physical problems. Buyers and their lenders were naturally concerned not to miss major defects in the house. Unfortunately, this usually only involved hiring a pest inspector—and pest inspectors rarely know about or checked the complex systems in the house (like electricity or plumbing) or structural defects unrelated to pests.

Sometimes, it later became obvious that the seller (and sometimes his or her agent) knew about a particular undiscovered defect but never said a word. California courts began to question this "find-it-if-you-can" system and started holding sellers and their agents financially liable for not disclosing known problems.

State and local laws now require sellers to provide specific information on the condition of the house as well as disclose potential hazards like floods, earthquakes, and environmental hazards.

The new statutes aren't the end of the story—California courts still require sellers to disclose any negative fact that could reasonably be expected to lower the value of the property. (See *Reed v. King*, 145 Cal. App.3d 261 (1983).) The sellers must even disclose any "psychological defects," or that the house is of "ill repute"—or else face liability. For example, in the *Reed* case, the sellers sold their house without revealing that it had been the site of a multiple murder ten years before—a fact that appraisers said brought the property's value down significantly. Courts in various states have looked to the *Reed* case to decide that sellers should have disclosed a previous suicide, neighborhood noise, groundwater contamination, and more.

Real Estate Transfer Disclosure Statement

State law requires sellers to tell you a lot about the condition of the house on a Real Estate Transfer Disclosure Statement form ("TDS" in real estate shorthand). (Civil Code § 1102.) The TDS includes three types of disclosures:

- items included in the property, such as a burglar alarm or trash compactor
- information on defects or malfunctions in the building's structure, such as the roof or windows
- a variety of special issues, such as the existence of a homeowners' association (and any CC&Rs), environmental hazards like asbestos and lead-based paint, whether remodeling was done with permits and met local building codes, and neighborhood noise problems or nuisances.

We include a sample TDS here (but not online; you'll receive it from the seller). The TDS you'll be handed as part of your purchase should contain the identical language, as the disclosures are specified by state law. (Civil Code § 1102.6.)

Real Estate Transfer Disclosure Statement

(California Civil Code § 1102.6)

THIS DISCLOSURE STATEMENT CONCERNS THE REAL PROPERTY SITUATED IN THE CITY OF _____, COUNTY OF _____, STATE OF CALIFORNIA, DESCRIBED AS _____. THIS STATEMENT IS A DISCLOSURE OF THE CONDITION OF THE ABOVE-DESCRIBED PROPERTY IN COMPLIANCE WITH SECTION 1102 OF THE CIVIL CODE AS OF _____, 20 _____. IT IS NOT A WARRANTY OF ANY KIND BY THE SELLER(S) OR ANY AGENT(S) REPRESENTING ANY PRINCIPAL(S) IN THIS TRANSACTION, AND IT IS NOT A SUBSTITUTE FOR ANY INSPECTIONS OR WARRANTIES THE PRINCIPAL(S) MAY WISH TO OBTAIN.

I
Coordination With Other Disclosure Forms

This Real Estate Transfer Disclosure Statement is made pursuant to Section 1102 of the Civil Code. Other statutes require disclosures, depending upon the details of the particular real estate transaction (for example: special study zone and purchase-money liens on residential property).

Substituted Disclosures: The following disclosures and other disclosures required by law, including the Natural Hazard Disclosure Report/Statement that may include airport annoyances, earthquake, fire, flood, or special assessment information, have been or will be made in connection with this real estate transfer, and are intended to satisfy the disclosure obligations on this form, where the subject matter is the same:

☐ Inspection reports completed pursuant to the contract of sale or receipt for deposit.

☐ Additional inspection reports or disclosures: _____

_____

II
Seller's Information

The Seller discloses the following information with the knowledge that even though this is not a warranty, prospective Buyers may rely on this information in deciding whether and on what terms to purchase the subject property. Seller hereby authorizes any agent(s) representing any principal(s) in this transaction to provide a copy of this statement to any person or entity in connection with any actual or anticipated sale of the property.

THE FOLLOWING ARE REPRESENTATIONS MADE BY THE SELLER(S) AND ARE NOT THE REPRESENTATIONS OF THE AGENT(S), IF ANY. THIS INFORMATION IS A DISCLOSURE AND IT IS NOT INTENDED TO BE PART OF ANY CONTRACT BETWEEN THE BUYER AND SELLER.

Seller ☐ is ☐ is not occupying the property.

A. The subject property has the items checked below (read across):*

☐ Range   ☐ Oven   ☐ Microwave   ☐ Dishwasher   ☐ Trash Compactor

☐ Washer/Dryer Hookups   ☐ Rain Gutters

☐ Carbon Monoxide Device(s)   ☐ Burglar Alarms

☐ Smoke Detector(s)   ☐ Fire Alarm   ☐ TV Antenna   ☐ Satellite Dish

☐ Intercom   ☐ Central Heating

☐ Central Air Conditioning   ☐ Evaporator Cooler(s)

☐ Wall/Window Air Conditioning   ☐ Sprinklers

☐ Public Sewer System   ☐ Septic Tank   ☐ Sump Pump   ☐ Water Softener

☐ Patio/Decking   ☐ Built-in Barbecue

☐ Gazebo ☐ Hot Tub ☐ Locking Safety Cover   ☐ Sauna ☐ Pool ☐ Child-Resistant Barrier

☐ Spa   ☐ Locking Safety Cover   ☐ Security Gate(s)

☐ Automatic Garage Door Opener(s)   ☐ Number of Remote Controls

☐ Garage: ☐ Attached ☐ Not Attached ☐ Carport

☐ Pool/Spa Heater: ☐ Gas ☐ Solar ☐ Electric   ☐ Water Heater: ☐ Gas ☐ Solar ☐ Electric

☐ Water conserving plumbing features

☐ Water Supply: ☐ City ☐ Well   ☐ Private Utility or ☐ Other_____

☐ Gas Supply: ☐ Utility ☐ Bottled (tank)

☐ Window Screens ☐ Window Security Bars ☐ Quick Release Mechanism on Bedroom Windows

Exhaust Fan(s) in _____ 220 Volt Wiring in _____ Fireplace(s) in _____

Gas Starter _____ Roof(s): Type: _____ Age: (approx.) _____

Other: _____

Are there, to the best of your (Seller's) knowledge, any of the above that are not in operating condition? ☐ Yes ☐ No. If yes, then describe. (Attach additional sheets if necessary.):

Installation of a listed appliance, device, or amenity is not a precondition of sale or transfer of the dwelling. The carbon monoxide device, garage door opener, or child-resistant pool barrier may not be in compliance with the safety standards relating to, respectively, carbon monoxide device standards of Chapter 8 (commencing with Section 13260) of Part 2 of Division 12 of, automatic reversing device stands of Chapter 12.5 (commencing with Section 19890) of Part 3 of Division 13 of, or with the pool safety standards of Article 2.5 (commencing with Section 115920) Chapter 5 of Part 10 of Division 104 of, the Health and Safety Code. Window security bars may not have quick-release mechanisms in compliance with the 1995 Edition of the California Building Standards Code.

B.   Are you (Seller) aware of any significant defects/malfunctions in any of the following?

☐ Yes   ☐ No.   If yes, check appropriate space(s) below.

☐ Interior Walls   ☐ Ceilings   ☐ Floors   ☐ Exterior Walls

☐ Insulation   ☐ Roof(s)   ☐ Windows   ☐ Doors

☐ Foundation   ☐ Slab(s)   ☐ Driveways   ☐ Sidewalks

☐ Walls/Fences   ☐ Electrical Systems   ☐ Plumbing/Sewers/Septics

☐ Other Structural Components (describe): _____

If any of the above is checked, explain. (Attach additional sheets if necessary):

_____

_____

C.   Are you (Seller) aware of any of the following?

☐ Yes   ☐ No   1.   Substances, materials, or products which may be an environmental hazard such as, but not limited to, asbestos, formaldehyde, radon gas, lead-based paint, mold, fuel or chemical storage tanks, and contaminated soil or water on the subject property.

☐ Yes   ☐ No   2.   Features of the property shared in common with adjoining landowners, such as walls, fences, and driveways, whose use or responsibility for maintenance may have an effect on the subject property.

☐ Yes   ☐ No   3.   Any encroachments, easements, or similar matters that may affect your interest in the subject property.

☐ Yes   ☐ No   4.   Room additions, structural modifications, or other alterations or repairs made without necessary permits.

☐ Yes   ☐ No   5.   Room additions, structural modifications, or other alterations or repairs not in compliance with building codes.

☐ Yes   ☐ No   6.   Fill (compacted or otherwise) on the property or any portion thereof.

☐ Yes   ☐ No   7.   Any settling from any cause, or slippage, sliding, or other soil problems.

☐ Yes   ☐ No   8.   Flooding, drainage, or grading problems.

☐ Yes   ☐ No   9.   Major damage to the property or any other structures from fire, earthquake, floods, or landslides.

☐ Yes   ☐ No   10. Any zoning violations, nonconforming uses, or violations of "setback" requirements.

☐ Yes   ☐ No   11. Neighborhood noise problems or other nuisances.

☐ Yes ☐ No 12. CC&Rs or other deed restrictions or obligations.

☐ Yes ☐ No 13. Homeowners' Association which has any authority over the subject property.

☐ Yes ☐ No 14. Any "common area" (facilities such as pools, tennis courts, walkways, or other areas co-owned in undivided interest with others).

☐ Yes ☐ No 15. Any notices of abatement or citations against the property.

☐ Yes ☐ No 16. Any lawsuits by or against the Seller threatening to or affecting this real property, claims for damages by the seller pursuant to Section 910 or 914 threatening to or affecting this real property, claims for breach of warranty pursuant to Section 900 threatening to or affecting this real property, or claims for breach of an enhanced protection agreement pursuant to Section 903 threatening to or affecting this real property, including any lawsuits or claims for damages pursuant to Section 910 or 914 alleging a defect or deficiency in this real property or "common areas" (facilities such as pools, tennis courts, walkways, or other areas co-owned in undivided interest with others).

If the answer to any of these is yes, explain (attach additional sheets if necessary):

_____

_____

D.

1. The Seller certifies that the property, as of the close of escrow, will be in compliance with Section 13113.8 of the Health and Safety Code by having operable smoke detectors(s) which are approved, listed, and installed in accordance with the State Fire Marshal's regulations and applicable local standards.

2. The Seller certifies that the property, as of the close of escrow, will be in compliance with Section 19211 of the Health and Safety Code by having the water heater tank(s) braced, anchored, or strapped in place in accordance with applicable law.

Seller certifies that the information herein is true and correct to the best of the Seller's knowledge as of the date signed by the Seller.

Seller _____ Date _____

Seller _____ Date _____

III
Agent's Inspection Disclosure (Listing Agent)

(To be completed only if the Seller is represented by an agent in this transaction.)

THE UNDERSIGNED, BASED ON THE ABOVE INQUIRY OF THE SELLER(S) AS TO THE CONDITION OF THE PROPERTY AND BASED ON REASONABLY COMPETENT AND DILIGENT VISUAL INSPECTION OF THE ACCESSIBLE AREAS OF THE PROPERTY IN CONJUNCTION WITH THAT INQUIRY, STATES THE FOLLOWING:

☐ Agent notes no items for disclosure.

☐ Agent notes the following items: _____

_____

_____

_____

_____

Agent (Broker obtaining the offer) _____

By _____
    (Associate Licensee or Broker Signature)

Date _____

IV
Agent's Inspection Disclosure

(To be completed only if the agent who has obtained the offer is other than the agent above.)

THE UNDERSIGNED, BASED ON A REASONABLY COMPETENT AND DILIGENT VISUAL INSPECTION OF THE ACCESSIBLE AREAS OF THE PROPERTY, STATES THE FOLLOWING:

☐ Agent notes no items for disclosure.

☐ Agent notes the following items: _____

Agent (Broker obtaining the offer) _____

By _____
    (Associate Licensee or Broker Signature)

Date _____

V

BUYER(S) AND SELLER(S) MAY WISH TO OBTAIN PROFESSIONAL ADVICE AND/OR INSPECTIONS OF THE PROPERTY AND TO PROVIDE FOR APPROPRIATE PROVISIONS IN A CONTRACT BETWEEN BUYER(S) AND SELLER(S) WITH RESPECT TO ANY ADVICE/ INSPECTION/DEFECTS.

I/We acknowledge receipt of a copy of this statement.

Seller _____ Date _____

Seller _____ Date _____

Buyer _____ Date _____

Buyer _____ Date _____

Agent (Broker Representing Seller) _____

By _____ Date _____
   (Associate Licensee or Broker Signature)

Agent (Broker obtaining the offer) _____

By _____ Date _____
   (Associate Licensee or Broker Signature)

SECTION 1102.3 OF THE CIVIL CODE PROVIDES A BUYER WITH THE RIGHT TO RESCIND A PURCHASE CONTRACT FOR AT LEAST THREE DAYS AFTER THE DELIVERY OF THIS DISCLOSURE IF DELIVERY OCCURS AFTER THE SIGNING OF AN OFFER TO PURCHASE. IF YOU WISH TO RESCIND THE CONTRACT, YOU MUST ACT WITHIN THE PRESCRIBED PERIOD. A REAL ESTATE BROKER IS QUALIFIED TO ADVISE ON REAL ESTATE. IF YOU DESIRE LEGAL ADVICE, CONSULT YOUR ATTORNEY.

Sample Letter Requesting Further Seller's Disclosure

February 22, 20xx

Dear _____:

I have received your Real Estate Transfer Disclosure Statement, dated _____ .
In item _____, you indicate that _____ .
Please explain this condition more fully. Specifically, I would appreciate
your letting me know in writing answers to the following questions:

1. _____

2. _____

3. _____

Also, please send me copies of any inspectors' reports that deal with any
aspect of the physical condition of the property, and copies of all home
insurance claim reports. Thank you for your cooperation.

Sincerely,

CAUTION

Exemptions from transfer disclosure statement. Certain properties,
including foreclosures and probate sales and buildings with more than four units,
are exempt from state disclosure laws. In these cases, be extra sure to get a professional home inspection before closing the deal.

Examining the Seller's Disclosure Statement

Sellers must provide you a copy of the Transfer Disclosure Statement "as
soon as practicable before transfer of title." (Civil Code § 1102.3.) It's to
your advantage to get a copy of the TDS as soon as possible; you don't
want to invest the time and money in the house-buying process only to
discover problems just before you close escrow.

Of course, you also need to remain alert to the possibility that the seller has not filled the form out thoroughly. That's why it's important to do your own inspections and other investigations. Look hard at any work done without permits, as well as signs of water damage.

Often, seller's disclosure forms are only cursorily filled out, and you'll need to ask questions for additional information. If the form you receive is sparse, you're confused about any of the seller's disclosures, or you simply want more details, make a written request for more information; send a copy to the seller's agent and keep a copy for yourself. Insist on a written response from the seller. See sample above.

In your request, ask not only for elaboration on the TDS, but also for any other recent inspection reports the seller may have authorized, such as a pest inspection (especially if you're in Southern California).

In addition, ask for copies of any home insurance claims reports. The key here is not merely to discover previous damage, but to see how much insurance claim activity took place. As discussed in Chapter 18, a history of "too many" claims can lead to high premiums on your policy, or even to an uninsurable house. Be particularly concerned if you see any past claims for water damage, which make insurance companies skittish.

Real Estate Agents' Disclosures

California law requires licensed real estate agents (brokers and salespeople) to conduct a "reasonably competent and diligent" visual inspection of property and to disclose to you anything that would affect the "value or desirability" of the property—that is, anything that would be likely to affect your decision to buy. (Civil Code §§ 2079, 2079.3.)

This obligation is on both your agent and the agent representing the seller. Agents do not have to inspect inaccessible areas (such as the sealed-off underside of the porch) or review public documents affecting title to or use of the property. Similarly, agents are not required to explain the legal ramifications of their disclosures.

Also, be sure to carefully read the visual disclosures made by your agent and the seller's agent. The seller may not notice obvious defects he or she has lived with every day (such as cuts in linoleum or spots of mold on the walls). Therefore, the agent might be the only one to mention these issues.

When to Go Beyond the Real Estate Transfer Disclosure Statement

In addition to considering at face value the information disclosed, examine the disclosure statement for clues to other problems, and follow up with a professional inspection.

For example, if the seller says that several windows won't open, they may simply be painted shut. But it's also possible that the house has settled and the window frames are no longer properly aligned. Similarly, cracks in the dining room ceiling may mean no more than that the plaster is old, or they may be a clue to significant earth movement or to an otherwise unstable foundation. In either case, have the foundation checked extra carefully.

CAUTION

The seller doesn't need to find out on your behalf whether gas transmission or hazardous liquid pipelines run near the property. This issue came to public attention after the 2010 explosion of a Pacific Gas & Electric pipeline in San Bruno, which caused eight deaths and destroyed dozens of homes. Local homeowners hadn't even known the pipelines were there. Under a California law passed in 2012, home sellers need only advise buyers to check a database for the existence of such lines; it's at www.npms.phmsa.dot.gov. (Of course, a seller who already happens to know about defective pipelines nearby should disclose that to you.)

Handling Problems With the Transfer Disclosure Statement

The law specifically allows buyers, in deciding whether and on what terms to buy the house, to rely on a seller's disclosure statement. Even if your offer was not contingent upon your approving inspection reports, state law allows a person to terminate an offer to purchase real property three days after personal delivery of a TDS (five days from mailing). (Civil Code § 1102.3.) (If, however, you signed off on the TDS before submitting the offer, there's no three-day right of rescission.) A buyer may alternatively decide to proceed with the sale and negotiate the cost of making repairs with the seller.

Although sellers and agents need disclose only defects within their personal knowledge, some sellers worry about being sued. They're afraid they won't be able to prove that they didn't know about a certain problem. In short, they now have a good reason to discover and disclose defects, just as do buyers.

A wise seller will disclose all possible (and sometimes even imagined) defects to protect against possible future lawsuits, often in a supplement to the TDS. On a supplementary form recommended by some San Francisco real estate agents, for instance, sellers are asked to answer if they are aware of any problems, such as damages caused by animals, neighborhood animal problems, criminal activities on the property, or diseased trees on the property.

Disclosures Required With FHA Loans

The Department of Housing and Urban Development (HUD) requires disclosures regarding home inspections for borrowers seeking Federal Housing Administration (FHA) financing. All FHA borrowers must be given a form, "For Your Protection, Get a Home Inspection." This form must be signed and dated by the borrower before the execution of the sales contract. For more information on FHA loans, see Chapter 11.

Not all sellers and agents are savvy enough to provide detailed disclosures. Some still try to cover up serious problems, hoping that you and your inspector won't find them. The seller is risking a lawsuit, but some sellers don't think this far ahead. (For handling these types of legal problems, see Chapter 21.)

Water Heater Bracing

If the property you are buying has had a new or replacement water heater installed since January 1, 1991, it must be braced, anchored, or strapped to resist falling or displacement during an earthquake. (Health and Safety Code § 19211.) Anyone selling property with such a water heater must certify in writing that the heater complies with the law.

As of July 1, 2011, California sellers of residential property must comply with the Carbon Monoxide Poisoning Prevention Act of 2010 (Cal. Health and Safety Code §§ 13260 and following; and §§ 17926 and following). This law addresses the problem of carbon monoxide poisoning, the leading cause of accidental deaths in the United States. The odorless gas is produced whenever fuel is burned, and can come from seemingly innocent sources, such as a gas stove, furnace, or woodstove, usually due to leakage, backdrafting, or poor venting.

The new law requires homeowners to have installed a carbon monoxide (CO) alarm (or a CO alarm combined with a smoke detector) by July 1, 2011. Of course, many have not done so. The disclosure form from your seller will state whether the house includes such alarms, but will also include a section explaining that installation is not a precondition or requirement of sale or transfer. However, if you see that the house lacks CO alarms, you could insist that they be installed as a condition of closing. Or simply plan to buy them yourself; they typically cost between $20 and $90 per detector. The Consumer Product Safety Commission recommends installing a CO alarm in the hallway near every separate sleeping area of the home.

Natural Hazard Disclosure Statement

The Transfer Disclosure Statement discussed in the previous section includes information on many hazards affecting the house, some of which require additional disclosures. Many of these are made on the Natural Hazard Disclosure Statement (NHDS), which indicates whether the property is in one of the following hazard zones (Civil Code § 1103.2):

- a flood hazard zone designated by the Federal Emergency Management Agency (FEMA)

- an area of potential flooding due to failure of a dam as identified by the Office of Emergency Services on an "inundation map" (Government Code § 8589.5)

- a very high fire hazard severity zone designated by a local agency (Government Code §§ 51178, 51179)

- a state-designated wildland fire area zone (Public Resources Code § 4125)

- a delineated earthquake fault zone as identified by the California State Geologist (Public Resources Code § 2622)

- a seismic hazards zone (area where landslides and liquefaction are most likely to occur) as defined under Public Resources Code § 2696, or

- an airport annoyance area or one subject to special tax assessments (Civil Code § 1103.4).

These designations are often puzzling, at least to a layperson. For example, San Francisco is not within an earthquake fault zone. That's because the fault line isn't in San Francisco—although San Francisco has certainly experienced the ravages of earthquakes.

Also, sometimes the available maps and information are not of sufficient accuracy or scale for a seller to determine whether the property falls inside a designated hazard zone, such as a high fire hazard severity zone. In this case, the law requires the seller to mark "Yes" on the NHDS —unless the seller has evidence, such as a report from a licensed engineer, that the property is not in the particular zone. (Civil Code § 1102.4.)

Natural Hazard Disclosure Statement

This statement applies to the following property: _____.

The transferor and his or her agent(s) or a third-party consultant disclose the following information with the knowledge that even though this is not a warranty, prospective transferees may rely on this information in deciding whether and on what terms to purchase the subject property. Transferor hereby authorizes any agent(s) representing any principal(s) in this action to provide a copy of this statement to any person or entity in connection with any actual or anticipated sale of the property.

The following are representations made by the transferor and his or her agent(s) based on their knowledge and maps drawn by the state and federal governments. This information is a disclosure and is not intended to be part of any contract between the transferee and the transferor.

THIS REAL PROPERTY LIES WITHIN THE FOLLOWING HAZARDOUS AREA(S):

A SPECIAL FLOOD HAZARD AREA (any type Zone "A" or "V") designated by the Federal Emergency Management Agency.

☐ Yes ☐ No ☐ Do not know and information not available from local jurisdiction

AN AREA OF POTENTIAL FLOODING shown on a dam failure inundation map pursuant to Section 8589.5 of the Government Code.

☐ Yes ☐ No ☐ Do not know and information not available from local jurisdiction

A VERY HIGH FIRE HAZARD SEVERITY ZONE pursuant to Section 51178 or 51179 of the Government Code. The owner of this property is subject to the maintenance requirements of Section 51182 of the Government Code.

☐ Yes ☐ No

A WILDLAND AREA THAT MAY CONTAIN SUBSTANTIAL FOREST FIRE RISKS AND HAZARDS pursuant to Section 4125 of the Public Resources Code. The owner of this property is subject to the maintenance requirements of Section 4291 of the Public Resources Code. Additionally, it is not the state's responsibility to provide fire protection services to any building or structure located within the wildlands unless the Department of Forestry and Fire Protection has entered into a cooperative agreement with a local agency for those purposes pursuant to Section 4142 of the Public Resources Code.

☐ Yes ☐ No

AN EARTHQUAKE FAULT ZONE pursuant to Section 2622 of the Public Resources Code.

☐ Yes ☐ No

A SEISMIC HAZARD ZONE pursuant to Section 2696 of the Public Resources Code.
☐ Yes (Landslide Zone) ☐ Yes (Liquefaction Zone) ☐ No ☐ Map not yet released by state

THESE HAZARDS MAY LIMIT YOUR ABILITY TO DEVELOP THE REAL PROPERTY, TO OBTAIN INSURANCE, OR TO RECEIVE ASSISTANCE AFTER A DISASTER.

THE MAPS ON WHICH THESE DISCLOSURES ARE BASED ESTIMATE WHERE NATURAL HAZARDS EXIST. THEY ARE NOT DEFINITIVE INDICATORS OF WHETHER OR NOT A PROPERTY WILL BE AFFECTED BY A NATURAL DISASTER. TRANSFEREE(S) AND TRANSFEROR(S) MAY WISH TO OBTAIN PROFESSIONAL ADVICE REGARDING THOSE HAZARDS AND OTHER HAZARDS THAT MAY AFFECT THE PROPERTY.

Signature of Transferor(s) _____ Date _____

Signature of Transferor(s) _____ Date _____

Agent(s) _____ Date _____

Agent(s) _____ Date _____

Check only one of the following:

☐ Transferor(s) and their agent(s) represent that the information herein is true and correct to the best of their knowledge as of the date signed by the transferor(s) and agent(s).

☐ Transferor(s) and their agent(s) acknowledge that they have exercised good faith in the selection of a third-party report provider as required in Civil Code Section 1103.7, and that the representations made in this Natural Hazard Disclosure Statement are based upon information provided by the independent third-party disclosure provider as a substituted disclosure pursuant to Civil Code Section 1103.4. Neither transferor(s) nor their agent(s) (1) has independently verified the information contained in this statement and report or (2) is personally aware of any errors or inaccuracies in the information contained on the statement. This statement was prepared by the provider below:

Third-Party Disclosure Provider(s) _____ Date _____

Transferee represents that he or she has read and understands this document. Pursuant to Civil Code Section 1103.8, the representations made in this Natural Hazard Disclosure Statement do not constitute all of the transferor's or agent's disclosure obligations in this transaction.

Signature of Transferee(s)_____ Date _____

Signature of Transferee(s)_____ Date _____

More and more sellers, however, don't even fill this form out on their own, but instead pay a few hundred dollars to a company that generates a report based on the lot and block number of the home in question (or using the street address, to make it even easier). The reports carry explanatory language about how the various zones are set up legally and what their designations mean.

We include a sample NHDS here so that you can familiarize yourself with this form. The NHDS you receive should contain identical language, as the disclosures are specified by state law (but it may contain extra language if prepared by an outside company).

Examine the Natural Hazard Disclosure Statement and follow up on any questions or problems. Also, check with the local planning department for more information on earthquake hazards in the area. And see Appendix A, "Welcome to California," which discusses areas of the state susceptible to various natural disasters and includes resources for more information.

TIP

Alternative disclosure form. A seller may provide these disclosures on a Local Option Real Estate Disclosure Statement, described under "Local Disclosures," below.

Earthquake and Seismic Disclosures

To help buyers make informed decisions, the seller must indicate on the Natural Hazard Disclosure Statement whether the property is in an earthquake fault zone or a seismic hazard zone. In addition, state law requires sellers to provide information on the safety of the house itself and its ability to resist earthquakes.

Residential Earthquake Hazards Report

The seller must tell you whether the property has any known seismic deficiencies, such as whether or not the house is bolted or anchored to the foundation and whether cripple walls, if any, are braced. (Government Code § 8897.) The seller is not required to hire anyone to help evaluate the house or to strengthen any weaknesses that exist. If the house was built in 1960 or later, oral disclosure is enough.

If the house was built before 1960, the seller must disclose in writing and sign the disclosure form, Residential Earthquake Hazards Report, included in a booklet called the *Homeowner's Guide to Earthquake Safety*. The seller must give the buyer a copy of this booklet and disclosure "as soon as practicable before the transfer." (Government Code § 8897.1.)

RESOURCE

The *Homeowner's Guide to Earthquake Safety* is available from the California Seismic Safety Commission (CSSC) at www.seismic.ca.gov. This booklet provides valuable information, including how to find and fix earthquake weaknesses.

Environmental Hazards

Item C.1 on the Transfer Disclosure Statement asks the seller to identify environmental hazards on the property, such as radon gas, contaminated soil, or mold. In addition, sellers should provide prospective home buyers a copy of *Residential Environmental Hazards: A Guide for Homeowners, Homebuyers, Landlords and Tenants*, by the California Department of Toxic Substances Control, which provides information on different environmental hazards that may be on or near the property, such as asbestos, formaldehyde, lead, and hazardous wastes.

Lead

HUD rules require that applicants for FHA mortgages be given a lead-based paint notice disclosure form before signing the final sales contract. Lead paint in homes financed by the FHA must be removed or repainted.

California law requires that a seller disclose lead-based paint hazards to prospective buyers on the Transfer Disclosure Statement. (Civil Code § 1102.6.) Furthermore, sellers of houses built before 1978 must comply with the federal Residential Lead-Based Paint Hazard Reduction Act of 1992 (42 U.S. Code § 4852d), also known as Title X (Ten). Sellers must:

- disclose all known lead-based paint and paint hazards in the house
- give buyers a pamphlet prepared by the U.S. Environmental Protection Agency (EPA) called *Protect Your Family From Lead in Your Home*
- include certain warning language in the contract, as well as signed statements from all parties verifying that all requirements were completed
- keep signed acknowledgments for three years as proof of compliance, and
- give buyers a ten-day opportunity to test the housing for lead.

If a seller fails to comply with Title X requirements, you can sue the seller for triple the amount of your resulting damages.

RESOURCE

Lead. The National Lead Information Center has extensive information on lead hazards, prevention, and disclosures, as well as the required pamphlet. For more information, call the center at 800-424-LEAD or check www2.epa.gov/lead.

Disclosure of Deaths

State law implies that the seller should disclose any death within the last three years that he or she knows occurred on the property. (Civil Code § 1710.2.) If a death occurred more than three years before, the seller need disclose it only if asked by the buyer—unless the circumstances of the death (for example, a multiple murder) would significantly lower the house's value.

A seller, however, need not disclose that an owner had, or died from, HIV/AIDS. But the property owner or agent should answer honestly any direct questions on this subject. (Civil Code § 1710.2.) The legislature didn't address any diseases other than AIDS; its concern was that the widespread fear and stigma around this disease would lead to sellers' having to disclose their private health information.

Disclosure of Military Ordnance

Sellers who know of any former federal or state ordnance locations (once used for military training purposes and potentially containing explosive munitions) within one mile of the property must provide written disclosure to the buyer as soon as practicable before transfer of title. (Civil Code § 1102.15.)

Disclosing Ghosts and Haunting

Do the sellers need to tell you if they think their house is haunted? Based on California's broad disclosure rules, most experts would say yes. You're not likely to see a seller boldly declare on the TDS form that the house is haunted—but if you see statements such as "dining room furniture tends to move around at night," "cats won't go near the attic stairs," or "unexplained vapors," you might want to ask further questions.

Local Disclosures

Many cities and counties have local disclosure requirements. To make sure the seller complies, check with the local city or county planning or building department for any local requirements. For example:

- Many municipalities require sellers to upgrade insulation before selling and take specific energy efficiency measures.

- Many coastal areas restrict owners from making structural modifications to their properties without a permit.

- Some communities adjacent to agricultural or timber production zones require sellers to disclose agricultural nuisances, such as noise, odors, and dust.

- Sellers of property in designated "community facilities" districts must disclose information on special taxes for police or fire departments, libraries, parks, and schools. (Civil Code § 1102.6b.)

Sellers in communities with local disclosure requirements passed after July 1990 may use a special form, the Local Option Real Estate Disclosure Statement. (Civil Code § 1102.6a.)

Inspecting the Property Yourself

At some point, you'll want to arrange professional inspections. Before you get this far, you should first take a close look at the house on your own—ideally, before you make a formal written offer so that you can save yourself the trouble should you spot serious problems.

Make a list of areas you can check out without needing expertise or having to climb around in dangerous places. Focus on items of particular importance to you and your family. For example, peer up at the roof (from inside and outside, if possible) to look for leaks, loose or missing shingles, or clogged gutters; check around the house for peeling paint and loose caulk and soil that slopes toward the house (likely bringing in water); check the bathroom for mildew, a shaky toilet, or loose grout; check the basement for rotting wood, termite tubes, and water stains; and so on. (A simple Internet search for "DIY home inspection" will bring up extensive material on this topic.) Bring along a note pad, tape measure, camera, and flashlight and a copy of the Ideal House Profile you prepared in Chapter 1. If you're buying a condo, be sure to visit the unit in the evening when neighbors are more likely to be home, to hear any loud noises.

CAUTION

Look hard at "do-it-yourself" home repair jobs. If you see signs that the previous owners took on major repairs or remodeling work without professional help, ask the inspector to take an especially hard look. Amateur home repair projects are notorious for violating codes and containing hidden—or not-so-hidden—defects. Be sure the work was done with permits, and that all the permits have been "finaled."

Special Considerations When Evaluating an Extensively Remodeled (Flipped) House

Considering a home that has been extensively remodeled, perhaps after the owner bought it as a fixer or at a foreclosure auction? Here are some important tips from co-author Ira Serkes:

- Make sure your lender will be able to make a loan on the property. Some lenders won't lend if the property was purchased very recently.
- Find out the contractor's track record in the area. Is it the contractor's first home (in which case you'll have no track record to go by) or has the company done several in recent years?
- Thoroughly inspect the home, compare recent inspections to earlier ones, and compile a "punchlist" of repair items for the seller to take care of prior to close of escrow.
- Find out what guarantee or warranty the seller provides.

Arranging Professional Inspections

In addition to inspecting the house yourself and examining the seller's disclosure and inspection reports, you'll want to hire a general contractor to inspect the property and a licensed structural pest control inspector to check for pest damage. (A few inspectors are qualified to do both.)

This is normally done after your written purchase offer has been accepted by the seller (which should be contingent upon your approving the results of one or more inspections). Make sure you have the seller's Transfer Disclosure Statement and Natural Hazard Disclosure Statement so that the inspectors can follow up on any problems identified therein. You may also want to arrange more specialized inspections.

Request Copies of Utility and Water Bills

While sellers are not required to tell you how much they pay the gas and electric company every month, ask to see past bills, especially for the winter months. Gas and electric bills can vary a lot, depending on a house's location, size, and insulation, and the type and age of the furnace and hot water heater.

If utility bills are high, ask the local gas and electric company to conduct an energy check or audit. Many do it at no charge, identifying the problems, recommended solutions, and costs. If your utility company won't help or will take too long, ask for the names of private companies that conduct energy audits.

With water bills, look for any sudden increase in water usage. In older houses especially, this may be a tip-off that main pipes are leaking.

Even if you are an expert, such as an architect or investor, don't forgo the professional home inspection. The inspector may find defects that you missed—and his or her report of the cost of repairs will be given more weight than your own estimate. That means the cost of the inspection can be readily offset by negotiating price concessions or repairs by the seller.

If, on the other hand, the seller is not willing to negotiate on price, the inspection contingency gives you a ready opportunity to back out of the sale. The most costly items to repair tend to be foundation, drainage, roof, pest, electrical, and heating.

 TIP

In a hot market, consider a professional inspection before you make an offer. This allows you to close the deal quickly, by waiving the inspection contingency, giving you an edge over the competition. Obviously, you'll need the seller's permission first to do a preoffer inspection (called a "preinspection"). And you may want to lower your offer price in light of what you find.

Structural Pest Control Inspection

An inspection by a licensed structural pest control inspector, covering infestation by termites and flying beetles, dry rot, and other fungal conditions, is almost always required by the lender. If you don't make it a condition of the contract, your lender may, particularly if you put down less than 20% of the purchase price.

If the seller had a pest report done before putting the house up for sale, you should still get your own done. Some inspectors are less picky than others, and the seller has a motive (wanting the deal to go through) to pick someone who won't be too fussy. Pest control reports range from about $150 to $250 for a typical single-family dwelling. In a condo, you may need an authorization from the homeowners' association for the pest control inspector to look at common areas.

> **RESOURCE**
> **More information on pest control inspection.** The Structural Pest Control Board keeps files of all pest control reports commissioned within the past two years and provides useful consumer information on pest control inspections and reports. The board can provide complaint information on individual pest control companies and help mediate disputes. Go to www.pestboard.ca.gov.

General Inspection

A licensed inspector (usually with a background as a general contractor) inspects all major house systems, from top to bottom. The inspector will examine the general conditions of the site, such as drainage, retaining walls, fences (some skip the fences—remind them to look), and driveways; the integrity of the structure and the foundation; and the condition of the roof, exterior and interior paint, doors and windows, and plumbing, electrical, and heating systems. A growing number of inspectors test for lead in water or radiation exposure around a built-in microwave.

As of 2011, California law allows you to request that your inspection include an energy-efficiency audit. You might also want to arrange specialized inspections, such as for seismic safety or asbestos hazards (described below). If you're concerned about toxic mold, make sure the inspector has expertise in finding and assessing it.

How to Find a Good Inspector

A reliable personal recommendation is the best way to find a house inspector and structural pest control inspector. Remember, you want someone who will be thorough and tough.

Ask your real estate agent for a referral to an inspector, but be sure to double-check any leads from your agent. Some agents are anxious that the deal go through and therefore may recommend an inspector not overly persnickety about identifying problems. The better agents, however, realize that referrals to tough inspectors work in everyone's interests—after all, most real estate lawsuits are filed by buyers against sellers as well as real estate agents, claiming that problems with the home weren't disclosed to them.

You can also get local referrals from two professional associations: the American Society of Home Inspectors (ASHI) or the California Real Estate Inspection Association (CREIA) (contact information below).

Get at least two or three specific proposals from recommended home inspectors and check the status of each individual's license and any outstanding complaints with the Contractors State License Board or the Structural Pest Control Board (contact information above). Ask for references from customers who have owned their homes for a few years, so that any problems the inspector didn't discover have had a chance to pop up. Ask the inspector about his or her liability insurance coverage, including "errors and omissions" (E&O) or malpractice insurance to cover negligence.

Recognizing that there is an inherent conflict of interest in inspecting and bidding on the same job, state law prohibits this practice. Home inspectors may not perform any repairs to a house on which the inspector, or the inspector's company, has prepared a home inspection report in the past 12 months. (Business and Professions Code §§ 7195, 7197.) Note, however, that this law only covers home inspectors. There's nothing to stop you from asking a general contractor to examine your roof or foundation and then prepare a bid to do any necessary work.

RESOURCE

For referrals to local inspectors and information on buying a home in good shape: Contact the American Society of Home Inspectors (ASHI), www.ashi. org, or the California Real Estate Inspection Association (CREIA), www.creia.org.

Inspections and Reports

The general inspection should take at least two to three hours, while the pest control inspection should take about an hour. Accompany the inspector during the examination. You will learn a lot and better understand the report the inspector will later write. You can also find out about the maintenance and preservation of the house and ask questions.

If a friend or relative has experience in any aspect of construction, bring him or her along. Another set of eyes that know what to look for is always a help. It's also a good idea to bring along a video camera to record the inspection (if the inspector permits it). You may want to view it years later to remind yourself about maintenance issues.

Expect to receive the general inspector's report after a short time (a few days or up to a week), and the pest control report within about five days. Both reports should detail the condition of all major components of the house inspected or checked for infestation and estimated repair costs. Many inspectors include photos in their reports, which can be useful both for identifying and understanding the issue, and for looking back at in later years, for home maintenance guidance. The inspector should point out any problems and indicate which are truly important and which are minor, and give a rough estimate of the costs involved for repairs. The inspector may also recommend additional specialized inspections such as those listed below.

House inspection contractors often worry about their liability should they fail to discover a serious defect. While this encourages thoroughness, it can also result in overly defensive inspecting. Here's how to filter out inspector paranoia while reading an inspection report:

- Don't focus on the long-winded disclaimers written by lawyers. While this boilerplate language may sound scary, it's usually not a tip-off that all sorts of problems are lurking just out of sight.

- Pay attention to statements describing the tests the inspector didn't conduct or areas not inspected. Were any areas or systems left out that shouldn't have been? (Sometimes, the seller will block off certain areas, for example by piling up boxes in the basement or attic, in which case you should insist that they be opened for reinspection.) Next, focus on what the inspector did discover. You'll have to decide whether the identified problems merit a specialized inspection (for example, by a structural engineer) and whether you still want to go through with the transaction, based on what the inspection revealed.

- Get a second opinion if a general contractor or pest control inspector discovers a potentially serious problem or doesn't inspect important areas. Arrange for the follow-up inspection to be conducted by a specialist.

Specialized Inspections Common in California

Some specialized inspections that may be necessary are described below.

Asbestos. Exposure to airborne asbestos has been linked to an increased risk of cancer. Normally, a separate asbestos inspection is not necessary unless you suspect problems (generally not the case with homes built since the mid 1970s). A general contractor should tell you if the house contains asbestos insulation around heating systems, in ceilings, or in other areas.

Ira Serkes notes, "If a home has asbestos ducting, it probably can be removed, and new ducting installed for a few thousand dollars."

RESOURCE

To check the license of an asbestos inspector: Check with the California Department of Industrial Relations, Division of Occupational Safety and Health (Cal/OSHA), www.dir.ca.gov (search for "asbestos contractor").

Electrical. If you or a general contractor suspects problems (more likely if the house was built 25 years ago or more), have an electrician or an electrical engineer do a specialized electrical report. Many general contractors don't have enough knowledge of electrical codes to do an adequate job on a large older house. Be sure to replace any fuse boxes with circuit breakers.

Electromagnetic radiation. If you're considering a home near high-voltage electrical power lines, you may be worried about possible health hazards. Although links between electromagnetic radiation and diseases such as cancer have not been proven, you may still want to call the local utility company for a test and evaluation of the electromagnetic radiation levels. Some general contractors can test for this as well.

Foundation, structure, and earthquake retrofitting. A general contractor can report on these; if the contractor suspects a problem, or you're concerned based upon the seller's disclosures, you'll want an expert to inspect the foundation and drainage. Be sure to have your house inspected for seismic safety, particularly if it has living space above a garage. (That's called a "soft story.") The general contractor may recommend a professional engineer to perform this evaluation.

Lead. Exposure to lead-based paint and lead water pipes may lead to serious health problems, especially for children. For information on home testing for lead hazards and a list of state-certified lead inspectors and testing laboratories, contact the California Department of Public Health, www.cdph.ca.gov (click the "Health Information" tab, then "Environmental Health," then "Hazards"). For state-by-state statistics on lead levels in children and other information, go to www.epa.gov/lead.

Mold. Recent concerns about mold's effect on human health have brought it into the public spotlight. The concern is not with the relatively benign mold that appears on shower tiles—it's with the layers of mold that develop around leaky pipes or other major moisture problems. These villains are reputed to cause everything from allergic coughs to brain damage and death. Some people have major reactions to mold, while others have none at all.

Regardless of your sensitivity level, if the house you're hoping to buy has a mold problem, you'll want to know about it. Your first step is to look closely when you visit the house yourself. Look not only for visible signs, but also for unpleasant smells or areas of obvious moisture or water damage. Unfortunately, not all molds have a smell, and mold may hide in air ducts, crawl spaces or ceilings, and attics. For this reason, you should choose a home inspector who has experience in identifying mold problems. Many of them attend special trainings. For more information, see the website of the California Real Estate Inspection Association, www.creia.org.

To further protect home buyers, the California Legislature passed the Toxic Mold Protection Act of 2001. (Health & Safety Code §§ 26100 and following.) This requires sellers to disclose any significant known or suspected mold problems. However, sellers are not required to test for mold (reliable tests haven't yet been developed). It's entirely possible the sellers won't notice any mold on their own.

> **RESOURCE**
>
> **Mold.** For information on the detection, removal, and prevention of mold, see the EPA website at www.epa.gov/learn-issues. Additional publications are available from the California Department of Public Health at www.cdph.ca.gov.

Plumbing. If the general inspector's report indicates plumbing problems, get an in-depth report from a plumber. Your local water department may provide some useful information regarding water pressure and hardness or softness of water. If a house is more than 50 years old, the main sewer line to the street may need replacing before long. General contractors typically do not inspect wells and septic tanks; you'll need to hire a specialist if you want these checked out.

Radon. Radon is a naturally occurring radioactive gas associated with lung cancer that enters and can contaminate a house built on soil and rock with uranium deposits or through water from some private wells. Radon concentrations tend to be highest in newer buildings, whose tight sealing doesn't allow the gas to escape. It is not a problem in most of California, but if you're concerned and want a test kit, contact the National Safety Council (NSC) Radon Hotline at 800-767-7236 or visit www.nsc.org. The California Department of Public Health (CDPH at www.cdph.ca.gov) can also provide information at 800-745-7236. The CDPH website also contains maps of areas' potential for radon hazards—and these maps are more up to date than the EPA one that you may receive along with your hazard reports from the seller. Go to www.cdph.ca.gov and click "Health Information," then "Radon," then "California Test Results."

Subsoil. If earth movement, especially subsidence or slippage, is a problem or possibility (or if the house is on fill), contact your local building or planning department for any soil reports on file. For information sources on earthquake study zones and hazardous landslide and flood areas in California, see Appendix A, "Welcome to California." In addition, you may want to consult a soils expert, who may recommend soil borings.

Which Inspections Do You Really Need?

Some very cautious buyers have different specialists check all major areas of the house, such as heating, plumbing, roof, and foundation. Involving specialists makes excellent sense if the house is old, large, expensive, or in obviously poor condition. But weigh the benefit against the cost. If you're buying a five-year-old house in apparently great shape, you have read up on inspections, and an experienced general inspector and pest control inspector have discovered no problems, spending any money on additional inspections is probably overkill. These guidelines should help you decide how many inspections you need:

- **Let your eyes and nose be your first guide.** The poorer looking the house's condition, or the worse the mildew smells, the more you should use a fine-tooth comb.

- **Age is a factor.** Houses deteriorate over time, and construction techniques (especially for foundations) weren't always the best years ago. So the older the house, the more it makes sense to examine it closely.

- **Mansions deserve a third look.** The more expensive the house, the more you want to be sure you're getting your money's worth.

- **In areas where the earth moves often, check the foundation and the subsoil carefully.** This is especially true for houses in landslide- or earthquake-vulnerable areas and houses built on landfill.

- **Look for evidence of seasonal problems.** If you buy a house in the middle of August, the roof won't be leaking or the basement flooding—but they may in December. So look carefully at ceilings, attic spaces, and basements for stains or water marks. If ceilings have recently been repainted, ask why. If you aren't satisfied with the answer, ask your inspector to check these areas extra carefully and the seller to state in writing that no problems have been covered up.

- **Question new construction.** If you have any questions about a room addition or any remodeling done on the house, check permits on file at the local planning department. Make sure that all the work was done with permits and that the final permits were issued.

Earthquake Reinforcements

Earthquakes in the late 1980s and 1990s have cast much new light on making houses earthquake safe. The time-tested advice to bolt a house to its foundation and install stiff plywood cripple walls in the basement proved to be helpful. These reinforcements typically cost only a few thousand dollars, won't trigger a reappraisal of your home for property tax purposes (Revenue and Tax Code § 74.5), and are frequently a condition of getting earthquake insurance.

Recent earthquakes have also focused attention on the possibility that vertical earth movements can make houses vulnerable to literally jumping off their foundations. To cope with this danger, it's best to secure the house to the foundation using steel ties, straps, and, in some cases, cables. You might also want the cripple walls strengthened with heavy-gauge metal fasteners and cross bracing. A basic retrofit of this type typically costs $2,000–$8,000 or more, depending on the size and age of the house, but should be done only after an earthquake expert is consulted.

In addition, it's important to repair termite and other structural damage, or else earthquake retrofit work can actually make a house more susceptible to earthquake damage. Earthquake retrofit services are advertised heavily; many people sound convincing but actually know so little that they are apt to make the problem worse.

Who Pays for Inspections?

A general inspection typically costs about $500–$800 for a single-family home, and more for a multiple-unit dwelling. Structural pest control inspections cost upwards of $150 for an average single-family house. Normally, the buyer pays for inspections required as part of the offer to purchase. This is custom, however, not law, and it's possible to negotiate an arrangement where the seller pays or shares in the cost of inspections. Just make sure that even if the seller pays, you choose the inspector.

Are the Repairs Really Needed?

If the inspection reports identify expensive repair needs, here are some questions to ask:

- **Should you get a second opinion?** Especially if the problem is serious or requires specialized knowledge, you might want one.

- **Has one inspector called for very different types of repairs from another?** If so, some work probably needs to be done, but you still need to figure out exactly what.

- **Is the problem real or potential?** Can the situation be monitored? Will less-expensive work solve the problem? Pest control inspectors must notify the person requesting the report that the information can be divided into two sections: corrective measures for damage from evident infestations and corrective measures for conditions deemed likely to lead to infestation and future problems. For potential problems, ask whether the expensive work needs to be done now.

- **Is the problem getting worse?** If so, it's an indicator that you'll probably have to take immediate steps to either repair it or at least prevent it from spreading.

Don't simply accept as gospel what the expert tells you. If the costs seem too high, get a second opinion from someone committed to helping you arrive at a less-expensive solution.

Who Pays for Defects?

If inspections turn up a laundry list of expensive defects, you and the seller will have to negotiate who pays what. If your offer is contingent upon your approving inspection reports, you have no obligation to proceed with the purchase until you approve of the plan to remedy the defects.

Thinking Green When Making Repairs or Replacements

Did your inspector recommend you replace your water heater? Do you need to repair the roof? Now's a great time to think green!

Consider replacing a 40-gallon water tank with a tankless unit. Instead of keeping 40 gallons of water hot all the time, the heater turns on only when you need hot water.

Or, if your new house will need a new roof, now's an excellent time to look into getting photovoltaic (PV) panels or shingles, which generate solar power. The best time to install a PV system is when you're replacing or repairing the roof.

Coauthor Ira Serkes says, "I installed a 24-panel PV system and now generate almost all the power we use up. I also installed two on-demand hot water heater units, which have greatly reduced our gas usage."

Ask for a Home Warranty

Several companies sell home repair warranty contracts. Typically, these service contracts cover the heating, air conditioning, plumbing, and electrical systems, as well as the water heater and built-in kitchen and laundry appliances. For an extra charge, the policy can also cover pools, spas, and even roofs.

A home warranty should not be confused with insurance. Under standard home warranties, if one of these systems fails during the warranty period (usually one year), the warranty company sends out a repairperson to fix or replace the item. You'll have to pay a fee of around $50 per visit, depending upon the particular policy. In addition, there may be a modest deductible.

> ⓘ **CAUTION**
>
> **Buying a newly built home?** It will normally come with a warranty between you and the builder, or purchased by the builder.

A number of sellers voluntarily include a year's service contract as part of the price of the house. If the seller doesn't offer you one, it doesn't hurt to ask. Depending on the size and age of the house, a home warranty contract might cost $300–$900. A seller may see this as a bargain if it clinches the sale.

Sometimes a buyer's real estate agent will provide a buyer with a home warranty—again, as incentive for the deal to close. Most houses sold in California come with a home warranty.

If no one offers you a warranty, you can buy one yourself (but must do so now, as part of your purchase transaction). The warranty usually begins at the close of escrow.

Here are some keys to finding a good home warranty:

- Be sure the contract covers preexisting conditions that were not known to the seller or discovered in an inspection.

- Be sure you're aware of all restrictions and dollar limits of coverage. For example, while a home warranty might cover the cost of repairing a burst pipe, secondary damage to furniture or carpeting typically won't be covered. You'll also be expected to perform various types of regular maintenance.

- Find out how disputes are handled and whether the warranty requires mediation or arbitration.

- If an appliance or system is still covered by its own warranty, don't bother including it in the home warranty unless the warranty that came with the appliance or system will expire shortly. Instead, ask for a fee reduction.

TIP

Don't worry—filing home warranty claims won't raise the price or availability of your homeowners' insurance coverage. Home warranty contracts are a different animal from regular homeowners' insurance. The offering companies don't even communicate with one another. And since home warranty claims don't tend to run into high dollar figures, the industry isn't paranoid about the number of claims you file per year—the typical amount per customer is two.

RESOURCE

Home warranties. The California Department of Insurance licenses home warranty firms and can provide information on the current status of a particular company's license. Check its website at www.insurance.ca.gov.

For a discussion of developers' warranties on new homes, see Chapter 7.

Legal Ownership: How to Take Title

One Unmarried Person...326

Two or More Unmarried People...326

    Joint Tenancy...327

    Tenancy in Common 330

Couple or Domestic Partners Owning Together..331

    Community Property With Right of Survivorship...331

    Joint Tenancy...334

    Tenants in Common 334

Married Person Owning Alone 335

Partnership...336

Avoiding Having the Property Go Through Probate 339

efore escrow closes on your new house, you'll need to choose how to take "title" (documented legal ownership). Title is evidenced by a deed recorded at the county recorder's office. The deed contains a description of the property and includes the name(s) of the seller(s) and buyer(s).

SKIP AHEAD

Owned a house before? If so, you may be familiar with your options and already know how you want to take title, and you can skip this chapter. If you're a first-time homeowner or new to California and its community property ownership system, however, read on carefully.

One Unmarried Person

If you're single, you simply take title in your own name. The title company may add "an unmarried man" or "an unmarried woman" to the deed. This isn't legally required, but helps dispel any later questions about whether there's a spouse out there with an ownership interest in the house.

The name to put on the deed is the one that appears on your checks, driver's license, passport, and other similar documents. This need not be your birth name. If you use more than one name, list the name you most commonly use for business purposes first, followed by A.K.A. ("also known as") and the other name.

Two or More Unmarried People

Unmarried people who purchase a house together may take title in one of four ways:

- joint tenancy
- tenancy in common
- partnership, or
- if you've registered as domestic partners, as community property.

The overwhelming majority of unmarried couples or groups own property in joint tenancy or tenancy in common. Partnership is typically appropriate only if you already own a business together and purchase the house as a business asset, or if you buy the house as a business investment to fix up for resale.

Joint Tenancy

If you take title to real property as joint tenants, all buyers will share property ownership equally and have the right to use the entire property. The key feature of joint tenancy is "the right of survivorship." When one joint tenant dies, his or her share automatically goes to the survivor(s), even if the deceased attempted to leave a portion of the house to someone else by will or living trust.

The right of survivorship lets the survivor take the property right after the other's death, without the expense and trouble of probate. Property left in a will must go through formal probate court before being transferred to the new owner (although there is a simplified procedure for property left to a spouse). If, however, you're the property's primary owner and just adding someone's name to the title to avoid probate, consider using a living trust instead; it allows you to change your mind later. See "Placing the Property in a Living Trust," below.

While the joint tenants are alive, any owner can end the joint tenancy by selling his or her share of the property, or by deeding it to him- or herself in tenancy in common. (Civil Code § 683.2.) This ends the joint tenancy and with it, the automatic right of survivorship.

Joint tenancy isn't a good choice for all unmarried couples or groups. First, it necessitates equal ownership shares, so if people want to own the house in unequal shares, joint tenancy won't work. Second, contrary to popular belief, joint tenancy won't necessarily protect a surviving owner from state tax authorities coming to reappraise the house's value after one owner dies. Although married couples and registered domestic partners are exempt from this reappraisal, unmarried couples are not. It's most appropriate for people in intimate, long-term relationships who wish to provide for each other after one dies.

Forms of Real Property Co-Ownership

	Tenancy in Common	Joint Tenancy	Partnership
Creation	Deed must transfer property to two or more persons "as tenants in common" or without specifying how title is to be held.	Deed must transfer property to two or more persons "as joint tenants" or "with right of survivorship."	Deed must transfer property to the name of the partnership, or partnership funds must be used to buy it.
Shares of co-owners	Shares may be unequal. (This is specified on the deed.)	All joint tenants must own equal shares.	Shares determined by partnership agreement or Uniform Partnership Act.
Survivorship	On co-owner's death, interest passes to heirs under intestate succession law or beneficiaries under will or living trust.	Deceased joint tenant's share automatically goes to surviving joint tenants.	Interests usually go to partner's heir or beneficiaries, but partnership agreement may limit this.
Probate	Interest left by will is subject to probate. Simplified procedure available if left to spouse or domestic partner.	No probate is necessary to transfer title to surviving joint tenants.	Interest left by will is subject to probate.
Termination	Any co-owner may transfer his or her interest or get partition order from court. Co-owners can change the form of ownership by signing a new deed.	Joint tenant may transfer interest to him- or herself or another as tenants in common, or may get partition order from court.	Transfer governed by partnership agreement or Uniform Partnership Act.

Forms of Real Property Co-Ownership (continued)

	Community Property	Community Property With Right of Survivorship
Creation	Deed must transfer property to a married couple or to registered domestic partners "as community property."	Deed must transfer property to married couple or to registered domestic partners as "community property with right of survivorship."
Shares of co-owners	Each spouse or domestic partner owns half.	Each spouse or domestic partner owns half.
Survivorship	Spouse or domestic partner can leave his or her half to anyone; if nothing to the contrary, goes to survivor.	When one spouse or domestic partner dies, survivor automatically owns entire property.
Probate	Simplified probate procedure is available to transfer title to survivor.	No probate is necessary to transfer title to survivor.
Termination	Both spouses or domestic partners must agree.	Both spouses or domestic partners must agree.

> ## Joint Tenants: What Your Deed Should Say
>
> If you want to take title as joint tenants, the deed should specify that you hold title as joint tenants with right of survivorship. You need not use a form with "Joint Tenancy Deed" printed on it, though it's fine if you do. A "Grant Deed" or a "Quitclaim Deed" will also form a legal joint tenancy as long as the proper legal language is used.

Tenancy in Common

Tenancy in common (TIC) is the appropriate way for many unmarried co-owners to take title to property, because co-owners need not own equal shares. For example, one person could own 70% of the property and the other person own 30%. If ownership is to be unequal, it's best to write a separate contract specifying each person's ownership percentage and what happens if one person wants to sell or dies.

Two Nolo books—*Living Together: A Legal Guide for Unmarried Couples,* by Ralph Warner, Toni Ihara, and Frederick Hertz, and *A Legal Guide for Lesbian & Gay Couples,* by Denis Clifford, Frederick Hertz, and Emily Doskow—contain tenancy in common (and joint tenancy) contracts as well as lots of other useful information for unmarried couples buying together. Regardless of the percentages, however, each person owns an undivided portion of the entire house, not a particular part of it.

Tenancy in common has no right of survivorship—when a tenant in common dies, his or her share passes to the person named in a will or living trust, or by intestate succession (the laws that govern who gets your property if you fail to specify whom you want to receive it). If you're doing an equity share (described in Chapter 3), you must, unless there is some compelling reason against it, hold title as tenants in common.

If you wish to provide for the survivor without going through probate when the first partner dies, you can hold property as tenants in common and each put your share into a revocable living trust. Simply name each other as beneficiary to receive the owner's share on the owner's death.

If you change your mind and decide not to leave your co-owner your share, change the trust beneficiary of the living trust.

Tenants in Common: What Your Deed Should Say

In California, a transfer of real property to two or more persons automatically creates a tenancy in common unless the deed says otherwise. No special words are necessary.

Couple or Domestic Partners Owning Together

Married persons (opposite sex or same sex) and registered domestic partners (RDPs) who wish to co-own may take title as joint tenants, tenants in common, or as community property with right of survivorship. The last one is the choice we recommend for most married couples and RDPs.

Community Property With Right of Survivorship

Taking title as community property with right of survivorship offers two advantages:

- avoiding formal probate when a spouse or partner dies, and
- easy qualification for a federal income tax break (for married couples only, not RDPs).

CAUTION

If you don't want to leave the property to your spouse or registered domestic partner, hold title a different way. If you and your spouse or partner own the property as "community property with right of survivorship," at your death your spouse or partner will inherit your half—even if your will contains instructions to the contrary. If you want the other advantages of community property without the automatic right of survivorship, you can hold title as plain "community property." Simply leave the words "with right of survivorship" off the deed. The deceased person's half of the property will then go to whoever is named in the will.

How Community Property Avoids Probate

When one spouse or partner dies, property held as community property with right of survivorship goes directly to the surviving person without formal probate. A surviving spouse or partner who inherits needs only to record a simple document with the county recorder. This can be done without a lawyer; the survivor avoids not only lengthy delays in transferring the property (and title), but also costly probate fees.

RESOURCE
The petition and instructions for completing and filing an affidavit with the probate court are included in *How to Probate an Estate in California,* by Julia Nissley (Nolo).

Tax Planning

Normally, if someone sells a house, taxable profits are determined by adding the price originally paid for the house to the cost of capital improvements, and then subtracting this total from the amount the house sells for less the costs of sale.

When title is held by a married couple as community property with right of survivorship, a surviving spouse who inherits the property automatically qualifies for a significant tax advantage. (One that's more difficult to achieve if the same property is held in tenancy in common or joint tenancy.) The cost basis of the entire property—the cost of the house and improvements—increases ("steps up") to the property's value at the deceased person's death.

Because the higher the cost basis is, the lower the taxable profit will be, a stepped-up basis can significantly reduce your overall tax liability if one spouse dies. If the property isn't community property, the basis of the survivor's share stays the same. Only the half inherited from the deceased spouse gets a stepped-up basis.

> ## Community Property With Right of Survivorship: What Your Deed Should Say
>
> For a married couple and registered domestic partners, the deed need simply say, "Fred Parks hereby grants to Mabel Rivera and Albert Riviera, [*either* "spouses" or "registered domestic partners"] as community property with right of survivorship, [*the legal description of the property*]."

EXAMPLE: Carmen and Al brought a house in 1976. In tax lingo, what Carmen and Al originally paid for the house ($60,000), plus the cost of improvements ($40,000), is their "adjusted cost basis" in the property ($100,000). If they sell for $850,000, their taxable profit would be $750,000: the selling price less the cost basis.

If, instead, Carmen dies, leaving everything to Al, and they owned their house as tenants in common, the cost basis on Carmen's half of the property would increase from $50,000 (half of the $100,000 adjusted cost basis) to $425,000 (half of the $850,000 value at the time of her death). The basis on Al's half remains $50,000; as owner of the entire property, his total cost basis becomes $475,000. If Al later sells the house for $975,000, his taxable profit will be $500,000.

But if Carmen and Al had taken title to the house as community property, Al would qualify for a 100% stepped-up federal cost basis, not just on the half of the house belonging to Carmen. Now, if Al sold the property for $975,000, he'd have no taxable profit from the sale, because his gain is less than $250,000.

It's possible to argue, even if you didn't hold title as community property, that the property was in fact community property, held in joint tenancy or tenancy in common "for convenience." But there are no drawbacks to holding title as community property, and you can save yourselves an argument with the IRS.

Joint Tenancy

What about holding co-owned property in joint tenancy? Some spouses need to do this, for example, because their bank or savings and loan insists on it, for separate reasons. Other than this type of situation, however, there is very little reason for a married couple to choose a joint tenancy. Community property with right of survivorship offers the same advantages and more.

What about qualifying for a stepped-up tax basis? Do you lose this big advantage if you hold title in joint tenancy? Not necessarily. If you want to put your co-owned property in joint tenancy and qualify for a stepped-up cost basis, too, you simply need to be able to convincingly document to the IRS that the property is community property. Some experts recommend that you place the words "community property held in joint tenancy" on the deed. Before taking property in joint tenancy, read the section above on joint tenancy for unmarried people.

Separate Versus Community Property

Separate property is property acquired by one spouse or registered domestic partner prior to marriage or registration, after permanent separation, or during marriage or registered partnership by gift or inheritance. If separate property is sold, and other property is bought with the proceeds, it, too, is separate property.

Community property is all money earned or otherwise acquired by either spouse or partner during the marriage or registered partnership (except for rents, dividends, interest, and the like earned on separate property). A spouse or partner can turn his or her separate property into community property by stating that intention in writing.

Tenants in Common

While married couples rarely hold property as tenants in common, it is occasionally done. If, for example, the house was bought with the separate property of the husband and the separate property of the wife, and they want to keep it in separate shares, tenancy in common makes sense.

Tenancy in common lets spouses own the property in unequal shares. The specific shares, however, must be identified in writing, and the document should be recorded with the county recorder. Otherwise, property held in tenancy in common is presumed to be community property if you die or divorce.

Marital Property Agreement #1, below, is a sample agreement for spouses who hold unequal shares of their house as tenants in common. This is a tricky area of law; have a real estate lawyer look at any agreement you draft.

Married Person Owning Alone

If a married person wants to own a house separately, title should be in that person's name alone, and the couple should sign and record (with the deed) an agreement declaring their intention that one spouse owns the house as separate property. Otherwise, if the couple divorces and disagrees about ownership, a court will characterize the house as community or separate property depending on what funds (community or separate) paid for it, not whose name is on the deed. Because most couples mix and spend separate and community funds without regard to type, what property was used to pay the mortgage, insurance, improvements, and taxes won't always be clear.

CAUTION

A house that starts out as separate property may easily become a mix of separate and community. For example, if Jeff and Maida, a married couple, buy a house using Jeff's premarital earnings for the down payment and then use income earned during marriage for the insurance, taxes, mortgage payments, and improvements, everything but the down payment is community property, no matter what the deed says. Jeff and Maida can change this only by signing a written agreement.

To put your understanding in writing, use an agreement like Marital Property Agreement #2, below.

> ⓘ **CAUTION**
>
> **Be careful if one spouse gives up property rights.** If you or your spouse or partner gives up valuable property rights in the agreement, a court might later conclude that that person was unduly influenced by the other. The court could throw out the whole agreement. To be safe, consult a lawyer—who may recommend that you each see separate lawyers.

Partnership

Partnership may be appropriate for people already in a business together who purchase a house as a business asset, or people buying a house purely as an investment to fix up and resell.

Property acquired with partnership funds is presumed to belong to the partnership, absent an agreement to the contrary. What the partners can do with the property once it's transferred to the partnership is governed either by their partnership agreement or, if they have no agreement, the Uniform Partnership Act. (Corp. Code §§ 16100 and following.)

Partnership: What Your Deed Should Say

When a partnership buys a house, the deed states the business name used by the partnership, or the partners' names themselves, such as, "Fred Parks hereby grants to the Stobert Partners, [*the legal description of the property*]."

Marital Property Agreement #1

Diane Holst and James Kelvin, wife and husband, agree as follows:

1. We purchased the house at 9347 24th Street, Laguna Niguel, California, using as a down payment Diane's separate property plus a small amount of community property.

2. We hold title to the house as tenants in common.

3. Diane agrees to pay mortgage payments and taxes from her separate property, with only a small amount of community property being used for improvements.

4. As a result, Diane owns 80% of the equity in the house, and James owns 20%.

5. We intend this document to rebut the presumption of Civil Code § 4800.2 that, at dissolution, property held in joint title is community property. We do not wish the property to be treated as community property if we dissolve our marriage.

Diane Holst   _9/30/17_
Diane Holst   Date

James Kelvin   _9/30/17_
James Kelvin   Date

State of California   }

County of _Orange_

On _September 30_, 20_17_ before me, _Nora Public, Notary Public_, personally appeared _Diane Holst_ and _James Kelvin_, personally known to me (or proved to me on the basis of satisfactory evidence) to be the persons whose names are subscribed to the within instrument and acknowledged to me that they executed the same in their authorized capacities, and that by their signatures on the instrument the persons, or the entity upon behalf of which the persons acted, executed the instrument.

WITNESS my hand and official seal.

Signature _Nora Public_

[SEAL]

Marital Property Agreement #2

We, Brian Morgan and Laura Stein, husband and wife, hereby agree that:

1. Brian Morgan holds title to a vacation cabin near Lake Tahoe, the address of which is 43566 Lake Tahoe Drive, Lake Tahoe, California, which he owned prior to our marriage as separate property.

2. Although the mortgage, maintenance, and improvements on the cabin have been, and will be, paid during our marriage with savings that are partially community property, we intend that Brian Morgan own the cabin as his separate property.

3. We make this agreement in light of the fact that Brian's earnings constitute a greater portion of our community savings, and that upon Brian's death, we both want the cabin to be inherited by Scott Morgan, Brian's son.

Brian Morgan	9/30/17
Brian Morgan	Date
Laura Stein	9/30/17
Laura Stein	Date

State of California

County of _Alameda_

On _September 30_, 20 _17_ before me, _Jon Dough, Notary Public_, personally appeared _Brian Morgan_ and _Laura Stein_, personally known to me (or proved to me on the basis of satisfactory evidence) to be the persons whose names are subscribed to the within instrument and acknowledged to me that they executed the same in their authorized capacities, and that by their signatures on the instrument the persons, or the entity upon behalf of which the persons acted, executed the instrument.

WITNESS my hand and official seal.

Signature _Jon Dough_

[SEAL]

RESOURCE

Partnership law. Home buyers don't usually form a partnership to purchase a house, so we do not discuss partnership rules in detail here. For more information on partnership law and written partnership agreements, see *Form a Partnership: The Complete Legal Guide,* by Denis Clifford and Ralph Warner (Nolo), and Nolo's *Quicken Legal Business Pro* (software), to create a partnership agreement.

Avoiding Having the Property Go Through Probate

Now is a good time to think about keeping the house from going through probate at your death. Probate is a long and expensive court process where assets are distributed by the terms of a will or, if there is no will, by the laws of the state.

TIP

Already taking title as joint tenants or as community property with right of survivorship? If so, the house will pass to the surviving spouse without probate anyway. Realize, however, that this doesn't cover you against all eventualities. You might, for example, want to think about avoiding probate in case both spouses die at once, or if you're both at a stage in life where you're planning who will inherit the house when you're gone.

Fortunately, avoiding probate is relatively easy. One possibility is to set up a revocable living trust, name yourself as the trustee (which means you keep control over the property), and name a beneficiary to receive the property when you die. The beneficiary can be anyone: a spouse, boyfriend/girlfriend, child, charity, or whoever. You prepare, sign, and record a deed transferring ownership from yourself to yourself as trustee of the living trust. When you die, the beneficiary takes title, usually in a few weeks, without probate.

Because you name yourself as trustee of your own living trust, you keep control over the property while you're alive. You can easily change the title to the house, sell the house, or change the trust beneficiary.

To create a living trust, you must prepare and sign the trust document papers. They appoint you as trustee and set out the terms of the trust, including how you are to manage the property, that the trust is revocable, and when ownership should be transferred to the beneficiary. We recommend Nolo's *Online Living Trust*, which allows you to create a legally valid living trust tailored to your wishes and the laws of California.

Before putting your house into a trust, however, check with the lender to see if changing title triggers any due-on-sale provision (requiring full payment when ownership changes) of your mortgage.

If you decide to create a living trust but don't have it ready when you buy your house, take title in your name or, if you own the house with someone else, in your name and the other person's name. After you create the trust, transfer title to the house (if you're the sole owner), or your share of the house, to yourself as trustee of the trust. If you are married, you'll need your spouse's consent to transfer your share of community property.

How Transfer-on-Death (TODs) Deeds Can Help Avoid Probate

If you don't want to go to the expense and trouble of creating a living trust, there's a new, easy, and effective alternative called a transfer-on-death (TOD) deed or beneficiary deed. It's like a regular deed used to transfer real estate, with a crucial difference: It doesn't take effect until your death. You retain ownership, responsibility, and control over the property during your life. After your death, ownership transfers to the beneficiary you name.

Nolo offers an online "California Transfer-on-Death (Beneficiary) Deed" for purchase.

If Something Goes Wrong During Escrow

The Seller Backs Out..342

The Seller Refuses to Move Out..342

You Back Out 343

The Seller Dies 344

You Discover a Defect in the Property..344

The House Is Destroyed by Natural Disaster (Fire, Earthquake, Flood)........345

House-Hungry Martians Take Possession of the House 345

Finding a Lawyer 346

The likelihood of a major disaster befalling your purchase—such as the seller dying or an earthquake destroying the house—is slim. But it's possible that during escrow something will go wrong. A missing or incorrect loan document or last-minute title problems may simply delay closing a bit. More serious problems may jeopardize the whole deal. This chapter presents a brief overview of what may happen if your deal threatens to unravel.

If you and the seller both agree to rescind the contract, simply complete the Release of Real Estate Purchase Contract form in Chapter 18. If either of you wants to continue forward and close the deal, however, you'll need quick help from an experienced real estate lawyer.

The Seller Backs Out

Your purchase agreement probably gives both you and the seller a number of outs—that is, legal excuses to drop out of the deal, such as if the other person fails to comply with a time limit or another obligation. If the seller backs out for one of these justifiable excuses, there's no breach of contract, and you can't really complain, much less sue for damages. We're not going to get into the whole panoply of justifiable reasons for the seller to back out. Some of these might be highly technical and need lawyers and courts to sort them out.

But suppose a seller backs out of the deal after you have met or waived all contingencies simply because he or she doesn't want to sell the house or gets another offer that looks better. Isn't that a clear breach of contract? Yes, and your remedy is normally to mediate or arbitrate (an option in many standard real estate contracts) or sue, demanding that the seller sell you the house and pay you damages based on your out-of-pocket costs.

The Seller Refuses to Move Out

In rare circumstances, the seller may refuse to move out, even though the house is legally yours. This is a particular problem in areas with rent or eviction controls. To force a "holdover" seller from your property, you must follow the same procedure as a landlord uses to evict a tenant—and file an unlawful detainer lawsuit in superior court. You can do this even if your purchase contract includes a mediation or arbitration clause, so long as unlawful detainers are listed as an exception to your dispute clause. Hire an attorney or see *The California Landlord's Law Book: Evictions,* by David Brown (Nolo), for step-by-step instructions and forms.

CAUTION

If the seller has already moved out, keep an eye on the property. An obviously empty house can be a target for thieves and vandals. Now might be a good time to start getting to know your neighbors—ask them to watch for any suspicious activity. If you can, drive by the house regularly. Though chances are you won't catch a crime in progress, you might prevent one. You'll be making your presence felt and can deal with any obvious signs of your absence—such as a pizza flyer on the front door that would otherwise stay there for days.

You Back Out

If you refuse to go through with the deal without a good reason, the seller can pursue mediation, arbitration, or a lawsuit, requesting you pay damages. Damages aren't always easy to determine, however, because the seller has a duty to try to limit (mitigate, in legalese) losses by selling the house to someone else. To avoid arguing over the amount of the loss, most house purchase contracts provide a specific dollar figure (liquidated damages) for the seller's maximum damages if you breach the contract.

A liquidated damages clause means that the maximum amount the seller is entitled to is the stated amount. Disputes are often settled by the buyer and seller agreeing to allow the seller to keep part, but not all, of the deposit. Canny buyers know that sellers who are under pressure to find another buyer and transfer clear title want to get a deal-gone-bad behind them and are therefore often willing to compromise on the amount of the deposit they get to keep.

The Seller Dies

Technically, a contract to buy a house is enforceable even if the seller dies, because a deceased person's estate is responsible for fulfilling that person's lawful obligations. But in reality, the title insurance and/or escrow company will put on the brakes and call in their attorneys if the seller dies.

The executor of the seller's estate, and possibly the seller's inheritors, may want to get out of the deal. This could be a blessing in disguise, because after a seller dies, completing a house purchase transaction often becomes more complicated and time-consuming than when the seller was alive, especially if the house is part of an estate that must be probated. If the seller's inheritors do want out, insist that they reimburse you for any expenses you've thus far incurred.

If you and the inheritors want to proceed, be patient and sensitive. Try to determine whether the sale is likely to go through without difficulty. (Talking to an estate planning lawyer should help.) If settling the estate will be simple, the delay with the sale will probably be short. If settling the estate will be more complicated (for instance, the estate must be probated and 17 people claim the seller owed them money), consider discussing with the lawyer the best way to get out of the deal so that you can look for another house.

You Discover a Defect in the Property

If you feel that a seller knew about a defect—such as a basement that floods in a heavy rain—before the sale and failed to disclose it, contact the seller and the seller's broker and ask for money to correct the problem. If they turn down your request, and you can document that the defect was longstanding and should have been known to the seller, you have a good chance of going to court and recovering damages.

You may sue both the seller and his or her broker in small claims court (up to $10,000). *Everybody's Guide to Small Claims Court in California*, by Ralph Warner (Nolo), shows how. If more money is involved or the situation is complicated, you'll need to obtain legal advice.

As long as the defect is disclosed, however, there is usually no legal liability. If the disclosure doesn't happen until late in escrow, however, you (the buyer) may have the right to get out of the deal or to be compensated. You may need to sue the seller or the title insurance company, depending on who was at fault. Again, you'll need legal advice for this type of situation.

The House Is Destroyed by Natural Disaster (Fire, Earthquake, Flood)

Destruction of the house before the closing is handled as follows: Only when you have either physical possession of, or legal title to, the property, are you responsible for its physical condition and insurance. Otherwise, the seller is responsible. Thus, the seller should make sure to have a homeowners' policy in force until the close of escrow, at which moment your policy goes into effect.

If, for example, the house is flooded three days before escrow closes, the seller can pay for the repairs and deliver the property in the condition it was in before the flood. If you want out of the deal, however, simply refuse to grant an extension to the seller to make the repairs.

House-Hungry Martians Take Possession of the House

While we don't expect your deal to be threatened by extraterrestrials, we include this heading to remind you that in this weird and wacky world of ours, all sorts of unexpected events can frustrate even the best plans. If you suddenly find your house purchase threatened from a totally unexpected angle (for example, the state announces that construction of a new freeway running through the house's kitchen will begin in a month), see an experienced real estate lawyer pronto.

Finding a Lawyer

This chapter points out a few instances when an attorney's advice or services may be useful. The best way to find a lawyer who specializes in real estate law is through a trusted person who has had a satisfactory experience with one. Your agent may have some suggestions (unless, of course, your legal problem involves your agent). Also check out Nolo's online "Lawyer's Directory," where you can view extensive biographies of real estate lawyers in your area. Go to www.nolo.com/lawyers.

Once you get a good referral, call the law offices that have been recommended and state your problem. Find out the hourly fee and cost of an initial visit. Most lawyers charge $200 to $450 an hour. If you feel the lawyer is qualified to handle your problem, make an appointment to discuss your situation.

Here are some things to look for in your first meeting:

- Will the lawyer answer all your questions about his or her fees and experience in real estate matters and your particular legal problem? Stay away from lawyers who make you feel uncomfortable.

- Is the lawyer willing (after the start of your lawyer/client relationship) to answer your specific questions over the phone and charge you only for the brief amount of time the conversation lasted? If the lawyer won't give you any advice over the phone despite your invitation to bill you for it, find someone else.

- Does the lawyer represent home sellers, too? Chances are that a lawyer who represents both buyers and sellers can advise you well on how to avoid many legal pitfalls of buying a house.

> **CAUTION**
>
> **Attorney's fees clauses.** If your purchase contract has an attorneys' fees provision, you are entitled to recover your attorney's fees if you win a lawsuit based on the terms of that agreement. There's no guarantee, however, that a judge will award attorneys' fees equal to your attorney's actual bill, or that you will ultimately be able to collect the money from the seller.

Getting Your Deposit Back

If the deal falls through, you and the seller should sign a Release of Real Estate Purchase Contract form (see Chapter 18 for a sample). If one of you refuses to sign within 30 days following a written demand to do so from the other, the person who refuses to sign may be liable to the other for attorneys' fees and damages of three times the amount deposited in escrow—no more than $1,000 and no less than $100. (Civil Code § 1057.3.)

True Story

Felicity and Melinda: Earthquake Jitters

We had contracts to buy one house and sell our existing one. The buyers of the house we were selling had the house inspected and signed off. Then a big earthquake hit. Our house suffered no damage, but the buyers wanted to pay less, claiming that the earthquake had generally lowered real estate values. After much haggling, we agreed to a small reduction in price, provided they increase their deposit to $4,000 and sign that it was nonrefundable.

Three weeks later, on the day the buyers got notice of their loan approval, they backed out.

The earthquake had scared them, and they changed their mind about living in California. Then they demanded that half of their nonrefundable deposit be refunded! A lawyer told us that going to binding arbitration or suing would be costly, risk clouding the title of the house, and prevent an easy sale to someone else. Nevertheless, we asked the lawyer to write a stiff letter demanding that we keep the full amount. As a result, the former buyers agreed to let us keep $3,000, which meant we ended up with $2,700 after our lawyer got his fee.

Welcome to California

Climate and Geography... 350

Natural Hazards 352

    Earthquake 352

    Fire 355

    Flood 355

    Drought 356

Pollution 357

    Water Pollution 357

    Toxic Waste 358

    Air Pollution 358

Nuclear Plants 360

Schools 360

Traffic 362

Crime 363

This appendix is intended primarily for house purchasers who are new to California, moving from one part of the state to another, or first-time purchasers. There are a number of unique aspects to life on the Pacific coast—and to California in particular.

RESOURCE

California online. We list many California-specific websites through-out this section (and the entire book) on everything from home listings to crime to earthquake hazards to schools. Be sure to see Appendix B, Real Estate Websites, for a complete list organized by topic.

Climate and Geography

Impressions of California are created by movie and television depictions of an endless summer. And why not? On New Year's Day, while you're snowbound in the East or Midwest, the Rose Bowl is being broadcast from Pasadena, where the temperature is invariably 80 degrees. You're forgiven for your initial view of California.

But reality, even California-style, tends to come without a suntan in January. If you doubt this, trade your sunglasses for reading glasses and look at a map of the United States. Notice how far California stretches from top to bottom—a state of such varied latitude just can't be uniformly warm and sunny year-round. Sure, you might tan in January in San Diego on a particularly nice day, but tanning is the last thing you'd do in Crescent City, near the Oregon border, which is as far north as Boston and gets significantly more wintertime precipitation.

The key to understanding California climate is in the word "variety." The state holds the U.S. records for highest and lowest summer tempera-tures and for greatest annual snowfall. Much of the San Francisco Bay Area (called "Northern" California, but really part of the middle coast) has a Mediterranean climate—temperate, dry summers and relatively mild, wet winters. Summers along the coast are kept cool by the high fog that rolls in at night—thus the remark attributed to Mark Twain,

"The coldest winter I ever spent was a summer in San Francisco." Twain could have found all the summer he ever wanted just a few miles inland, though, where 100 degree temperatures abound.

To the far north, the coast is practically a rain forest, where California's famous redwoods grow, and rainfall can exceed 100 inches a year. Inland, in the far north of the state, snow-capped Mount Shasta is often viewed as a symbol for the mountain regions of the state.

Most 14,000-foot peaks are in the Sierra Nevada mountain range, far to the south, and along the eastern side of the state. The Sierra not only is the source of much of the state's water, but also provides much of its power. Happily for all who love its spectacular natural beauty, it is within a reasonable drive of many of the state's population centers.

In Southern California, the climate is semiarid; Los Angeles has dry, pleasant winters and warm summers, which attract flocks of people. Southeastern California is a desert (the best-known city is Palm Springs), inhabited by cacti and retired actors. It's within a few hours' drive of most of the southern part of the state.

More locally still, the weather within one city's limits can change considerably from neighborhood to neighborhood: Summer in San Francisco's Sunset District, for instance, is far cooler and foggier than in the warmest neighborhood, the Mission, just a few miles to the east.

How close your house is to the coast is a big factor in determining the weather you'll be enjoying—or complaining about. Hills and valleys are also important: West-facing slopes generally get more rain and lower temperatures than east-facing ones. So, however sunny a weather picture a real estate broker paints for you, listen with a drop of skepticism. If you can, ask a local resident what the weather is like.

TIP

Wondering how sunny the house is? There's an app for that! Called "LightTrac," it will show, for any location and day of the year, sunrise, sunset, and sun position. Available at www.lighttracapp.com.

Natural Hazards

California still seems to be getting more than its share of natural disasters. The four major natural hazards you'll find in California are earthquakes, fires, floods, and droughts.

Earthquake

There have been some devastating earthquakes as well as many smaller ones and likely will continue to be in the next 50 years. And in a state where faults underlie the land like a capillary system and the most populated cities are on the coast, the area of highest fault activity, there are no areas where you are completely safe from earthquakes. (Take a look at the fault map below.) While the odds of a quake shaking your home are unfortunately significant, you can take steps to minimize the risk of severe damage.

How Safe Is the Site?

Surprisingly, proximity to a major fault is not the primary factor that affects how well a house will hold up during an earthquake, according to seismic experts. Instead, other geologic and geographic factors should be examined, as should the structure of the house itself:

- **Avoid houses on unstable hillsides.** An unstable hillside is not a good place to be if an earthquake hits, because of the potential for landslides. In the San Francisco Bay Area, for example, experts predict that a sizable quake on the Hayward fault (one of the state's most dangerous), which runs through the Oakland and Berkeley hills on the east side of San Francisco Bay, will result in more homes being damaged from landslides than from shaking. The danger of a slide depends on the soil condition—rock is preferable to unconsolidated dirt. Flat, solid ground is even better.

- **The worst place for a house to be built is on fill.** Artificial fill is common along many California bays and rivers including, most notably, the San Francisco Bay. Some newer types of fill are sturdier than older ones. In a strong quake with a lot of vigorous shaking, older fill and bay mud may have a tendency to lose cohesiveness and liquefy. A house built on fill won't necessarily sink, but it could tilt.

- **Don't buy a house downstream from a dam.** Some dams in California will fail (leak or even break) in a really strong earthquake. This can sweep a whole town away in minutes.

A geologist or soils engineer can evaluate the site and give you an opinion on its safety. Seismic maps may also help you evaluate the earthquake hazards of a particular area. (See "Resource: Earthquakes," below.)

How Safe Is the Structure?

Even more important than where a house is built is what it's made of. Wood frame houses are quite flexible and, if properly secured to their foundations, will shake but not break. Masonry houses are significantly less earthquake resistant than wood frame houses. An unreinforced brick house a few stories tall is considered extremely dangerous.

RESOURCE

Earthquakes. The California Seismic Safety Commission, which publishes *The Homeowner's Guide to Earthquake Safety*, can be reached at 916-263-5506, or www.seismic.ca.gov.

The California Department of Conservation, in particular the State Mining and Geology Board, publishes seismic hazard data and fault zone maps. They are at 916-322-1082 or www.conservation.ca.gov/cgs. Similar information may be available from your city or county planning department.

The California Governor's Office of Emergency Services (CalOES) provides local and regional earthquake maps and a wide variety of material on earthquake preparedness; contact 916-845-8510, or go to www.caloes.ca.gov.

Peace of Mind in Earthquake Country, by Peter Yanev (Chronicle Books), is the best book around on earthquake preparedness.

The Building Education Center is a nonprofit organization that offers all-day seminars and publications on earthquake retrofitting. It's in Berkeley, California, at 510-525-7610, or www.buildingeducator.com.

California Fault Map

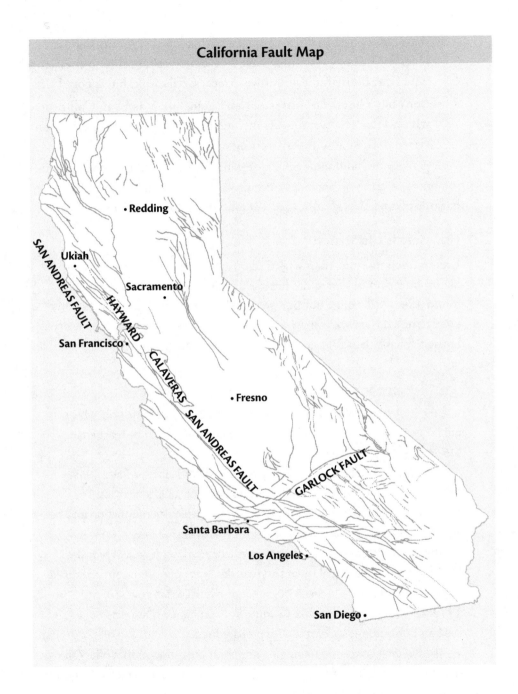

Fire

The fires that pose the greatest threat to houses are grass and brush fires, most common in dry Southern California, where large areas of parched brush and chaparral spark easily to flame. But these fires aren't limited to Southern California. Fires begin in dry canyons all over the state. And once started, they can spread incredibly quickly, destroying thousands of homes, especially when fanned by hot winds that blow from the interior valleys toward the coast.

If you are considering buying a house near a wild canyon or hill area, look at whether you can reduce the risk of fire by clearing a wide area around it. Pay attention to what the house is made of; shake roofs and wood shingles are far more dangerous than tile roofs and stucco. Some cities have outlawed wood shingles for new construction.

If the house you're considering is in an area that has been identified as a high fire hazard zone, or is even a replacement house for one that burnt, any recent building probably had to comply with state standards. The roof, for example, should meet safety specifications, and there will have to be a minimum vegetation clearance around the house itself. (If the landscaping looks sparse, don't count on filling it in.) Ask the sellers for details.

RESOURCE

Wildfires. For fire safety information, call your city's fire department or the nearest Office of Emergency Services. Many cities and counties in high-risk areas have implemented special programs to reduce fire danger and improve fire department response to wildfires.

Flood

It hardly seems fair, but the same hills and canyons that make fires so hard to control in the summer are prone to dangerous floods and mudslides in the winter. The steep canyons in the San Gabriel mountains above Los Angeles are notorious for the torrents of water, mud, and boulders that have demolished many expensive homes over the years.

Houses by the ocean are also vulnerable to flood damage. Every year, Pacific storms combine with normal high tides to produce huge waves that roll over the beaches. The Russian and Sacramento rivers in Northern California have flooded so often that locals know where the danger spots are. So, if you're considering buying a house near a stream or river, ask someone who has lived in the area for many years about floods. If you're told that the area flooded 40 years back or just last year, consider buying a bit higher up, because floods can recur at any time.

RESOURCE

Floods and landslides. The National Flood Insurance Program (NFIP) publishes hundreds of flood zone maps for California. For information on NFIP flood insurance policies, call 800-621-3362 or check the Federal Emergency Management Agency (FEMA) website at www.fema.gov/national-flood-insurance-program.

The U.S. Geological Survey Earth Sciences Information Center can supply information about landslide susceptibility in California; see earthquake.usgs.gov.

Drought

Droughts in California are regular occurrences. As this book went to print, nearly half of California was experiencing "extreme" drought conditions.

Rationing programs vary according to the severity of the drought. But they also vary depending on where you live—some water districts may be harder hit than others.

For many homeowners, watering the landscaping is one of the first things that must go in a drought. Fortunately, California's native plants are accustomed to dry conditions. You may well want to lose the lawn as soon as you move in, and replace it with drought-tolerant, native options—many of which flower beautifully and attract hummingbirds and butterflies. For more information and lists of appropriate plants, see www.californiagardens.com, or the book *Plants and Landscapes For Summer Dry Climates*, published by the East Bay Municipal Utility District, and available at bookstores and www.ebmud.com.

Pollution

Like any other state, California has its environmental problems. Some make a place unpleasant; others make it unhealthy, especially if you're particularly sensitive to environmental contaminants.

Water Pollution

Many towns and cities in California get drinking water good enough to bottle and sell. It comes straight from mountain river reservoirs. Other parts of the state are not so lucky. Southern California, Los Angeles included, must import most of its water, often from as far away as the Colorado River. The water is not as pure, and tastes bad, too.

"Where does it come from?" is the most important question to ask in determining the quality of a water supply. In general, water from aboveground sources is good water. Water pumped from ground aquifers can be just as good but can also be polluted with health-threatening substances, such as toxic waste from industrial sources or agricultural chemicals. In a number of California areas, water quality isn't too different from that in developing countries. People who can afford to do so buy a filtration system or drink bottled water.

The key to determining water quality is to find out the source for a particular town. Often, one part of a county—Santa Clara, for example —will have excellent water piped in from the mountains, while a few miles away the water will be wretched.

RESOURCE

Water quality and water pollution. Ask the local water district where the water comes from. If it's pumped from the ground or comes from a river, demand information on recent water quality tests.

The best source for candid information on all pollution is private environmental groups, such as Communities for a Better Environment (CBE) (www. cbecal.org). They do their own studies and can tell you if a known pollution problem exists in your neighborhood. CBE has offices in Oakland, 510-302-0430, Wilmington, 310-952-9097, and Huntington Park, 323-826-9771.

Ask your regional office of the State Water Resources Control Board about pollution (www.swrcb.ca.gov). Or check water.epa.gov/drink. These agencies, however, have limited information—they generally report only complaints received, unless a particular area has been tested recently. If so, ask for the results.

Toxic Waste

No one in his or her right mind would knowingly buy a house next door to a toxic waste dump. Unfortunately, the presence of toxic waste may not be obvious. Many toxic dumps are buried; other locations have yet to be disclosed. And some dumps may pose broader health threats if their contaminants leak into groundwater supplies.

Reports by the California Legislature have stated that most solid waste landfills in California leak. Almost one third of California's ground water has been chemically polluted, from this and other sources. Aquifers, which store water, are not naturally flushed. Once one becomes polluted, it stays that way. The situation is so bad that several communities in California whose aquifers became contaminated have been rendered uninhabitable.

RESOURCE

Toxic waste. The California Office of Environmental Protection, Department of Toxic Substance Control, 800-728-6942, maintains the Hazardous Waste and Substances Sites list of problem sites in California. (For more information, see www.dtsc.ca.gov.)

See also "Scorecard," a nonprofit website that provides information on toxic waste and environmental pollutants by community, at www.scorecard.org.

Air Pollution

The air quality in California varies about as much as the weather, as the two are closely related. Residents breathe easier near the coast, where the air circulates regularly, keeping the smog from ever getting really thick.

Unfortunately, if you enjoy hot weather, you'll have to learn to like polluted air. Anywhere the air sits still long enough to really warm up, pollution collects, particularly in the summer. Areas of the state east of the coastal range are blocked from the cleansing incursions of sea air. The Central Valley is often thick with smog, as are the San Gabriel and San Fernando valleys in Southern California. Ditto the Livermore Valley, east of San Francisco.

Los Angeles has some of the most polluted air in the United States. Despite efforts to convert to cleaner fuels, the situation is expected to worsen in coming years as more cars and industry fill the area. The Pacific winds blow much of L.A.'s smog inland to the rapidly developing Riverside and San Bernardino counties. L.A.'s coastal communities, such as Pacific Palisades, Santa Monica, Venice, and Palos Verdes, have relatively clean air, as well as the most expensive houses in the L.A. metropolitan area.

Many people consider air pollution more of a nuisance than a hazard, but recent studies show that airborne toxins pose a threat to anyone living near industry, including the "clean" computer industry. One survey linked exposure to air toxins with high cancer rates near Contra Costa County's petrochemical plants. If you're sensitive to air pollution, you'll want to move close to the coast or the Sierra foothills and avoid most areas in between, although there are still many rural parts of Northern and central California where the air is relatively clean.

RESOURCE

Air pollution. Communities for a Better Environment (www.cbecal.org) can tell you if a known pollution problem exists in your neighborhood. Also see www.scorecard.org.

A local or regional air quality district such as Bay Area Air Quality Management District (415-749-4900 or 800-HELP-AIR, www.baaqmd.gov) and www.sparetheair. org; South Coast Air Quality Management District (909-396-2000, www.aqmd.gov); or San Joaquin Valley Air Pollution Control District (209-557-6400 in Modesto, 559-230-6000 in Fresno, and 661-392-5500 in Bakersfield, www.valleyair.org) will tell you more about the air where you live. A city manager's or mayor's office should be able to refer you to a specific air quality district, or check the Air and Waste Management Association's website at www.awma.org for the nearest district.

Nuclear Plants

Atomically speaking, California is in better health than many other states. While four commercial nuclear power plants have been built, only one is operational—the Diablo Canyon plant in San Luis Obispo, 200 miles north of Los Angeles. Pacific Gas and Electric Company (PG&E) has announced plans to close the Diablo Canyon plant in 2025, ending atomic energy's more than half-century history in the state.

Many people believe it makes sense to avoid buying a house near any of the power plants, as serious safety questions have been raised about all four. These questions often center on whether the plants will withstand a strong earthquake, although operations problems (at the plant up and working) also arise.

If you decide to live near a nuclear plant, a house to the north or west will be safer from possible releases of radioactivity than a house to the south or east, as winds in California blow toward the south and southeast 80% of the time.

 RESOURCE
Nuclear plants. The Nuclear Information and Resource Service has helpful information at www.nirs.org.

Schools

California has many excellent public schools —the problem is finding them. The solution is to look yourself, not to simply ask your real estate agent, "How are the schools around here?"

Since California's Proposition 13 cut taxes, schools have had less money. Some schools are in worse shape than others, but all have had to cut back programs, usually in sports, art, music, languages, and drama. At some schools, where parent interest is high and financial resources available, parents pay to keep "nonessential" programs going.

To learn about average class size, course offerings, instructional practices, and available services, start by calling and visiting local schools and school districts. Obtain the *School Accountability Report Card* (or SARC), which each school must prepare annually. This report covers a range of important topics, including expenditures per student and types of services funded; class sizes and teaching loads; student achievement and progress toward meeting academic goals; and much more. A searchable list of SARCs is available at http://sarconline.org.

Arrange to visit schools you're considering. Observe the atmosphere by sitting in on classes and talking to some parents or teachers. And look for locally produced publications, such as a school newsletter or parent handbook.

The State Department of Education in Sacramento can also provide useful information. Up until 2013, student performance in California was measured by a series of standardized tests, known as "STAR" tests (Standardized Testing And Reporting). In July of 2013, the STAR program was replaced by the California Assessment of Student Performance and Progress (CAASPP) System. For information about these tests and how California's students are scoring, see the Department of Education's Standards and Assessments Office website: star.cde.ca.gov.

The Educational Demographics Unit provides much data for schools and districts, including enrollment figures, racial and ethnic information, language census data, and even dropout rates. Call them in Sacramento at 916-319-0800. The Department of Education's website is www.cde.ca.gov.

Check out local resources at public libraries. Look under "Schools" in the index of local newspapers at a public library for articles on how active the district PTA is and how well attended parent open houses are. Local civic groups, such as the League of Women Voters or PTA, often publish ratings of local schools. Ask a reference librarian for help finding these.

Contact EdSource, a nonprofit resource center that distributes impartial statewide information. EdSource publishes numerous impartial pamphlets discussing school budgets and finances, the ramifications of state education legislation, demographics, and bilingual education. If EdSource doesn't have what you need, they can help you find it. Contact them at 510-433-0421 or at www.edsource.org.

Additional online resources. Look in regional directories for a specific city or county, and then search the "schools" area for a particular school or district. Also, see "The School Report," www.homefair.com (look in the left sidebar). This contains useful information on and maps of school districts throughout California. Another website offers detailed reports for a fee: School Match, www.schoolmatch.com. Also see the summaries of schools provided at www.greatschools.org (a nonprofit organization).

Traffic

In California cities, traffic is a favorite topic of conversation; as more people move here, traffic gets worse. In the San Francisco Bay Area, people in the North Bay and East Bay commonly arise before dawn and drive hours to reach major urban centers. Los Angeles has seven of America's ten busiest freeways. Traffic typically crawls from morning to midnight.

Before you buy a house in California, figure out how you are going to get to work. Is driving reasonable? Will it still be in ten years?

Consider the availability of public transportation. As traffic continues to worsen, rapid transit may be the only alternative. And, of course, if you live near your job, you can avoid a commute altogether. If you work in the city, a house there may cost more, but this extra cost is increasingly likely to balance against your commuting (and sometimes parking) costs. This is a popular approach in L.A., where people are "rediscovering" downtown and the advantages of living close to work.

 RESOURCE

Transportation. Check the nearest office of the California Department of Transportation (Caltrans) for information on ride sharing and transportation planning, or call the state office. Call Caltrans at 916-654-2852, or check www.dot.ca. gov. Also, city traffic departments may be of some help.

Crime

Picking an area that is reasonably safe is a major concern when purchasing a house, especially if you have children. Understand that a substantial percentage of the crime that occurs in any neighborhood is committed by people who live there—often teenagers and others who feel alienated, bored, or angry. There is no way to escape this type of crime except by taking home security precautions and working with others as part of neighborhood groups designed to help local teenagers channel energy into healthier activities.

Still, it's sensible to be aware of a neighborhood's crime level when buying a house. Here are a few suggestions:

- Some cities have far less crime than others. The California Attorney General's Office publishes statewide statistics adjusted by population in *Crime in California*. It's available from the Criminal Justice Statistics Center in Sacramento at 916-227-3509 or online at oag. ca.gov/cjsc/pubs.

- You can check on crime types and frequency with the local police department. Although they may not keep statistics on a block-by-block basis, you may be able to get numbers for the general neighborhood you are considering. Also check out Sperling's Best Places at www.bestplaces.net, which offers crime-risk indices down to the zip code level.

- Neighborhoods with active, effective neighborhood watch groups, where residents understand the importance of keeping their eyes on the street and maintaining good communication among neighbors, are usually much safer than those that remain unorganized.

- If you are seriously worried about crime, you may want to live in a community secured with walls and guards. But check with residents before you assume security is tight—some of these communities have become targets for burglars who easily evade lax security systems or unguarded front gates.

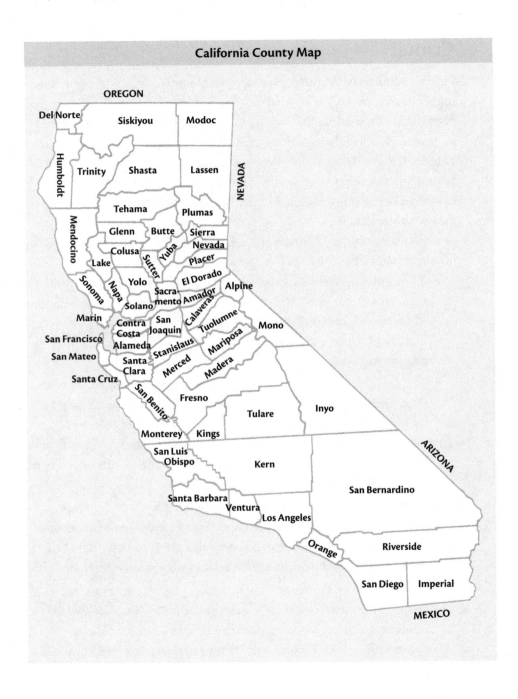

California County Map

- Upscale suburban areas next to very poor ones are almost always targets for robbery and burglary. So before you buy, drive 20 blocks in every direction. Look for graffiti, broken windows, bars on doors, or boarded-up buildings. If you find yourself rolling up your window in your car, you'll likely need a burglar alarm and maybe bars on the windows at home.

- In California cities, neighborhood safety changes block to block, driven by many factors, most of which are invisible to newcomers. Ask long-time local residents in what areas they would feel safe walking the dog at 10:00 p.m. Then confirm what you hear by talking to patrol cops. ●

Real Estate Websites

Top Real Estate Websites 368

How to Find a California Statute Online 375

There are hundreds of thousands of real-estate-related websites, with more added every day. That's a lot of surfing for home buyers! To make your online research easy, we've chosen the 100 or so websites of specific value to California home buyers. Our list is organized in alphabetical order by topic, with reference to specific chapters for more information. This appendix also includes some general advice on doing real estate searches online, including how to find a California statute without setting foot in a law library.

Be sure to check Nolo's website at www.nolo.com for real estate calculators and other useful information and resources.

Top Real Estate Websites

From air pollution to title insurance, here are useful websites for California homebuyers.

Air Pollution (App. A)
Air and Waste Management Association: www.awma.org

Scorecard: www.scorecard.org

Asbestos Hazards and Inspections (Ch. 19)
American Lung Association: www.lungusa.org

California Department of Industrial Relations, Division of Occupational Safety and Health (Cal/OSHA): www.dir.ca.gov

Community and Relocation Information (Ch. 6)
California Home Page: www.ca.gov

HomeFair: www.homefair.com

National Association of Realtors®: www.realtor.com

Sperling's Best Places: www.bestplaces.net

Comparable Sales Prices (Ch. 15)

National Association of Realtors: www.realtor.com

Trulia: www.trulia.com

Zillow: www.zillow.com

Contractors (Ch. 7 and 19)

Contractors State License Board: www.cslb.ca.gov

Credit Bureaus and Reports (Ch. 2)

Equifax: www.equifax.com

Experian: www.experian.com

TransUnion: www.transunion.com

Annual Credit Report service: www.annualcreditreport.com

Credit Counseling (Ch. 2)

National Foundation for Credit Counseling: www.nfcc.org

National Consumer Law Center: www.nclc.org

Credit Scores (Ch. 2)

Fair Isaac: www.myfico.com

Crime (App. A)

California Attorney General's Office, Criminal Justice Statistics Center:
   oag.ca.gov/cjsc/spereq

Earthquakes and Seismic Hazards (Ch. 19 and App. A)

Seismic Safety Commission: www.seismic.ca.gov

California Governor's Office of Emergency Services: www.caloes.ca.gov

California Department of Conservation, State Mining and Geology Board:
   www.conservation.ca.gov/smgb

Escrow Companies (Ch. 18)

California Department of Business Oversight: www.dbo.ca.gov

Floods (Ch. 19 and App. A)

Federal Emergency Management Agency (FEMA): www.fema.gov

U.S. Geological Survey: www.usgs.gov

Foreclosures (Ch. 3)

www.realtytrac.com

www.ushud.com

See Government Loans and websites of individual lenders.

Government Loans (Ch. 11)

Veterans Affairs (VA): www.benefits.va.gov/homeloans

Federal Housing Administration (FHA): www.hud.gov/buying

California Housing Finance Agency (CHFA): www.calhfa.ca.gov

CalVet: www.cdva.ca.gov

Homes for Sale (Ch. 6 and 7)

California Living Network: ca.realtor.com

California Living Network's Spanish-language equivalent, Sucasa:
www.sucasa.net

HomeBuilder: www.move.com

HomeFinder: www.homefinder.com

For Sale By Owner: www.forsalebyowner.com

Owners' Network: www.owners.com

Realtor.com: www.realtor.com

Trulia: www.trulia.com

Zillow: www.zillow.com

Also, see websites of local papers, individual real estate brokers, and mortgage lenders.

Home Inspections (Ch. 7 and 19)

American Society of Home Inspectors (ASHI): www.ashi.org

Contractors State License Board: www.cslb.ca.gov

California Real Estate Inspection Association (CREIA): www.creia.org

Homeowners' Associations (Ch. 7)

Community Associations Institute: www.caionline.org

Executive Council of Homeowners: http://echo-ca.org

Homeowners' Insurance (Ch. 18 and 19)

California Department of Insurance: www.insurance.ca.gov

Insurance News Network: www.insure.com

Housing Discrimination (Ch. 6)

California Department of Fair Employment and Housing: www.dfeh.ca.gov

Lead Hazards, Inspections, and Disclosures (Ch. 19)

National Lead Information Center: www.epa.gov/lead

Lenders (Complaints) (Ch. 13)

California Bureau of Real Estate: www.dre.ca.gov

California Dept. of Consumer Affairs: www.dca.ca.gov

Mold

California Dept. of Public Health; Indoor Air Quality Program: www.cal-iaq.org

E.P.A.: www.epa.gov/iaq

Mortgage and Financial Calculators (Ch. 2, 3, 8, 9, and 13)

Bankrate: www.bankrate.com

HomeFair: www.homefair.com

MortgageCalc: www.mortgagecalc.com

Nolo: www.nolo.com/legal-calculators

Also, see websites listed under "Mortgage Rates and Loans," and "Rent Versus Buy Decisions," below.

Mortgage Rates and Loans (Ch. 2, 8, 9, and 13)

E-Loan: www.eloan.com

Interest.com: www.interest.com

The Mortgage Superstore: www.superlender.net/home

QuickenMortgage: www.quickenloans.com

LendingTree: www.lendingtree.com

MSN Real Estate: www.msn.com/en-us/money/realestate

HSH Associates: www.hsh.com

Mortgage Marvel: www.mortgagemarvel.com

Mortgage-Net: www.mortgage-net.com

Also, search for individual lenders, and see "Homes for Sale," above.

Moving Companies (Ch. 3 and App. C)

American Moving and Storage Association: www.moving.org

California Public Utilities Commission: www.cpuc.ca.gov/puc

Moving.com: www.moving.com

New Homes (Ch. 7)

Homeowners Against Deficient Dwellings: www.hadd.com

Homeowners for Better Building: www.hobb.org

J.D. Power Consumer Center: www.jdpower.com

NewHomeGuide.Com: www.newhomeguide.com

Nuclear Plants (App. A)

Nuclear Information and Resource Service: www.nirs.org

Pest Control Inspections (Ch. 19)

California Structural Pest Control Board: www.pestboard.ca.gov

Radon (Ch. 19)

California Department of Public Health: www.cdph.ca.gov (search for "radon")

National Safety Council: www.nsc.org

Real Estate Agents and Brokers (Ch. 5 and 13)

California Association of Realtors: www.car.org

California Bureau of Real Estate: www.dre.ca.gov

HomeGain: www.homegain.com

Ira Serkes: www.berkeleyhomes.com

Council of Residential Specialists: http://crs.com

Real Estate Buyer's Agent Council: www.rebac.net

National Association of Realtors: www.realtor.com

RealtyTimes: www.realtytimes.com

Real Estate Law (Ch. 5)
California Association of Realtors: www.car.org

California Bureau of Real Estate: www.dre.ca.gov

Refinancing Calculators (Ch. 9)
HomeFair: www.homefair.com

E-Loan: www.eloan.com

Nolo: www.nolo.com/legal-calculators

Remodeling (Ch. 3)
ImproveNet: www.improvenet.com

National Association of the Remodeling Industry: www.nari.org

Building Education Center: www.buildingeducator.com

Remodeling Magazine: www.remodeling.hw.net

Rent Versus Buy Decisions (Ch. 3)
HomeFair: www.homefair.com

E-Loan: www.eloan.com

Also, see other websites listed under "Mortgage Rates and Loans," above.

Safe Drinking Water (App. A)
EPA Office of Water: www.epa.gov/aboutepa/about-office-water#ground

Communities for a Better Environment: www.cbecal.org

State Water Resources Control Board: www.swrcb.ca.gov

Schools (App. A)

Ed Source: www.edsource.org

The School Report: www.homefair.com/real-estate/school-reports

School Match: www.schoolmatch.com

Great Schools: www.greatschools.org

California State Department of Education: www.cde.ca.gov

   Also, see websites listed in "Community and Relocation Information," above.

Secondary Mortgage Market (Ch. 2 and 4)

Fannie Mae: www.fanniemae.com

Freddie Mac: www.freddiemac.com

Tax Information (Ch. 4, 8, and 14)

IRS: www.irs.gov

State Franchise Tax Board: www.ftb.ca.gov

Title Insurance (Ch. 18)

California Land Title Association (CLTA): www.clta.org

American Land Title Association (ALTA): www.alta.org

Toxic Waste (App. A)

California Office of Environmental Protection, Dept. of Toxic Substance
   Controls: www.dtsc.ca.gov

Scorecard: www.scorecard.org

Transportation (App. A)

California Department of Transportation: www.dot.ca.gov

Water Pollution (App. A)

Communities for a Better Environment: www.cbecal.org

State Water Resources Control Board: www.swrcb.ca.gov

How to Find a California Statute Online

Using this book is a good way to educate yourself about the laws that affect the home-buying process. In some cases, you may want to read the exact California statute that we refer to in the text. This is easy to do online. Go to Nolo's site at www.nolo.com/legal-research. Click "State Law Resources," then "California," then "California Code."

There you'll find a list of statutes, also called codes, grouped by subject matter (for example, the Civil Code, Business and Professions Code, and so on).

There are two ways to find statutes; both are free:

- If you know the subject matter of the code (for example, real estate agents), you can enter these "keywords" into the Text Search box and you'll get a list of codes that include this phrase.

- You can also "browse" the codes by clicking through to the Table of Contents for each Title. As you look down the list, you may see the statute that interests you.

The state's Legislative Counsel also provides current legislative information, at www.leginfo.ca.gov. You can read the text of any pending bill, the analyses prepared by assembly and senate members, voting records, and lists of sponsors. You can also ask to be notified via email any time there is legislative action on a bill that you want to follow.

RESOURCE

Legal research. For more information, see *Legal Research: How to Find & Understand the Law*, by Attorney Stephen Elias and the Editors of Nolo (Nolo). This book gives easy-to use, step-by-step instructions on finding legal information.

Planning Your Move

Tax-Deductible Moving Expenses and Costs of Sale 378

Moving Checklist: Two Weeks Before Moving 379

Things to Remember While Packing 380

Who Should Get Changes of Address 381

Things to Do After Moving In 382

n terms of stress, studies show that moving ranks right up there behind divorce and the death of a loved one. But, with intelligent planning, you can at least minimize this stress. The following will help you plan your move.

Tax-Deductible Moving Expenses and Costs of Sale

You may deduct job-related moving expenses—such as travel, transportation, and storage costs—from your gross income on your federal tax return if all of the following are true:

- Your move is within one year of starting your new job.
- The distance from your old home to your new job is at least 50 miles more than the distance from your old home to your old job.
- The distance from your new home to your new job is less than the distance from your old home to your new job; this test need not be met if your employer said moving was a condition of your employment, or if you'll spend less time or money on your new commute.
- You were fully employed for 39 weeks out of the year following the move; and, if you're self-employed, you also worked for 78 weeks out of the two years following the move.

You may also deduct certain costs of selling and/or buying a home such as points and other loan fees.

RESOURCE

Tax-deductible expenses. For information on tax-deductible moving expenses, see IRS Publication 521, *Moving Expenses*.

For tax rules that apply when you sell a house, see IRS Publication 523, *Selling Your Home.*

These publications and related forms are available at 800-829-1040 or www.irs.gov.

Moving Checklist: Two Weeks Before Moving

Not all items on this list will apply to you. If you're moving within the same town, you probably won't have to transfer your kids to a new school or have your car serviced for travel. Just focus on the applicable items.

- ☐ Check with your childrens' new school about what records and transcripts are needed, and arrange for their transfer.
- ☐ Close or transfer bank and safe deposit box accounts.
- ☐ Change your address for deliveries (newspaper, magazines—including alumni bulletins and nonprofit newsletters—as well as diapers, and laundry).
- ☐ Cancel utilities (gas, electric, cable, phone, water, garbage); transfer services (if possible) or arrange new services; request deposit refunds.
- ☐ Get recommendations for (or find in advance, especially if a medical condition needs regular attention) new doctors, dentist, and veterinarian; arrange for transfer of medical records.
- ☐ Get reference letters if you'll need to find a job.
- ☐ Cancel membership (and transfer membership, if relevant) in religious, civic, and athletic organizations.
- ☐ Have car serviced for travel.
- ☐ Buy travel insurance.
- ☐ Get maps.
- ☐ Line up storage facility.
- ☐ Arrange for moving pets, including a safe place for them to stay while the moving van is being loaded—a common time for animals to escape.
- ☐ Finalize arrangements with moving company. (Get bids and make preliminary arrangements weeks in advance.)
- ☐ Tell close friends and relatives your schedule and contact information.
- ☐ If your email account is with a local provider, sign up with a national service such as Gmail or Hotmail.

RESOURCE

Moving companies. It's worth doing careful research before choosing a moving company. Complaints about them are skyrocketing. Customers report long delays, broken goods, and even having their possessions held "hostage" until an extra, unexpected cash payment is handed over. Ask friends for referrals, and get bids from at least three companies before choosing—while being wary of any exceptionally low bids. Good sources of information include the American Moving and Storage Association (a trade group, at www.moving.org) and the Web-based company Moving.com (www.moving.com).

Things to Remember While Packing

☐ Inventory your possessions before packing them, in case things get lost in the move. Take photos of the more valuable items.

☐ Label boxes on top and side—your name, new city, room of house, contents.

☐ Assemble moving kit—hammer, screwdriver, pliers, tape, nails, tape measure, scissors, flashlight, cleansers, cleaning cloths, rubber gloves, garbage bags, lightbulbs, extension cords, step stool, mop, broom, pail, vacuum cleaner.

☐ Keep the basics handy—comfortable clothes, toiletries, towels, battery-powered alarm clock, disposable plates, cups and utensils, can opener, one pot, one pan, sponge, paper towels, toilet paper, plastic containers, toys for kids.

☐ Carry jewelry, extremely fragile items, currency, and important documents.

☐ Make other arrangements if moving company won't move antiques, art collections, crystal, other valuables, or plants.

TIP

How to pack a truck like a pro. If you're handling your own move, minimize damage to your possessions—and your spine—by first placing extra-long items such as mattresses and framed art works along the walls of the truck, then putting in the heaviest objects (always keeping appliances upright), then piling the lighter objects on top. Use some rope to tie the doors on your appliances and dressers, and rent some blanket-style furniture pads to protect surfaces.

Who Should Get Changes of Address

- ☐ Friends and relatives
- ☐ Subscriptions
- ☐ Government agencies you regularly deal with—VA, IRS, Social Security Administration, and so on
- ☐ Charge and credit accounts
- ☐ Installment debt—such as student loan or car loan
- ☐ Frequent flyer programs
- ☐ Brokers and mutual funds
- ☐ Insurance agent/companies
- ☐ Medical providers—if you'll be able to use them after moving
- ☐ Catalogs you want to keep receiving
- ☐ Arts and theatre groups you wish to continue receiving information from
- ☐ Charities you wish to continue donating to
- ☐ Post office. (If you're trying to get off catalog and other direct mailing lists, only have first-class mail forwarded. Give your new address to those catalog companies on whose lists you want to remain, and tell them not to trade or sell your name.)

Things to Do After Moving In

- ☐ Open bank accounts and safe deposit box account.
- ☐ Begin deliveries: newspaper, diapers, laundry.
- ☐ Register to vote.
- ☐ Change (or get new) driver's license.
- ☐ Change auto registration.
- ☐ Install new batteries in existing smoke and carbon monoxide detectors; buy fire extinguisher.
- ☐ Hold party for your house scouts and moving helpers, and take yourself out for a congratulatory dinner! ●

Using the Downloadable Forms

Editing RTFs 384

List of Forms 385

This book comes with interactive files that you can access online at:

www.nolo.com/back-of-book/BHCA.html

To use the files, your computer must have specific software programs installed. Here is a list of types of files provided by this book, as well as the software programs you'll need to access them:

- **RTF.** You can open, edit, print, and save these form files with most word processing programs such as Microsoft *Word*, Windows *WordPad*, and recent versions of *WordPerfect*.

- **MP3.** You can listen to these audio files using your computer's sound system. Most computers come with a media player that plays MP3 files, or you may have installed one on your own.

Editing RTFs

Refer to the book's instructions and sample agreements for help about what should go in each blank of a form. Here are some general instructions about editing RTF forms in your word processing program:

- **Underlines.** Underlines indicate where to enter information. After filling in the needed text, delete the underline. In most word processing programs you can do this by highlighting the underlined portion and typing CTRL-U.

- **Bracketed and italicized text.** This text indicates instructions. Be sure to remove all instructional text before you finalize your document.

Every word processing program uses different commands to open, format, save, and print documents, so refer to your software's help documents for help using your program. Nolo cannot provide technical support for questions about how to use your computer or your software.

> CAUTION
>
> **In accordance with U.S. copyright laws,** the forms provided by this book are for your personal use only.

List of Forms

Form Title	File Name
Ideal House Profile	IdealHouse.rtf
House Priorities Worksheet	PrioritiesWorksheet.rtf
House Comparison Worksheet	ComparisonWorksheet.rtf
Family Financial Statement	FinancialStatement.rtf
Directions for Completing the Family Financial Statement	FinancialStatementDirections.rtf

Index

A

Adjustable rate (ARM) mortgage
  assumability, 165
  defined, 148
  fixed rate mortgages vs., 162
  hybrid type, 148, 165–166
  indexes and margins, 162–163, 165
  interest costs, 159
  interest-only, 149
  interest rates, 148, 149, 162
  loan payments, 148–149, 162
  projected income increases and, 152
Adjustable rate (ARM) mortgage caps,
  163, 164
Adjustable rate (ARM) mortgage,
  choosing an
  assumability factor, 165
  cautions, 162
  good reasons for, 162
  guidelines for, 166
  projected time for ownership and,
  156
  questions to ask before, 166
  refinancing plans, 156, 162
Adjustable rate (ARM) mortgage
  terminology
  adjustment period, 164
  caps, 164
  fully indexed rate, 164
  index, 164
  life-of-the-loan cap, 164
  margin, 164
  overall cap, 164
  periodic cap, 164

Adjustment period, defined, 164
Advertisements
  classified ads, translating real estate
  terms in, 108
  for fixer-uppers, 48
Affordability
  basics of, 16, 18
  calculating, 24–26
  California Association of Realtors
  (CAR) on, 18
  Family Financial Statements to
  determine, 18–21
  moving for, 43
Affordability, buying strategies for
  auctions, 67–69
  cohousing or cooperative
  arrangements, 65–67
  condominiums, 63
  desirable houses in marginal areas,
  45–46
  equity sharing, 55–56
  fixer-uppers, 47–48
  foreclosures, 52–55
  investors, 57–58
  lease option, 60–63
  leveraging, 43
  marginal houses in desirable areas,
  44–45
  marginal houses in marginal areas,
  47
  nonresident equity sharing, 57–58
  probate sales, 49–51
  rent out part of the house, 58
  small houses with expansion
  potential, 48–49

structural problems, 51–52

tenant-in-common (TIC) interest, 64

town houses, 64

Affordability, components of

amount needed to borrow, 24

annual income ratio, 16

closing costs, 22

down payments, 16, 21–22

fixed monthly debt, 25

house-related expenses, 25

insurance and property taxes, 24

lender qualification, 25

monthly gross income needed, 25

monthly mortgage payment, 24, 26

mortgage interest rate, 23–24

reserve money, 22, 211

Airbnb, 60, 139

Air conditioning in new construction, 128

Air pollution, 358–359

American Arbitration Association (AAA), 237

American Land Title Association (ALTA) policy, 281

American Society of Home Inspectors (ASHI), 314, 315

Amortization chart, 26

Appraisal fees, 150, 193–194, 284

Appraisals, 77, 168, 171, 194

Appreciation, 63, 76

Artificial fill, earthquake damage and, 352–353

Asbestos hazards and inspections, 316, 368

Assessment bonds, 228

Assessments, property taxes and, 283

Assumability

ARM mortgages, 165

FHA loans, 165

fixed rate mortgages, 159

VA loans, 165

Assumption fees, 284

Attorneys, working with during escrow, 346

Attorneys' fees, 229, 237, 346–347

Auctions

affordablility option, 67–69

foreclosures, 53–54

probate sales, 49

B

Backup offers, 248, 252–253

Beneficiary deed, 340

Beneficiary statement, demand or request for, 258

Bidding

competing bids, counteroffers and, 248

on foreclosures, 53

initial bids, increasing, 248–249

preemptive bid strategy, 246

on probate sales, 49

the seller has received a higher bid, 248

the seller is waiting for other bids, 247

Bidding wars, 210–211, 242

Bond liens, 230

Buydowns, 125–126, 149, 150–151

Buyer's (cold) market, 214–215, 241

Buyer's agent, 85, 90–91, 101–102

Buying
  additional expenses post-, 211
  online resources, 370
  timing your purchase, 104, 115
  See also Dream home, finding your
Buying now, options to
  remodeling, 39–41
  renting, 36–38, 373
  save and wait, 42
Buying while owning
  between buying and selling, 197, 200–203
  bridge loans, obtaining, 202–203
  buying first vs. selling first, 196
  closings, delaying, 198
  down payments, raising, 197, 200, 202
  equity line of credit, obtaining, 202
  financing contingency, 200
  if you need more time to move, 198
  market conditions and, 197–200
  possession dates, 198
  real estate commissions, saving on, 200
  rent-backs, 198, 201–202
  renting out your old house, 202
  selling your house contingency, 198, 199
  wipe-out clauses, 199

C

California
  city, community, and neighborhood information, 115
  climate, 350–351
  county map, 364
  crime, 363, 365
  fault map, 354
  geography, 350–351
  house prices, 36–37
  nuclear plants, 360
  online resources, 350
  pollution in, 357–359
  schools in, 360–362
  statutes online, 375
  toxic waste, 358
  traffic, 362
California, natural hazards in
  drought, 356
  earthquakes and seismic, 306–307, 352–354, 369
  fire, 355
  floods, 133, 355–356, 370
  online resources, 356
California Bureau of Real Estate (CalBRE), 91
California Housing Finance Agency (CalHFA), 72, 172
California Land Title Association (CLTA) policy, 281
California Real Estate Inspection Association (CREIA), 314, 315
CalVet, 72
Capital gains tax, 203
Caps
  ARM, 163
  defined, 164
  life-of-the-loan cap, 163, 164
  overall cap, 164
  periodic cap, 163, 164
Carbon monoxide (CO) alarms, 302
Carbon Monoxide Poisoning Prevention Act, 302

Carpets in new construction, 128

Carrying costs, 16

Cash
  available for emergencies, 37, 75
  converting assets to, 27

Certificate of Reasonable Value
    (CRV), 168

Classified ads
  for fixer-uppers, 48
  translating real estate terms in, 108

Climate, California, 350–351

Closing (close of escrow)
  dates of, 228, 286–287
  defined, 258
  forms required to sign, 286–287
  possession at, 227, 235
  rental agreements post-, 227
  repairs required prior to, 264–265
  See also Escrow

Closing at a distance, 259

Closing costs
  affordability and, 22
  assumption fees, 284
  defined, 258
  escrow costs, 229, 261–262,
    284–285
  homeowners' insurance, 285
  interest on the loan, 285
  physical inspection reports, 284
  private mortgage insurance (PMI),
    285
  property taxes, 285
  purchase price relation to, 211, 261,
    284
  recording and filing fees, 285
  survey fees, 285
  tax service fee, 285

title search and title insurance, 285
  transfer tax, 285
  verifying ability to pay, 228

Closing statement, defined, 258

Cohousing arrangements, 65–67

Cold (buyer's) market, 214–215, 241

Commissions, saving on, 114, 200

Communities, intentional, 65

Community property
  creation of, 329
  probate, 329
  separate property vs., 334
  shares of co-owners, 329
  survivorship, 329
  termination, 329

Community property with right of
    survivorship
  creation of, 329
  deeds, 333
  probate, 329, 332
  shares of co-owners, 329
  survivorship, 329
  taking title, 331–333, 339
  tax planning, 332
  termination, 329

Comprehensive Loss Underwriting
    Exchange (CLUE), 217

Condition of property
  defects, paying for, 321
  disclosure laws, 290–302
  home warranties, 322–323
  things to check for, 302
  transfer disclosure statement,
    291–300
  utility and water bills, requesting,
    311
  See also Disclosures; Inspections

Condominiums
  affordablility option, 63
  buying considerations, 123
  CC&Rs, 134, 137–139
  earthquake insurance, 63
  homeowner's associations, 136
  homeowners' insurance, 274, 276
  town houses vs., 64
Confirmation of Real Estate Agency
  Relationships, 90
Consumer credit counseling, 32, 369
Contingencies
  counteroffers, 249
  defined, 226
  failure to meet, 268–270
  financing, 200, 249, 265
  inspections, 142, 262–265
  new construction, 142
  offers and, 222
  preliminary title approval, 280–281
  on receiving financing, 200
  releasing, 233, 267–268
  seller's responses to, 245
  selling your house, 198, 199
  time to meet, extending, 265–266
  wipe-out clauses, 268
Contingency clauses in purchase
  agreements
  appraisals, 234
  hazard insurance, 234
  home warranties, 234
  inspections, 233
  selling your house, 232
  time allowed for removing, 233
  title contingency, 233–234
Contingency Release form, 267–268

Contractors
  experienced, using to assess quality,
    122
  general contractor report, 230
  online resources, 369
Contractors State License Board
  (CSLB), 122
Contracts
  cancelling, 140, 263, 268–270
  lease option, 62
  legally binding, 208, 224
  new construction, 119
  requirements for, 208
  revoking, 301
  seller obligations, 208
  sex offender information in, 232
  shared equity contracts, 56
  time to closing, 256
  wipe-out clauses, 199
Contracts, steps post-signing
  escrow holder, finding and working
    with, 260–261
  homeowners' insurance, obtaining,
    271–274, 276–278
  open escrow, 256–257
  ordering title insurance, 261
  post-inspection tour, 282–283
  title insurance and title reports,
    279–281
Contract to Purchase Real Property
  form, 245
Convenient to shopping, interpreting
  ads featuring, 108
Cool market, 214
Cooperative housing, 65–67
Counter counteroffer, defined,
  223–224

Counteroffer form, 249–250
Counteroffers
  competing bids, 248
  contingencies, 249
  defined, 223
  escrow holders, 260
  financing provision, 249
  initial bid, increasing the, 248–249
  inspection provision, 249
  negotiating, 248, 250–251
  occupancy provision, 249
  price provision, 248–249
  revoking, 252
  walking away, 249
  wipe-out clauses, 249
Court-supervised probate sales, 50, 51
Covenants, conditions, and restrictions (CC&Rs)
  checking the, 138
  condominiums, 63, 134, 137–139
  insurance requirements, 274, 276
  obtaining copies of, 137
  on parking, 138
  rentals, 139
  resources, 139
  reviewing, 138
  variances, obtaining, 134
Cozy, interpreting ads featuring, 108
Credit advisory groups, 32
Credit bureaus, online resources, 369
Credit counseling, online resources, 32, 369
Credit rating
  checking, 29–30
  loan qualification, effect on, 17, 146
  online resources, 369
  rebuilding your, 31–33
Credit reports
  closing costs and loan fees, 284
  copies, obtaining, 17, 30–31
  cost of, 31, 285
  down payment relation to, 73
  errors in, 30–31
  online resources, 369
  for private loans, 180
Crime, 363, 365, 369
Customers, borrowing a down payment from, 82

D

Damages, liquidated, 343
Dams, earthquake damage and, 353
Deaths, disclosures of, 308–309
Debt
  affordability and, 25
  borrowing a down payment and, 80
  cancelled, as income, 32
  fixed monthly, calculating, 25
  paying off, 25, 27
  See also Financial profile
Debt-to-income ratio, 18, 25, 180–181
Deed of trust, 182
Deed preparation fee, 229
Deeds
  community property with right of survivorship, 333
  joint tenancy, 330
  partnership, 335–336
  recording costs, 261
  transfer-on-death (beneficiary) deed, 340

Demand for beneficiary statement, defined, 258

Desirable houses in marginal areas, affordability option, 45–46

Developers, choosing, 121–122

Disclosure Regarding Real Estate Agency Relationships, 90, 235

Disclosures
deaths, 308–309
earthquakes and seismic hazards, 306–307
environmental hazards, 307
FHA loans and, 301
foreclosures and, 53–54
gas transmission pipelines, 300
ghosts and hauntings, 309
hazardous liquid pipelines, 300
lead, 308
local requirements, 309–310
military ordnance, 309
natural hazards, 51, 303–306
probate sales and, 50
purchase agreement clauses, 237–238
sex offenders in proximity, 232

Disclosure statement
additional information, asking for, 298–299
examining the, 298–299
insurance claims, asking for, 299
natural hazards, 51, 303
problems, handling, 301–302
real estate transfer, 51, 291–300

Discrimination in housing, 109, 249, 250, 371

Dispute arbitration, 236–237

Dispute mediation, 236

Division of expenses, 228, 229–230

Documentary transfer tax, 229

Dogs, homeowner's insurance and, 272

Do-it-yourself home repair jobs, inspecting, 310–311

Domestic partners owning together, taking title, 331–333

Doors, new construction interior, 128

Down payment assistance (DAP) programs, 172, 173–174

Down payments
affordability factor, 16, 21–22
defined, 225
FHA loans, 77, 152, 170
investors/nonresident equity sharing, 57
large, reasons for making, 75–77
lender choice and, 152
low down payment loans, 72–73, 153, 173
mortgages, factors in choosing, 152–153
for multi unit buildings, 58–60
no down payment plans, 72
owner occupancy and, 123
PMI and, 73–75
raising between buying and selling, 197, 200, 202
recordkeeping to show source of funds, 28
self-employed borrowers, 29
VA loans, 169

Down payments, options for obtaining
borrowing from family and friends, 80, 197, 202

buying PMI, 153

equity, using for, 77

401(k) plans, 81

gifts, 29, 77–80

IRA withdrawals, 82

private lenders, 180

two mortgages, 153

Drainage defects in new construction, 141

Drapes in new construction, 128

Dream home, finding your

absolute no ways list, identifying, 8

hopes to have list, identifying, 7–8

House Comparison Worksheet, 11–12, 385

House Priorities Worksheet, 8–11, 116, 385

Ideal House Profile, 5–8, 385

must haves list, identifying, 7–8

tips on searching new places, 5

wrong house, compromising on the, 4

Dream homes

affordability gap, 4

staged homes vs., 10

Drinking water, safe, 357–358, 373

Driveways, choosing a building lot and, 132

Drought hazard, 356

Dual agent, 85, 90, 92

Duplexes, affordability option, 58–60

E

Earnest money deposit

defined, 225

liquidated damages provision, 236

See also Escrow deposit

Earthquake hazard, disclosing, 306–307

Earthquake insurance, 63, 273–274, 279, 320

Earthquake retrofitting, 317, 320

Earthquakes

causes of damage from, 352–353

fault map, 354

online resources, 353, 369

Electrical inspections, 316–317

Electrical outlets in new construction, 128

Electromagnetic radiation inspections, 317

Energy-efficiency audits, 311, 313

Energy efficient new construction, 128

Entryways, new construction, 128

Environmental hazards, disclosing, 307

Equity building, 67

Equity contracts, shared, 56

Equity sharing, affordablility option, 55–56

Escrow

cost of, 229, 261–262, 284–285

termination of, 270

See also Closing (close of escrow)

Escrow, problems during

buyer backs out, 343

defects in the property discovered, 344–345

deposit, return of, 343, 347

destruction by natural disaster, 345

disputes, 261

lawyers, working with, 346

seller backs out, 342

seller dies, 344
seller refuses to move out, 342–343
suing the seller, 344–345
the unexpected, 345
Escrow company
choosing an, 227
complaints against, filing, 287
escrow fees, 284
online resources, 369–370
Escrow credit, 264–265
Escrow deposit
liquidated damages provision, 236
post-contract step, 252
return of the, 268–271, 343, 347
Escrow holders
interpleaders by, 261
responsibilities of, 261, 280
Escrow terminology
close of escrow (closing), 258
closing costs, 258
closing statement, 258
demand or request for beneficiary
statement, 258
final title report (final), 258
funding the loan, 258
legal description (legal), 259
loan commitment, 259
opening escrow, 259
preliminary, prelim, pre, 259
taking title, 259
Estate tax, 79
Eviction
additional resources, 55, 343
protections, 231
of seller's post-closing, 343
of tenants post-closing, 55, 226
See also Occupancy

Extending Time to Meet
Contingencies, 266
Extension of Offer to Purchase Real
Property, 246

F

Family
borrowing from, 29, 80, 197, 202
gifts from, 29, 77–80
as house scouts, 111–112, 116
Family Financial Statement
accuracy in preparing, 21
assets and liabilities categories, 20
downloadable forms, 21, 385
income and expenses categories, 19
purpose of preparing, 21
Fannie Mae HomeReady Program,
72
Federal Home Loan Mortgage
Corporation (FHLMC) (Freddie
Mac), 147
Federal Housing Administration
(FHA) foreclosures, bidding on,
54
Federal Housing Administration
(FHA) loans
assumability, 165
disclosure requirements, 301, 308
down payments for, 77, 152, 170
fair market value appraisal
requirement, 171
for fixer-uppers, 171
gifts for down payment provision,
77
loan limits, 170
low down payment loans, 72

mortgage insurance requirement, 171

obtaining, requirements for, 171

online resources, 170, 171

physical condition approval, 171

processing time, 171

qualifying for, 170

For Your Protection, Get a Home Inspection form, 301

Federal Housing Administration (FHA) Rehabilitation Loan Program, 171

Federal National Mortgage Association (FNMA) (Fannie Mae), 147

FICO Mortgage Score, 17

Filing fee, 285

Final title report (final), defined, 258

Financial calculators online, 213, 371

Financial profile, improving your
borrow from friends or family, 29

convert assets to cash, 27

emphasize imminent income raises, 28

if you work for yourself, show a profit, 28–29

pay off debts, 25, 27

recordkeeping to show source of funds, 28

remove delinquencies, 31–32

satisfaction of judgements, 32

See also Credit rating

Financing
contingencies, 200, 249, 265

direct financing subsidies, 125–126

new construction, 124–126

offers, seller's response, 244

options, 147

See also Loans

Fire hazard resources, online, 355

Fire insurance, 230

Five percent down payment loans, 73

Fixed rate mortgages
advantages, 156

amortization chart, 26

assumability, 159

defined, 148

factors in choosing, 156–158

interest costs, 156, 159

interest rates, 148, 149, 162

loan payments, 148, 149, 156–157

monthly payments by interest rate, 157

refinancing, interest rates and, 157

short-term, prepaying vs., 158–159

Fixed rate mortgages, factors in choosing
assumability, 159

lower interest rates projected, 157

PMI premiums, 157

points-interest rate relationship, 158

refinancing plans, 156

time projected for ownership, 156

Fixer-uppers
affordability option, 44–45, 47–48

FHA loans for, 48, 171

how to find, 48

interpreting ads featuring, 108

Flipped houses, inspecting, 311

Flood hazard, 133, 355–356, 370

Flood insurance, 273–274

Floors, new construction, 128

Foreclosures
affordablility of, 52–54

bidding on, 53–54
by homeowner's associations, 135
clear title, obtaining, 54
disclosure requirements, 53–54
government agencies, 54
liens, checking for, 54
online resources, 52, 370
real estate-owned (REO), 53
short sales, 52–53
tenant rights, 54–55
Foreign Investment in Real Property
    Tax Act (FIRPTA), 262
For Your Protection, Get a Home
    Inspection form, 301
Foundations and foundation defects,
    128, 141, 317
401(k) plans, 81
Framing defects in new construction,
    141
Fraud
  auctions, 68
  by real estate salespeople, 91
  gifts vs. loans, 80
Friends
  borrowing from, 29, 80, 197, 202
  as house scouts, 111–112, 116
Fruit trees, interpreting ads featuring,
    108
Fuller, Kathy, 152
Fully indexed rate, defined, 164
Funding the loan, defined, 258
Furnishings, cost of, 211

G

Gas transmission pipelines, disclosure
    of, 300
General contractor report, 230

Gentrification, desirable houses in
    marginal areas, 46
Geography, California, 350–351
Geologic reports, 133
Ghosts and hauntings disclosures,
    309
Gift letter, 78–79
Gifts
  for down payments, 29, 77–80
  loans vs., 80
  for real estate agents/brokers, 102
  seasoned, 78–79
Gift taxes, 79
Government-assisted loans, 170–174,
    370
  See also Federal Housing
    Administration (FHA) loans;
    Veterans Affairs (VA) loans
Government housing programs, 125

H

Half-bath, interpreting ads featuring,
    108
Handyman special, interpreting ads
    featuring, 108
Hazardous liquid pipelines, disclosure
    of, 300
High-balance conforming loan
    limits, 148
Home-based businesses, 272
Home equity loans, 75
Homeowner's associations
  advantages, 136
  assessments, 138
  checking out, 138
  condominiums, 136

disputes, avoiding, 135
fees, 135, 138
finances, 137–139
foreclosure actions by, 135
insurance coverage, 138, 274, 276
legal trouble or litigation, 138
mismanaged, 136
new construction, 121, 135–137
online resources, 371
role of, 135
*Homeowner's Guide to Earthquake
Safety*, 307
Home ownership
buying first vs. selling first, 196
buy vs. rent decision, 38, 373
financial advantages, 37, 38, 75
maintenance requirements, 275
planning length of, mortgages and,
152, 153
prior to retirement, 76
timing your purchase, 104, 115
wrong house, compromising on the,
4
See also Dream home, finding your
Home warranties
asking for, 322–323
claims against, 324
financial responsibility for, 230
new construction, 143–144, 170,
323
online resources, 324
purchase agreement contingency,
234
VA loan requirement, 170
Hot (seller's) market
bidding wars, 210–211

buying a house when you already
own one, 198
defined, 213
determining a, 214–215
inspections prior to offer, 311
preemptive bid strategies, 246
House Comparison Worksheet,
11–12, 385
House hunting
the best time to look, 104
city, community, and neighborhood
information, 115
mapping, 105
MLS, taking advantage of the, 110
neighborhood canvass, 112
new construction, 106, 116
online resources, 105–106, 108,
112, 115
open houses, 109
organizing, 104–105
personal contacts, using, 111–112,
116
real estate ads, translating, 108
the seller and, 105, 110, 114
sellers' agents, contacting, 105
timing your purchase, 115
tips, 107
when you're new to an area,
114–115
where to look, 105
on your own, 105, 112, 114
See also Foreclosures; Lease option;
Probate sales
House Priorities Worksheet, 8–11,
116, 385
House Scout letter, 113

Housing discrimination, 109, 249, 250, 371

Hybrid adjustable rate (ARM) mortgage, 148, 165–166

I

Ideal House Profile, 5–8, 385

Immigrant occupancy, affordability indicator, 46

Impound accounts, 74

Imputed interest, 177

Income

  affordability and, 25

  cancelled debt as, 32

  down payment plans for low and moderate, 72

  projected, emphasizing, 152

Indexes

  ARM mortgages, 162–163, 165

  defined, 164

Inflation guards, homeowner's insurance, 273

In-law units, affordability and, 58–60

Inspection reports, 284, 315–316

Inspections

  advantages of, 290

  for asbestos, 316

  by buyers, 310–311

  contingencies, 142, 220, 262–265

  cost of, 311

  counteroffer provisions, 249

  do-it-yourself home repair jobs, 310–311

  earthquake retrofitting, 317

  electrical, 316–317

  electromagnetic radiation, 317

  financial responsibility for, 230

  flipped houses, 311

  foundations, 317

  general, 313–314

  lead, 317

  mold, 317–318

  necessary, 319–320

  negative, emphasizing the, 52

  new construction, 130, 142–143, 170, 320

  online resources, 315, 370

  options when problems are found, 263–265

  paying for, 321

  pest control, 311, 313, 315

  physical condition approval, 171, 176

  plumbing, 318

  post-disclosure, 300

  post-inspection tour, 282–283

  pre-offer in a hot market, 311

  of probate sales, 51

  professional, arranging, 311–312

  radon, 318–319

  recording, 315

  repairs, identifying necessary, 263–265, 267–268, 321

  repairs post-, negotiating, 263–265, 267–268

  structural, 317

  subsoil, 318–319

  time required for, 315

  timing of, 233

Inspectors

  access requirements, 263

accompanying, 263, 315

good, finding, 314–315

online resources, 315, 316

paying directly, 285

questions to ask, 314

Insulation "R" factor, 128

Insurance

CLUE reports, 217

disability, 181

life, 181, 278

tenants, 227

Insurance, homeowner's

affordability and, 24

CC&Rs, 274, 276

claims against, 275, 278, 299

comprehensive, 271–273

condominiums, 274, 276

dogs effect on, 272

earthquakes and floods, 273–274

home-based businesses, 272

impound accounts for, 74

inflation guards, 273

lender requirement, 271

mold claims, 278

moral hazard, 277

obtaining, 217

online resources, 279, 371

policy renewal, 275

qualifying for, 277–278

shopping for, 276–277

typical coverage, 271–273

warranty claims effect on, 324

Insurance industry, discrimination in
the, 277

Interest

imputed, 177

prepaid, 285

Interest costs

ARM vs. fixed rate mortgages, 159

fixed rate mortgages, 156

short-term mortgages, 158

tax-deductible interest, 76

Interest-only ARM, 149

Interest rate caps, 163

Interest rates

affordability and, 23–24

ARM mortgages, 148, 149, 162

buydowns, 149, 150–151

CalVet loans, 173

choosing a mortgage and, 157

developer subsidies, 125

estimating the, 23–24

fixed rate mortgages, 148, 149, 162

forecasting, online resources, 154

indexes and margins, 163, 165

jumbo loans, 148

locking in, 140, 193–194

for private loans, 176, 179

refinancing and, 153

seller financing, 183

Interpleaders, 261

Investing, money available for, 76

IRS

foreign investor rules, 262

gift tax returns, 79

online resources, 378

See also Taxes

J

Joint tenancy

creation of, 328

deeds, 330

probate, 328, 339

right of survivorship, 327
shares of co-owners, 328
survivorship, 328
taking title, 327, 339
termination, 328
Judicial Arbitration and Mediation
Services, Inc. (JAMS), 237

K

Kitchen, interpreting ads featuring a
modern, 108
Kitchen cabinets, new construction,
128

L

Landscaping
additional resources, 356
drought tolerant, 356
low-maintenance yard, interpreting
ads featuring, 108
screening with, 44
street noise, reducing with, 44
Landslides, 355–356
Lead-based paint disclosure
requirement, 308
Lead hazards, inspections, and
disclosures, 308, 317, 371
Lease option, 60–63
Legal description (legal), defined, 259
Legally binding contract, defined,
224
Lender fees, 176, 284
Lenders
commitment by, obtaining, 193
developer's, 124–125
interviewing, 191

online resources, 371
private, 179–181
private, minimizing risk to, 180
See also Loans
Leverage, down payments and, 77
Liar loans (stated income loans), 30
Liens
checking, for foreclosures, 54
defined, 280
Life insurance, 181, 278
Life-of-the-loan cap, 163, 164
Limited equity housing cooperative
(LEHC), 65, 66–67
Liquidated damages, 343
Listing agent, 85
Living trusts, 330–331, 339–340
Loan applications
accuracy in, 21, 32
complaints, filing, 194
fees, 176, 284
Loan commitment, defined, 259
Loan discounts, 151
Loans
approval, time required for,
192–193
documents required, 34
financing options, 147
interest rate, estimating the, 23–24
interest rates, locking in, 193–194
mortgage payments in reserve for,
22, 211
new construction, 123, 124–125
online resources, 189, 371–372
preapproved, 33–34, 192, 219
prequalification, 34

secondary mortgage market, 147–148

See also Federal Housing Administration (FHA) loans; Lenders; Mortgages; Veterans Affairs (VA) loans

Loans, costs of
application fees, 150, 284
appraisal fees, 150, 193–194
general fees, 150
impound accounts, 74
lender fees, 176, 284
loan fees, 284
lowering, 75
points, 18, 73, 149, 150–151, 158
third-party fees, 150
title insurance, 150
transaction costs, 38
up-front costs, 74
See also Closing costs

Loans, qualifying for
credit scores effect on, 17, 146
debt-to-income ratio, 18, 25
down payment size and, 146
favorable, factors in obtaining a, 146
owner occupancy and, 123
private mortgages, 176
proof of employment, 28
prospective rental income, 58

Loans, types of
employer, 28
government-assisted, 54
home equity, 75
jumbo, 148
low down payment loans, 72, 73, 153, 173

no-down-payment loans, 72, 173
remodeling, 40
standardized, 147–148
stated income loans (liar loans), 30
See also Federal Housing Administration (FHA) loans; Mortgages, private; Veterans Affairs (VA) loans

Loan terms, defined, 225

Low down payment loans, 72, 153, 173

Low-maintenance yard, interpreting ads featuring, 108

M

Maintenance, requirements for, 275

Making an offer, defined, 223

Margin
ARM mortgages, 162
defined, 164

Marginal houses, affordability of
in desirable areas, 44–45
in marginal areas, 47

Marital Property Agreements
married person owning alone, 337
tenancy in common, 337

Market conditions
cold (buyer's) market, 214–215, 241
considering when buying, 197–198
cool market, 214
determining, 199, 213–214
hot (seller's) market, 198, 210–211, 213, 246, 311
offers and, 213–215, 241–242
online resources, 154

Married persons
  Marital Property Agreements, 337
  owning alone, taking title, 335–336, 338
  owning together, taking title, 331–333
Megan's Law, 232
Military ordnance, disclosure of, 309
Mold, online resources, 318, 371
Mold inspections, 313, 317–318
Moral hazard, 277
Mortgage brokers, 148, 189–190
Mortgage calculators online, 27, 371
Mortgage loans. *See* Loans
Mortgage payments
  affordability and, 25
  amortization chart, 26
  ARM mortgages, 148–149, 162
  builder buydowns, 125–126
  estimating, 24
  fixed rate mortgages, 148, 149, 156–157
  interest-only ARM, 149
  interest rate buydowns and, 149, 150–151
  in a lease option, 61
  lowering, 75
  private mortgages and, 176
  in reserve, 22, 211
Mortgage rates
  online resources, 189, 371–372
  researching, 188–189
Mortgages
  for down payments, 153
  factors in choosing, 152–153
  fixed rate vs. adjustable, 149

market trends, online resources, 154
online calculators, 24, 27
online resources, 148, 159
prepaying, 159
shopping for, 188–191
See also Loans
Mortgages, private
  advantages, 176
  considerations, 177
  credit reports for, 180
  deed of trust, 182
  down payments, borrowing, 80
  finalizing the loan, requirements for, 182
  lenders, potential, 178–181
  option of, 147
  promissory notes, 182
  for second mortgages, 182–185
  shared equity transactions, 182
Mortgages, types of, defined
  adjustable rate (ARM), 148
  fixed rate, 148
  interest-only ARM, 149
Mortgage transference, 63
Moving
  affordablility and, 39, 43, 211
  after moving in, things to do, 382
  allowing sellers time for, 218
  changes of address, 381
  checklist, two-weeks prior, 379
  expenses, tax deductible, 378
  packing, tips for, 380–381
  remodeling vs., 39
  rentals and, 38
Moving companies, online resources, 372, 380

Mudslides, 355–356
Multiple counteroffer, defined, 223
Multiple listing service (MLS), taking advantage of the, 84, 110
Multi-unit buildings, affordability option, 58–60

N

National Association of the Remodeling Industry, 41
National Foundation for Credit Counseling (NFCC), 32
Natural disaster destruction during escrow, 345
Natural Hazard Disclosure Statement, 51, 128, 303–306
Natural hazards
    disclosures, 51, 128, 303–306
    drought, 356
    earthquakes and seismic, 306–307, 352–354, 369
    fire, 355
    floods, 133, 355–356, 370
    online resources, 356
    soil instability, 277, 318–319
Needs tender loving care, interpreting ads featuring, 108
New construction
    add-ons and upgrades, 126–127, 129–132
    advantages of, 120–121
    buying considerations, 118–120, 130
    CC&Rs, 121, 134, 136–139
    choices in, 118
    defects common in, 141

delivery date and delays, 119, 139–141
    energy efficiency, 121, 128
    financing, 118, 123, 124–126, 170
    green builders, 122
    guarantees, 143–144
    homeowner's associations, 121, 135–137
    home warranties, 143–144, 170, 323
    inspections, 130, 142–143, 170, 320
    online resources, 122, 372
    real estate agents/brokers, using, 123–124
    repairs and maintenance, 121
    Supplementary Agreements, 131
    written agreements for add-ons and upgrades, 131, 132
New construction, costs of
    add-ons and upgrades, 118, 126–127, 129–130
    getting a good deal, 116
    lemons, 119
    negotiating the, 124, 126, 130
    prices, 119, 120
New construction, identifying elements of good
    air conditioning, 128
    building sites soils and engineering report, 128
    carpets, 128
    doors, interior, 128
    drapes, 128
    electrical outlets, 128
    energy efficiency, 128
    entryways, covered, 128
    floors, 128

foundations, 128
kitchen cabinets, 128
soundproofing, 129
watering systems, underground, 129
New construction contracts
  cancelling, 140
  closing contingencies, 142–143
  refunds on add-ons and upgrades,
    129
  written to benefit the seller, 119
New construction developers,
  choosing, 121–122
New construction lots, considerations
  when choosing, 132–134
No-down-payment loans, 72, 173
Noise, choosing a building lot and,
  132
Not a drive-by, interpreting ads
  featuring, 108
Notary fees, 229, 261
Nuclear plants, 360, 372

O

Occupancy
  counteroffer provisions, 249
  loans, qualifying for, 123
  possession dates, 198, 227, 235,
    342–343
  post-closing, 227, 342–343
  purchase agreement clauses,
    226–228
  seller's right of, 140, 342–343
  See also Eviction
Occupancy rates, 123
Offer conference, 242

Offer price, factors in determining
  the
  additional expenses post-moving,
    preparing for, 211
  the advertised price, 209–210
  amount you are willing to pay,
    216–217
  comparable recent sales, 211–213
  market conditions, 214–215
  online valuations, 212–213
  personal value of the house, 216
  seller's needs, 215–216
Offers
  accepted, steps following, 252
  attractive to the seller, creating,
    218–220
  backup offers, 248, 252–253
  contingencies, 222
  final price decision, 217
  inspections prior to, 311
  legally valid, 222
  limiting the acceptance time for,
    220
  market conditions and, 241–242
  open-ended, 220
  presenting, 243–244
  revoking, 222, 245, 252–253
  strategies to avoid, 220
  take-it-or-leave-it, 246
  See also Bidding; Counteroffers
Offers, responses possible
  acceptance, 245
  to contingencies, 245
  counteroffers, 245–246, 248–251
  financing information, 244
  more time requested, 246
  to price offered, 244

rejection, 245–246

Offer terminology
counter counteroffer, 223–224
counteroffer, 223
legally binding contract, 224
making an offer, 223
multiple counteroffer, 223

Off-market listings, access to, 86

Off the beaten path, interpreting ads featuring, 108

Open houses, 109

Opening escrow, defined, 259

Overall cap, defined, 164

P

Paint defects in new construction, 141

Partnerships
additional resources, 339
creation of, 328
deeds, 335–336
probate, 328
shares of co-owners, 328
survivorship, 328
taking title, 335–336, 339
termination, 328

Payroll deductions, for down payments, 81

Periodic cap, 163, 164

Personal property, purchase agreement clause, 232

Pest control inspections, 311, 313, 315, 372

Pest control reports, 230, 313

Pets, condominiums and, 63

Photovoltaic roof systems, 322

Physical condition approval, 171, 176

PITI (principal, interest, taxes, and insurance), 16

Plumbing inspections, 318

Points
costs of buying, 158
defined, 18, 158
for low down payments, 73
online calculators, 151
paying to lower interest rates, 149, 150–151
for private loans, 176
refinancing and, 153
tax deductions, 151
See also Margin

Pollution
additional resources, 357–358
air pollution, 358–359
online resources, 359, 368
toxic waste, 358
water pollution, 357–358

Possession dates, 198, 227, 235, 342–343

Power of attorney, 259

Pre/prelim/preliminary, defined, 259

Price, counteroffer provision, 248–249

Priced to sell, interpreting ads featuring, 108

Privacy
choosing a building lot, 132
screening with landscaping for, 44

Private mortgage insurance (PMI)
canceling, 75
closing costs and loan fees, 285
cost of, 74
down payments and, 73–75
estimating, 25

impound accounts, 74
for private loans, 176
requirements for, 73, 75
tax deductible, 74
VA loans, 169
Probate
additional resources, 332
avoiding, 327, 339–340
community property, 329
community property with right of
survivorship, 329, 332
joint tenancy, 328, 339
partnerships, 328
tenancy in common, 328
Probate sales, affordability and,
49–51
Promissory notes, private mortgages,
182
Property taxes, 24, 74, 204, 228, 283,
285
Property valuation, 213, 283, 291
Proposition 13, 204
Protecting Tenants at Foreclosure Act
of 2009, 54
Purchase agreement clauses
addenda containing other terms and
conditions, 238
agency disclosure and confirmation,
235
arbitration of disputes, 236–237
assessment bonds, 228
attorneys' fees, 237
backup offer, 235–236
broker compensation, 235
buyer's signature, 238
condition of property, 234, 235
disclosures, 237–238

division of expenses, 228, 229–230
entire agreement, 237
final walk-through and possession,
235
fixtures included in the sale,
230–231
insurance prorations, 228
liquidated damages, 236
mediation of disputes, 236
occupancy, 226–228
opening section, 224–225
personal property included in the
sale, 232
property tax prorations, 228
seller's acceptance of offer, 238
seller's rejection of offer, 238
time is of the essence, 237
title, 234
when offer expires, 236
Purchase agreement clauses,
contingencies in
appraisal, 234
hazard insurance, 234
home warranties, 234
inspection, 233
sale contingent on selling your
property, 232
time allowed for removing, 233
title contingency, 233–234
Purchase agreement clauses, financial
terms
deposit increases, 225
down payments, 225
earnest money deposit, 225
loan terms, 225
time limits and contingencies, 226

total, 226

Purchase agreements, contingency
clauses in
appraisals, 234
hazard insurance, 234
home warranties, 234
inspections, 233
selling your house, 232
time allowed for removing, 233
title contingency, 233–234

Purchase contracts. *See* Contracts

Q

Quaint, interpreting ads featuring,
108

R

Radon, 318–319, 372
Real estate ads, translating, 108
Real estate agency relationships
confirmation of, 90
disclosure regarding, 90, 235
Real Estate Agency Relationships
form, 235
Real estate agents/brokers
commissions and other
compensation, 86, 87, 235, 265
disclosure responsibilities, 299–300
duty of care, 90, 92
filing complaints against, 91
firing, 100–102
first meetings, 98
legal duties, 88
legal representation by, 90–93
licensing of, 91, 100

new construction and, 122,
123–124
online resources, 372–373
positives of working with, 84–86,
110
pressure from, 88–89
suing, 344
Real estate agents/brokers, hiring
by the hour, 93, 95
gifts for, 102
good, finding, 93–94, 96, 109–111
licenses, checking for, 100
steps in, 84
technical skills, 110–111
things to avoid, 98–100
tough questions to ask, 97
Real estate law, online resources, 373
Real estate-owned (REO)
foreclosures, 53
Real estate sales people, types of
agents, 85
agents hired by the hour, 101
brokers, 85
buyer's agent, 85, 90–91, 101–102
commissioned sales reps, 118, 120
dual agent, 85, 90, 92
listing agent, 85
real estate professional, 85
realtor, 85
relocation specialists, 115
salesperson, 85
seller's agent, 90, 92–93
selling agent, 85
Real estate tax, 230
Real Estate Transfer Disclosure
Statement, 51, 237, 291–300

Real estate websites, 368–374
Real property co-ownership, forms of
  community property, 329, 334
  community property with right of
    survivorship, 329, 331–333, 339
  joint tenancy, 327, 328, 330, 339
  partnership, 328
  tenancy in common, 328, 330–331
Recording fees, 229, 285
Redecorating, costs of, 211
Refinancing
  choosing an ARM and, 156
  fixed rate mortgages, 157
  interest rates and, 153, 157
  online calculators, 151
  points and, 153
  reasons for, 75
Refinancing calculators online, 373
Release clauses, 199
Release of Real Estate Purchase
    Contract form, 270, 347
Relocation resources, 115, 368
Remodeled (flipped) houses,
    inspecting, 311
Remodeling
  buying now, options to, 39
  costs, estimating, 39–40
  costs vs. value, 41
  fixer-uppers, 47–48
  moving costs vs., 39
  online resources, 41, 373
  reasons against, 40–41
  resale value, effect on, 40
  small houses with expansion
    potential, 48–49
Rental property, purchasing, 231
Rent-backs, 201–202, 227

Rent control, 38, 226, 231
Renting
  Airbnb and VRBO, 60, 139
  between buying and selling,
    201–202
  buy vs. rent decision, 36–38, 373
  CC&Rs, 139
  part of the house out, 58
Repairs
  green, 322
  inspections identifying needed,
    263–265, 267–268, 321
  new construction vs., 121
  post-inspection, negotiating,
    263–265, 267–268
  prior to closing, 264–265
Request for beneficiary statement,
    defined, 258
Reserve, money in, 22, 211
Residential Earthquake Hazards
    Report, 306–307
Residential Environmental Hazards,
    307
Residential Lead-Based Paint Hazard
    Reduction Act, 308
Revocation of Offer to Purchase Real
    Property, 245, 252–253
Right of survivorship
  community property with, 329,
    331–333, 339
  joint tenancy, 327
  tenancy in common, 330
  See also Survivorship
Roofs
  inspections, 230
  leakage, in new construction, 141
  replacing, 322

S

For Sale by Owner, 105
Sales, comparable, 211–213, 369
Schools
  in California, 360–362
  desirable houses in marginal areas,
    46
  resources about, 361–362, 374
Secondary mortgage market, 374
Seismic hazards, 306–307, 369
Self-employed borrowers, 272
Sellers
  acceptance of offer, 238
  backing out during escrow, 342
  canny, 210
  deaths of, 344
  discrimination by, 250
  financing by, 183
  foreign investors, 262
  the house hunt and, 105, 110, 114
  inspection reports from, relying on,
    290
  letters to, 219
  occupancy rights, 140, 342–343
  optimistic, 209
  refusal to return your deposit, 269
  straightforward, 209
  stuck-in-the-past, 209
  suing, 344–345
Seller's (hot) market
  bidding wars, 210–211
  buying a house when you already
    own one, 198
  defined, 213
  determining a, 214–215
  inspections prior to offer, 311

  preemptive bid strategies, 246
Sellers, offers to
  full-price, obligations, 209, 210
  notifying of, 240–241
  rejection of, 238
Seller's agent, 90, 92–93
Seller's Demand for Removal of
    Contingencies, 268, 269
Selling
  comps when, 211–213, 369
  resources, 196
  tax breaks, 203–204
  underpricing, 209–210
Selling agent, 85
Separate property, community
    property vs., 334
Sex offenders, 232
Shared equity contracts, 56
Shares of co-owners
  community property, 329
  community property with right of
    survivorship, 329
  cooperative housing, 66
  joint tenancy, 328
  partnership, 328
  tenancy in common, 328
Short sales, 52–53
Small business owners, 28–29
Small houses with expansion
    potential, affordablility option,
    48–49
Soil instability, 277, 318–319
Soils and engineering reports, 128
Soundproofing in new construction,
    129
Staged homes, 10

Starter house, interpreting ads featuring, 108
Stated income loans (liar loans), 30
Structural inspections, 317
Structural problems, affordability of houses with, 51–52
Subsoil inspections, 318–319
Survey fees, 285
Survivorship
  community property, 329
  community property with right of survivorship, 329
  joint tenancy, 328
  partnership, 328
  tenancy in common, 328
  See also Right of survivorship

T

Taking title
  community property with right of survivorship, 331–333, 339
  deeds, 326
  defined, 259
  domestic partners owning together, 331–333
  joint tenancy, 327, 334, 339
  married person owning alone, 335–336, 338
  married persons owning together, 331–333
  one unmarried person, 326
  partnerships, 335–336, 339
  tenancy in common, 330–331, 334–335, 337
  two or more unmarried people, 326–327

Tax assessment rates, 204–205
Tax deductions
  loan discounts, 151
  mortgage interest, 76
  moving expenses, 378
  points, 151
  private mortgage insurance (PMI), 74
Taxes
  affordability and, 24
  capital gains tax, 203
  estate tax, 79
  on gifts, 79
  gifts amounts free of, 79
  interest income reporting, 177
  online resources, 374
  property taxes, 228, 283
  real estate tax, 230
  seller financing, 183
  transfer tax, 229, 285
  withholding, 82
  See also IRS
Tax planning, community property with right of survivorship, 332
Tax service fees, 285
T-bills (Treasury Bills), 162
Tenancy in common (TIC)
  additional resources, 330
  affordability and, 64
  creation of, 328
  probate, 328
  right of survivorship, 330–331
  shares of co-owners, 328
  survivorship, 328
  taking title, 330–331, 334–335, 337
  termination, 328

Tenants
  liability for, 139
  rights of, 54–55, 141, 226
Tenant's insurance, 227
Ten percent down payment loans, 73, 153
Time is of the essence, 237
Title fees, 261, 285
Title insurance, 261, 279–281
Title insurance companies, 150, 287
Title insurance fees, 150, 229, 261, 285
Title insurance policies, 261, 374
Title report fees, 261
Title reports, 279–281
Titles
  contingencies, 233–234, 280–281
  final, defined, 258
  foreclosures and, 54
  preliminary approval, 280–281
  See also Taking title
Title search fee, 229, 285
Total, defined, 226
Town houses, 64
Toxic Mold Protection Act, 317–318
Toxic waste, 358, 374
Trading up, 77
Traffic in California, 362, 374
Transaction costs, 38
Transfer Disclosure Statement, 128
Transfer-on-death (beneficiary) deed, 340
Transfer tax, 229, 285
Transportation
  desirable houses in marginal areas, 46
  online resources, 362, 374

traffic in California, 362, 374
Triplexes, affordability option, 58–60
Trulia, 106

U
Underpricing, 209–210
Unlawful detainer lawsuits, 343
U.S. government-assisted loans, 170–174, 370
  See also Federal Housing Administration (FHA) loans; Veterans Affairs (VA) loans
U.S. government housing programs, 125
Utility bills, 128, 311, 313

V
Veterans Affairs (VA) foreclosures, bidding on, 54
Veterans Affairs (VA) loans
  assumability, 165
  Certificate of Reasonable Value (CRV), 168
  down payments, 72, 169
  fees, 169
  loan limits, 168
  low down payment plans, 72
  for new construction, 170
  online resources, 169
  PMI, 169
  qualifications, 168, 169
VRBO, 60, 139

W
Water bills, 311
Water damage, claims for, 278, 299

Water heaters
bracing, 302
replacing, 322
Watering systems, new construction, 129
Water pollution, 357–358, 373, 374
Wildfires, 355

Window leakage in new construction, 141
Wipe-out clauses, 199, 249, 268

Z
Zillow, 106, 213

⚖ NOLO *Online Legal Forms*

Nolo offers a large library of legal solutions and forms, created by Nolo's in-house legal staff. These reliable documents can be prepared in minutes.

Create a Document

- **Incorporation.** Incorporate your business in any state.
- **LLC Formations.** Gain asset protection and pass-through tax status in any state.
- **Wills.** Nolo has helped people make over 2 million wills. Is it time to make or revise yours?
- **Living Trust (avoid probate).** Plan now to save your family the cost, delays, and hassle of probate.
- **Trademark.** Protect the name of your business or product.
- **Provisional Patent.** Preserve your rights under patent law and claim "patent pending" status.

Download a Legal Form

Nolo.com has hundreds of top quality legal forms available for download—bills of sale, promissory notes, nondisclosure agreements, LLC operating agreements, corporate minutes, commercial lease and sublease, motor vehicle bill of sale, consignment agreements and many more.

Review Your Documents

Many lawyers in Nolo's consumer-friendly lawyer directory will review Nolo documents for a very reasonable fee. Check their detailed profiles at **Nolo.com/lawyers**.